Dedication

To Maria and Jim, who have been like
Eris and Pluto in my own life.

Thanks to Amy Shapiro and Deane Driscoll
for their advice in preparing the book.

Special thanks to Johonet Carpenter, who at age 91
was a better proofreader than some younger people.

Final special thanks to ROLAND A. TREMBLAY,
who provided last-minute proofreading and help with
the Index, even though he doesn't believe in the
material presented in the book.

**Also by
Thomas Canfield**

Eris, in Signs, Houses and Aspects

Uranus, in Signs, Houses and Aspects

Yankee Doodle Discord
A Walk with Planet Eris through USA History

Brother Pluto, Sister Eris
Aspects Between the Dwarf Planets
Through 800 Years of History

First Edition, first printing 2018

Cover and Book Design
by Maria Kay Simms

International Standard Book Number
978-1-934976678

Library of Congress Control Number
2018902155

ACS Publications
An imprint of Starcrafts LLC
68-A Fogg Road
Epping, NH 03042

Chapter 13
Eris Steps on the Gas, or the Race of the Thirty Years War —Eris semi-sextile Pluto 99

Chapter 14
Eris in the Lead—The Glorious Revolution & Queen Anne's War— Eris sextile Pluto.............................111

Chapter 15
The War of Polish Succession—Eris semi-sextile Pluto 129

Chapter 16
Welcome to World War One—Eris Conjunct Pluto.............137

Chapter 17
Revolutionary Wars—Eris semi-sextile Pluto 151

Chapter 18
Theirs Not to Reason Why—Eris sextile Pluto.................. 171

Chapter 19
World War 1/4? —Eris square Pluto 191

Chapter 20
The Big One: WW2—Eris trine Pluto.................................. 203

Chapter 21
Honkin' on the Tonkin—Eris quincunx Pluto (and Neptune and Uranus) 219

Chapter 22
The Plan for Afghanistan?—Eris opposing Pluto 233

Chapter 23
The Gulf War—Eris quincunx Pluto 245

Chapter 24
The War Against Dandruff—Eris trine Pluto 259

Chapter 25
Conclusion: Some Glimpses Into the Future 279

Bibliography: each chapter 1-24, has at it's end its own bibliography.

INDEX 286

That there are men in all countries who get their living by war, and by keeping up the quarrels of nations, is as shocking as it is true; but when those who are concerned in the government of a country, make it their study to sow discord and cultivate predjudices between nations, it becomes the more unpardonable.

—Thomas Paine

Persephone/Kore being abducted by Hades/Pluto

VIII. *Brother Pluto, Sister Eris*

Chapter 1
An Interplanetary Crime Scene

Whenever a series of murders takes place, one of the police tactics is to photograph the people at the crime scene. It is known that some murderers will come back to the scene of the crime, if only to witness the bafflement of the authorities. Now, suppose it was noticed that in the various pictures of crime scenes, there were two persons in particular who kept showing up. A man and a woman could be seen witnessing the investigation and the cleaning up operations. What makes their presence especially odd is the angular position they have to each other, which can be demonstrated through the hands of a clock.

When there has been a crime involving treachery and back-stabbing, the man and woman appear together, like the hands of a clock at the Noon position. When there has been a crime involving a brutal frontal assault and overwhelming force, the man and woman are a little apart, like the hands of a clock at 1 o'clock. When there have been mass murders involving extreme bloodshed, the man and woman are at a 2 o'clock position. When there have been crimes involving deception, chicanery, and confidence tricks, the man and woman are at a 3 o'clock position. When there have been great crimes like the rise and fall of empires or the collapse of leaders, the man and the woman have been at a 4 o'clock position. When there have been surprising deaths, like a "David versus Goliath" scene, the man and woman have been at a 5 o'clock position. Finally, when the man and woman are like both hands are pointing to opposite sides of the clock, the crime scene is one of confusion and chaos, leaving the investigators to scratch their heads and wonder what the outcome of such an action would be.

If such a man and woman did keep making appearances, the police would consider them to be "persons of interest," and then try to locate them for questioning. After apprehending the man and the woman, the police would have to determine whether they were involved with the crimes, or were they just persons with a vulture mentality who enjoyed looking upon scenes of death and horror? The police would start to investigate their backgrounds and assemble a dossier on each person.

The man would come up with the identity of Pluto, a short, dark and sinister looking figure. He was known for his underworld connections and his threatening demeanor. Rumor had it that he was married, but that he had abducted his wife. He lived an isolated life, not known for getting around very much. His whole appearance would bring up images of death, decay, and destruction.

The woman would come up with the identity of Eris, another short, dark, and sinister looking figure. She was known for being a smooth talker and a bit of a troublemaker. She was usually seen watching bar fights, street fights, and brutal sporting events. She would act like a cheerleader for both sides, trying to make the fighting last as long as possible. She reportedly had a fascination for victims of fights who were dying, and rather than call 911, she would sit and listen to the moans and groans of the suffering people.

The police might try to play off one against the other, possibly by offering secret deals or even just playing the "good cop, bad cop" game. However, Pluto and Eris are too clever for tricks like that. Pluto goes silent, and invokes his right to remain silent. Eris, on the other hand, keeps talking, and within a short time she has turned the "good cop" against the "bad cop." All cooperation breaks down, and the case does not seem to be getting anywhere. More background information is obviously needed on the suspects!

Pluto—A Dark Dossier

Pluto is the Roman name for Hades, Greek God of the Underworld. According to Greek Mythology, Hades/Pluto was the eldest child of the Titan Rhea and her brother/husband Kronos (aka Saturn). When Hades/Pluto was born, his father feared that he would overthrow his rule. So, Kronos/Saturn swallowed the child whole, and Hades/Pluto grew up in the belly of his father. He was soon joined by four other siblings, but they were all released when a sixth sibling, Zeus/ Jupiter, administered a drug to Kronos/Saturn. This caused him to vomit up his children, who then joined Zeus/Jupiter in a war against Kronos/Saturn.

With the defeat of Kronos/Saturn, it came time to divide up the world. Zeus/Jupiter set up his home on Mount Olympus and ruled over the lands of the earth. Poseidon/ Neptune was given the seas and oceans to rule. Hades/Pluto was given the land of the dead and moved to the underworld. He might have remained an obscure deity until one day he fell in love with Kore/Persephone, the daughter of the Earth goddess Demeter/Ceres.

There are differing accounts to the story of this relationship. One version said that Kore/Persephone was walking across a field, and Hades/Pluto suddenly burst through the soil and dragged her down to the underworld. Another version said that Kore/Persephone was bored with her domineering mother, and that she willingly ran off with bad-boy Hades/Pluto. Whatever the cause, Demeter/Ceres was so upset by the loss of her daughter, she withdrew her blessings from the Earth. The result was that the world became covered with ice and snow, leading to the fear that the population of the planet would freeze to death.

The situation became so dire that Zeus/Jupiter had to intervene, and he ordered that Hades/Pluto had to release the girl. However, the laws of the underworld declared that anyone who had eaten any food in the underworld had to remain there. Kore/Persephone had eaten six pomegranate seeds. It looked like she would have to remain with Hades/Pluto, until a compromise was agreed upon. It was finally decided that Kore/Persephone would return to Demeter/Ceres for six months, and then go back to the underworld for six months. Thus, the ancients explained the change in seasons from summer to winter.

After that, Hades/Pluto was a bit player in Greco-Roman mythology. He would confront various Greek heroes such as Orpheus, Theseus, and Hercules, who dared to venture into the underworld. Apart from those appearances, he did not interact with the other deities. There are no stories about Hades/Pluto chilling out on Mount Olympus, or demanding mass worship from mortals. There are no colorful or picaresque tales told about him as there were for Mercury, Venus, or Mars. In the end, the afterlife just seemed to be a boring place, filled with eternal sameness. It would take the coming of Christianity to heat things up in the underworld.

Pluto—The Planet

In the late 19th century and early 20th century, astronomers were searching for a planet beyond Neptune. They had noticed strange variations in the orbits of Neptune and Uranus, and concluded that another distant planet must be exerting a gravitational pull. The leading astronomers of the age started searching for "Planet X," and the American astronomer Percival Lowell constructed an observatory in Flagstaff, Arizona for the purpose of locating the new planet. Ironically, on March 19, 1915, the Lowell Observatory photographed two faint images of "Planet X," but it would be many years before astronomers figured out what the images were.

After the death of Percival Lowell in 1916, his legacy for the observatory was tied up by lawsuits filed by his widow. It was not until 1929 that the Lowell Observatory began operating again. The assignment of finding "Planet X" was given to a 23-year-old Kansas farm boy. Clyde Tombaugh had constructed his own telescopes, and had impressed the staff of the Lowell Observatory with his drawings of Mars and Jupiter. Tombaugh was put in charge of the "blink telescope," which photographed sections of the sky over a period of days. By flashing the photographs of the same sector, filmed several days apart, a body in motion appeared to "blink" in the picture.

On February 18, 1930, Tombaugh finally saw an image "blink" on two plates taken between January 23 and 29. Including a plate taken on January 21 added to the "blink." After more confirmation plates were made, the Lowell Observatory wired the Harvard College Observatory on March 13 about the discovery. The news made headlines all over the world, and a debate began over what to name the new planet.

The christening of the new planet was done by an English student of the classics, Venetia Burney. She thought that Pluto, as the lord of the dead who owned a helmet of invisibility, fit this new body. She mentioned it to her grandfather, who was a librarian at Oxford University. He passed the name on to an astronomy professor, who then contacted astronomers in America. On March 24, the staff at Lowell Observatory unanimously voted on the name "Pluto," and an official announcement was made on May 1, 1930. Adding to the popularity of the new name was the fact that the first two letters were the initials of the man who made the discovery possible, Percival Lowell.

For 75 years, there was a certain amount of national pride in that an American had discovered "Planet X." However, in 2006, a controversy began over whether Pluto should be considered a planet because of its diminutive mass. The International Astronomical Union decided to downgrade Pluto by giving it the new classification of "dwarf planet." The IAU decision was not universally popular, and there remain a number of astronomers who continue to see Pluto as a regular planet.

Pluto in Astrology

Although Pluto was discovered in 1930, it took astrologers a while to figure out what to do with this new planet in their readings. Looking backward, the opinion was that Pluto had an unsavory reputation because of the events taking place at the time of its discovery. Pluto had just entered Cancer at the time of World War I. One major result of the war was the political loss by most of the royal families in Europe. Also, millions of other families were shattered by the war and the 1918 influenza epidemic. Following the war, the criminal underworld gained immense power because of the folly of Prohibition and the illegal demand for alcohol. In Europe, fascist regimes rose up in Italy and Germany, and in Russia the power of the government was seized by Joseph Stalin, who purged all of his rivals. It was also a time when the atom was split and nuclear energy was considered to be a power source for the future.

The discovery of Pluto took place at the beginning of the Great Depression, when an economic upheaval wracked the nations of the world. Social aid programs, such as those presented in the New Deal, offered new chances for the population. However, the rise of militarism and the threats of another World War brought a pall of pessimism to the public. It was from this period that astrologers finally decided that Pluto was the ruler of Scorpio, and was symbolic of death, destruction, upheaval, and transformation. It was noted that when Pluto passed through a sign, it brought about major restructuring of the elements ruled by that sign.

Pluto in Cancer during World War I had marked an end to personal security, as warring armies ruined the homes of millions in Europe. In America, government raids against pro-German or pro-Communist organizations made people fear a loss of constitutional rights against illegal search and seizure. Prohibition also increased government power against privacy by raiding homes being used for bootlegging. In the middle of the Great Depression, houses and family farms were being foreclosed by the banks. By the time Pluto was getting ready to leave Cancer, families were finally able to settle down in their homes with protection against foreclosure and no more raids from Prohibition agents.

Pluto in Leo saw an end to egotistical dictators, and a need for cooperation. Following the carnage of World War II, great powers banded together for mutual protection, and put aside self-serving, national interests to support the needs of the international community. The formation of the United Nations helped bring relief to impoverished areas of the world, though some traditionalists lamented the perceived loss of national sovereignty. A more subtle conflict arose with the coming of the Cold War, in which national differences took the form of ideological opposition between the largest powers. Warfare became restricted to nationalist struggles, and after World War II was limited to local conflicts rather than international invasions.

During the 1960's, Pluto was in Virgo, and conjunct Uranus in the middle of the decade. It was a time of social upheaval as people began questioning the established order. The wisdom of institutions such as the FBI, the military, and the Presidency were questioned and exposed to analysis. Protest movements rose up to challenge the segregation laws, as well as the draft laws that sent young men to fight in Vietnam. Major institutions, including big corporations and ivy-league colleges also experienced the upheaval at this time, and a spirit of iconoclastic change went through the national identity. "Make Love, Not War" became the theme of the youth culture.

In the 1970's, Pluto went through Libra, and as a continuation of the breakdown of rules and moral codes from the 1960's, there were major changes in the area of love and relationships. Larger numbers of young people started "living together" and even started families without the benefit of a wedding ceremony. In the world of the arts, adult movies and magazines went into mass production, creating a whole culture of sexual expression. Gay liberation moved out of the closet to become a political movement, and talks of love and eroticism became major topics, as opposed to the days when "decent people didn't discuss such things."

From such public sexual discussion, more secretive matters came to light in the mid-1980's when Pluto entered Scorpio. When celebrities like Rock Hudson and Liberace died from AIDS, that dreaded disease became a major social and political cause. Previously, it had been dismissed as "Gay cancer," but then there was a realization that heterosexual people could get the HIV virus as well, either through an infected partner or blood transfusion. AIDS had a transformative effect on the Gay community. Previously, the Gays had met at parties or bath houses. During the AIDS epidemic, Gays socialized more at funerals. This period of Pluto in Scorpio also marked the Iran-Contra scandal, in which secret deals made by a shadow government were exposed to public scrutiny, and there began a lot of questioning about who was really in charge of things. In Eastern Europe, questioning of government authority would lead to the breakdown of Communist regimes, best symbolized by the smashing of the Berlin wall. New nations and new governments rose up, and new power structures began to assert themselves.

In the mid-1990's, Pluto's entry into Sagittarius brought about a collapse in religious authority. There had been religious sex scandals before, but the Roman Catholic Church suffered a major loss of prestige with the revelations of massive cover-ups of activity by pedophile priests. Documents which were released by the church showed that bishops and cardinals knew about the sexual predators in the priesthood, but they chose to hide the knowledge rather than alert the parishes. The breaking of the scandal in Boston caused Bernard Cardinal Law to flee the USA and reside in exile at the Vatican. The wealth of the church diminished as law suits were filed around the country.

Also weakening the religious grip at the time was the rise of the Internet, which exposed more young people to cosmopolitan views on religion. Yet, there were factions that descended into a fundamentalist mindset, and their messages of hate would be reported in the media. The Westboro Baptist church became known as the "God Hates Fags" church, and they became infamous for protesting at funerals. From the Middle East, Islamic fundamentalism expressed itself in the terrorist group Al-Qaeda, which attacked American interests abroad, and finally culminated in the September 11, 2001 attack against the USA. The terrorist attacks helped inspire a "God and Country" mentality, leading to a new militarism in the "War on Terror."

Such flag-waving militarism drew attention away from what banking firms were doing with junk bonds and toxic investments. By the time of Pluto's entry into Capricorn in 2008, the financial situation of the leading banks was ready for a melt-down. The government offered a bail-out program, which saved the banks, and gave bonuses to the bankers. However, the bail-out did not protect the housing market, and thousands of foreclosures were made on homes as banks tried to recoup losses. For homeowners who invested their savings, it was a grim time of loss and upheaval. Adding to the difficulty was more layoffs and down-sizing of corporations.

Pluto will enter Aquarius in 2024, and it has not been in that sign since the American Revolution. One wonders if the excesses and incompetence of the Pluto in Capricorn years will spark another Revolution. Adding to that threat is the fact that the USA will be having its third Uranus Return in 2027. The previous Uranus Returns took place just before the Civil War in 1860 and just before the D-Day invasion in 1944. So, between Pluto and Uranus, it may not be a quiet time.

Eris—A Discordant Dossier

Once upon a time, in the realm of Greek mythology, there was a minor goddess named Eris. Her mother was Nyx, goddess of the night. Her father was supposed to have been Zeus/Jupiter, but there were also stories that she was spawned by parthenogenesis. As a goddess, she was not as powerful, nor as attractive as the Olympian gods, and she was forced to live by herself. The reason for this ostracism was due to the nature of her power. Eris had the ability to inflame spirits of men so they would go out and kill one another, or in the case of nations they would march off to war. Because of this disturbing power, the only deity who would associate with her was her half-brother, Ares (aka Mars), because he was the god of war, and you can't have a war without some good warmongering.

The leading legendary exploit of Eris was that she was blamed for starting the Trojan War. This was because Eris was not invited to the wedding of the sea goddess, Thetis. For revenge, Eris took a golden apple, inscribed it with the words, "For the Fairest," then threw it into the court of Olympus. It attracted the attention of three major goddesses, Hera, Athena, and Aphrodite. They began arguing over the golden apple, each declaring herself to be the "fairest." They asked Zeus to adjudicate the matter, but Zeus was not going to touch that issue. They finally decided Paris, Prince of Troy, should make the judgment.

Paris chose Aphrodite as the fairest of them all, and she rewarded Paris by giving him the love of Helen, the most beautiful woman in the world. Unfortunately, Helen was already married to Menelaus, the king of Sparta. When Paris and Helen ran off to Troy together, Menelaus organized the Greek states into a punitive war that lasted ten years. It was a decade of bloodshed, slaughter, and massacre. Needless to say, Eris loved every minute of it. It was said she got her pleasure by walking the battlefield after the battle and listening to the groans of the dying men.

Another legend of Eris involves one of the stories about Hercules. One day, Hercules was walking through a narrow canyon, and he saw a golden apple on the ground in front of him. He decided to smash the golden apple with his club. However, when he hit the apple, instead of it splattering, the apple grew twice as large. When Hercules hit the apple again, it grew larger again. He kept hitting it until it grew so large that it blocked the canyon. Hercules was wondering how to get around the giant apple, when he suddenly had a visitation from the goddess Athena. She explained to him that he was dealing with the golden apple of discord, and to strike the apple was to make it grow. Athena advised the best way to deal with discord was to leave it alone. Hercules backed away from the apple, and after a while it began to shrink so that he was able to get past it and continue on his journey. It may be said that Eris craves that kind of attention through the desire to make trouble, and the only way to foil her is to leave her alone.

Eris—The Planet

In the early years of the 21st century, astronomers were exploring the Kuiper Belt, the area of gas and debris beyond Pluto, which may contain the building blocks of the Solar System. The conventional wisdom was that there were no planets out in the Kuiper Belt.However, astronomers from the Palomar Observatory began finding large bodies in the area, some of which were more than a thousand miles across. Instead of reporting on them right away, they began compiling records of their discoveries, saving the announcement for when they had the time to write a scientific paper.

On January 5, 2005, at 11:20 am, the Palomar astronomers (Michael Brown, Chad Trujillo, and David Rabinowitz) received computer confirmation that the Palomar telescope had located a body in the Kuiper Belt that was thought to be slightly larger than Pluto. The discovery was treated with a sense of anti-climax, and the new body was classified as UB-313 and added to the growing list of found bodies in the Kuiper Belt. No public announcement was made, and the public might not have known of the new discovery for years, if it had not been for a Spanish observatory, which was about to release news of Kuiper Belt discoveries in July, 2005.

It was at that point when Palomar astronomers realized they had to reveal their findings, or the Spanish observatory would get all the credit and the publicity. Information was hastily presented to the press that large bodies had been found in the Kuiper Belt. When asked why this was not mentioned before, the Palomar astronomers said they were waiting to complete their paper on the subject. As it turned out, their paper on the Kuiper Belt bodies wasn't completed until November, 2005.

When UB-313 was revealed, the discoverers wanted to name it "Xena" after "Xena: Warrior Princess." When a tiny moon was found around the planet, they wanted to name it "Gabrielle" after Xena's sidekick. The astronomical community shot down these names, saying that planets had to be named after deities from classic mythology. Michael Brown suggested the Hindu goddess "Lilah," which was similar to the name of his daughter. However, the astronomers insisted they would be the ones to determine the name of the new planet after lengthy debate.

Before the name was decided, there began a debate over the subject of what constituted a planet. Astronomers stuck to the conventional wisdom that there were no "planets" out in the Kuiper Belt. Yet, here was a body possibly larger than Pluto. This made the astronomers question whether Pluto could be considered a planet. If Pluto was not a planet, then what was it? A planetoid? A large asteroid? A lost moon? Finally, the International Astronomical Union, meeting in Prague in 2006, came up with a new classification for Pluto, calling it a "dwarf planet."

The definition of a "dwarf planet" was any spherical body which orbited the Sun, but did not have sufficient mass to clear other bodies out of its orbit. Pluto sometimes went inside the orbit of Neptune, but did not have the mass to clear Neptune out of the way. Ergo, Pluto was a dwarf planet. Of course, the same definition could be applied to Neptune, since it had not cleared Pluto out of its orbit, but no one has started a campaign to make Neptune a "dwarf planet." The newly discovered UB-313 was classified as a "dwarf planet," and to everyone's surprise, the asteroid Ceres was reclassified as "dwarf planet,"since it was spherical and it orbited the Sun.

At this point, the astronomical controversy boiled over into the world of Astrology. Maria Simms was getting ready to release the new edition of *The American Ephemeris 2000-2100 at Midnight*. She decided that Pluto was not going to be taken out of the ephemeris—no way! She instructed programmer Rique Pottenger to add Ceres to the daily planetary placements, so Ceres was inserted into the grid between Mars and Jupiter. The asteroids Juno, Vesta, and Pallas were given monthly positions on each page. Rique wanted to add monthly positions for the new body UB-313, but he needed a name to put into the ephemeris.

Just before the ephemeris was about to go to print, the International Astronomical Union (IAU) named the new planet, Eris, after the goddess of discord in Greek Mythology, because of arguments among them during the process of her discovery. The moon of Eris was named Dysnomia, after a daughter of Eris who ruled a lawless state.

Michael Brown, the astronomer who led the team that discovered Eris, said he was pleased by the name because astronomers had been in a state of discord since the planet was found. Also, the fact that Dysnomia ruled over a "lawless" state was an oblique reference to *Xena, Warrior Princess*, The title role of Xena was played by Lucy Lawless!

Rique Pottenger added the name Eris to the ephemeris and the book went to press. The astrological symbol for Eris, a Mars pointing down, was later devised by Henry Seltzer, and was then adopted by Astro Computing Services for use in charts, and also by companies that publish astrological software such as *Solar Fire*, *Intrepid* and *Time Passages*.

Eris in Astrology

Because Eris has an orbit of approximately 550 years, there was some question as to whether the body would be significant in the charts of individuals. A better prospect for study was in the area of Mundane Astrology, dealing with the rise

and fall of nations. Plotting the course of Eris was a bit difficult, because the body is about 45 degrees off the ecliptic. It sometimes travels inside the orbit of Pluto, and when it moves closer to the Sun, it starts moving faster than Pluto. Currently, Eris is the sign of Aries and will remain in Aries until 2048, taking about 125 years to go through the sign. Back in the 1600s, Eris took only 16 years to go through the sign of Leo.

When I began studying Eris, I decided to examine it in the chart of the USA, figuring that the dwarf planet of discord would show some upheavals by transit to the USA chart. I used the Wolfstar USA chart which put the Ascendant at 8° Scorpio. I felt this was appropriate because of the Scorpio elements of transformation have always been part of the American dream of "the land of opportunity." The reason why immigration has been such a hot issue during American history is because millions of immigrants have wanted better lives for themselves and their families in coming to the USA. The national mythology has been one of the "great melting pot" in which ancestral difference could be melted down to form a homogeneous nation.

I began looking at the transits of Eris to the USA chart, and the first transit to hit was an opposition to the USA Sun in 1782. Now one would expect that if a planet of discord is opposing the Sun of a nation, there would be a collapse of government and a breakdown of authority, yet 1782 was a quiet year. The American Revolution had essentially ended with the battle of Yorktown in

1781, and the final peace was being negotiated. The major event of the year was the creation of the Great Seal of the United States. Since the Middle Ages, a seal represented the power of the state, and any document bearing such a seal was meant to have the full force of government behind it. For the Congress of the United States to create a Great Seal was a statement that the power of the USA was here to stay.

Looking at the next Eris transit, in 1783, Eris was square Saturn in the USA chart. One would think that a planet of discord squaring Saturn would mark a breakdown of discipline and a loss of control. It almost happened, when George Washington's troops nearly rebelled and marched against Congress. Fortunately, Washington was able to talk them out of it. Order was restored, and when the final peace was declared, he returned his commission to Congress, and then went home to Mount Vernon. So, it appeared that Eris square the USA Saturn did not have much of a discordant rule.

At that point, I decided to look at the year 1812, and found that transiting Eris was trine the USA Uranus. This seemed to fit, because the War of 1812 had

---

The astrological symbol for Eris, a Mars symbol pointing down (as shown), was devised by Henry Seltzer, adopted by Astro Computing Services, and by the companies that produce Solar Fire, Intrepid, and other astrological computer programs.

---

been called "The Second War of Independence." However, the aspect seemed to be unusual for astrological interpretation. Why should Eris in square and opposition not mark major discord, but Eris trine Uranus has a war break out? That was when it hit me regarding the nature of Eris. In Greek Mythology, Eris causes the greatest trouble when she pretends to be your friend. The best example would be the start of the Trojan War, which began when Eris presented her Golden Apple "for the fairest." '

I began running charts for major events in USA history, as well as charts for USA leaders. What I found was that the charts with the most discord had Eris in cooperative aspects to other planets (trine, sextile, semi-sextile.) The charts with the least discord had Eris in challenging aspects to other planets (opposition, quincunx, square). Conjunctions tended to turn thing topsy-turvy, but there could be a good outcome. The most amazing find was that George Washington had Eris exactly conjunct his Mars. This seemed appropriate when you considered the rag-tag army he had during the Revolutionary War, which was little better than an armed mob. Yet they managed to win the war.

On the positive side, challenging Eris aspects could signify motivational times, causing a person or a nation to take steps towards progress and self-improvement. For example, in 1898, transiting Eris was quincunx the USA Neptune, just in time for the Spanish-American War. It was a conflict that

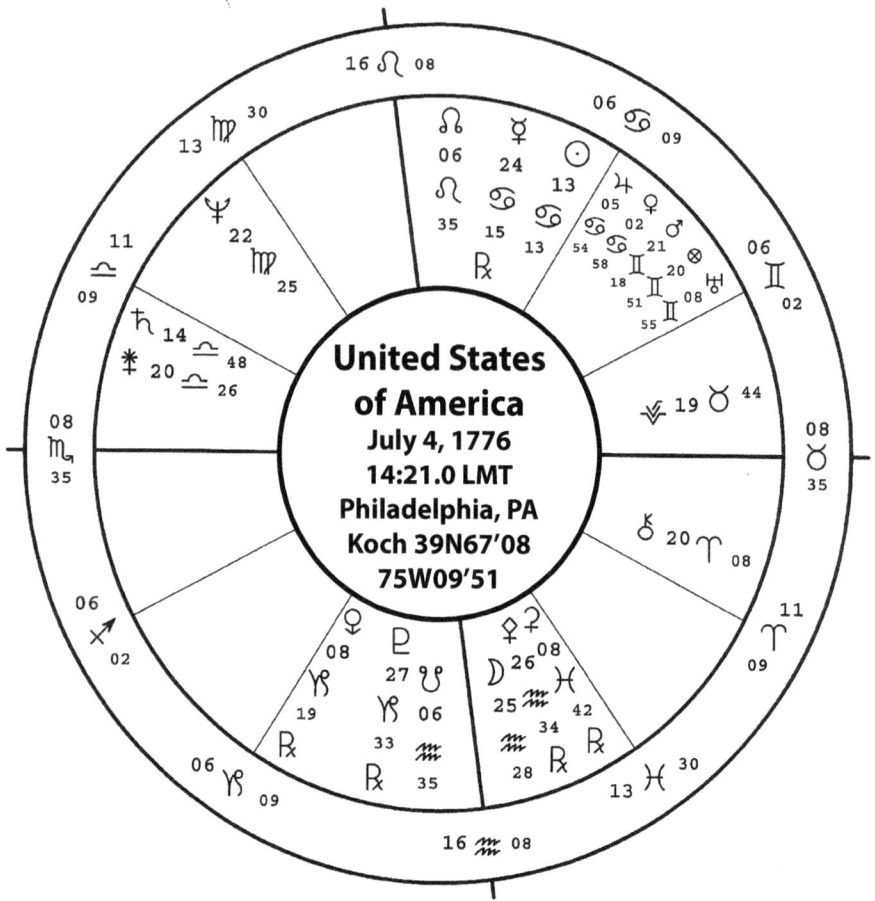

Chart: United States of America, July 4, 1776, 14:21.0 LMT, Philadelphia, PA, Koch 39N67'08 75W09'51

signaled the rise of the USA as an international power, utilizing the strength of a modern navy to establish new bases and commonwealths abroad. The war lasted only a few months and did not have the the carnage of the Civil War, which had taken place with transiting Eris conjunct the USA Ceres, sextile the USA Eris position and trine the Ascendant of the Wolfstar Scorpio Rising chart.

From all these charts, I wrote my first book, *Yankee Doodle Discord*, examining the charts from Independence to the third USA Uranus return. I began to see generational issues in the positions of Eris to the outer planets. One striking aspect was that Eris was trine Pluto during the years of World War II. This prompted me to study other angular connections between Eris and Pluto, and what I found was a strange dance of death, warfare and upheaval. Starting with Eris-Pluto positions in the 14th century, I found certain historical themes repeating themselves as the two dwarf planets were in aspect to each other:

Eris conjunct Pluto: Treachery. Misperception. Distortion. Covetousness. Victims of false propaganda. The collapse of international power.

Eris semi-sextile Pluto: A great battle that sets the tone for decades to come. A struggle which may be spurred on by events at this transit. A weakening of a great power.

Eris sextile Pluto: Mass destruction. Violent passions leading to a crusading spirit. A determination to win at any cost. Military victory on an epic scale, worthy of legends.

Eris square Pluto: events which seem to bring peace and reconciliation, but which serve for later, more violent encounters; a period of arms buildup, which can be manipulated by rulers; a delayed reaction; actions which show a lack of wisdom by leaders, best typified by saying, "It seemed like a good idea at the time."

Eris trine Pluto: The fall of empires and the rise of greater empires. New players upon the international scene. Impressive victories that change the balance of power.

Eris quincunx Pluto: Overwhelming victories brought about by underwhelming judgement. A David versus Goliath situation. Turning back the power of a superior nation by a smaller nation. An opponent who has been underestimated and misjudged.

Eris opposition Pluto: A confusing political and military situation, which could cause some people to scratch their heads in wonderment. An unstable and backbiting governing structure which can cause problems for years afterward. As Walt Kelly once wrote, "We have met the enemy and he is us."

As we travel through history for 800 years, we will see these scenes of murder and mayhem played out on battlefields and through political and military strategy. There have always been wars and battles between nations. However, the most worthy struggles seem to take place around the time of Eris-Pluto aspects. This is why the description of an interplanetary crime scene has been used to represent Eris-Pluto transits.

Where death and destruction appear, Eris and Pluto may be near.

NOTES:

In examining charts with Eris aspects, I use a four degree orb for natal or event charts, and a one degree orb for transits. This is because of the slow movement of Eris, and even a one degree aspect can last for a while in a transit. This is a matter of personal preference, and others may use whatever orbs they consider likely.

Regarding the ACS charts, all charts done for dates before the year 1500 are automatically set for the Julian calendar. All charts done for 1500 and after are set for the Gregorian calendar, though not every country used the Gregorian calendar until the 20th century.

All chart data with recorded birth times were from Astrodatabank at www.astro. com, a good resource for historical study.

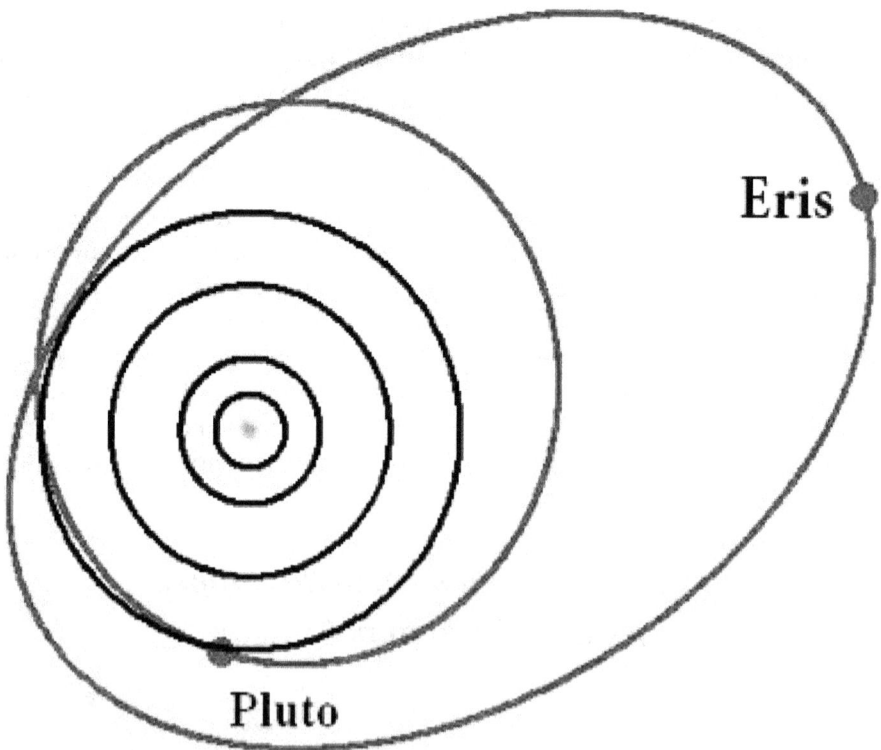

Bibliography - Chapter 1
Internet Sources

Discovery of Pluto
https://en.wikipedia.org/wiki/Pluto

Mythology of Pluto
https://en.wikipedia.org/wiki/Pluto_(mythology)

Kore/Persephone
https://en.wikipedia.org/wiki/Persephone#Abduction_myth

Discovery of Eris
https://en.wikipedia.org/wiki/Eris_(dwarf_planet)

Mythology of Eris
https://en.wikipedia.org/wiki/Eris_(mythology)

Legends of Eris
https://www.greeklegendsand myths.com/eris.html

Book Sources

George, Llewellyn, A to Z Horoscope Maker, St. Paul, MN, Llewellyn Publications, St. Paul, MN, 1972

Pottenger, Rique, *The New American Ephemeris for the 21st Century 2000-2100 at Midnight: Michelsen Memorial Edition*, Epping, NH, Starcrafts LLC, 2006

Murphy, Simonne, *Pluto in Signs, Houses, and Aspects*, ACS Publications, Epping, NH, 2015

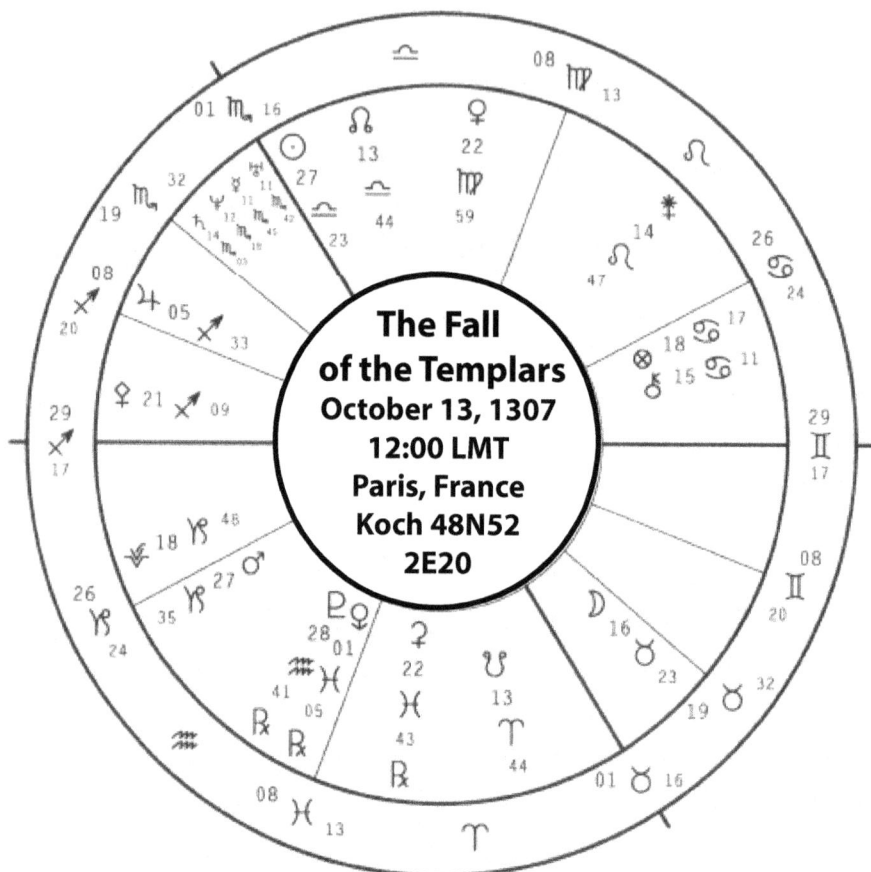

The Fall
of the Templars
October 13, 1307
12:00 LMT
Paris, France
Koch 48N52
2E20

For the benefit of those who may have a bit of difficulty in identifying the positions of the four tiny planet glyphs that you see in house 10, here they are, in order from the Midheaven:

♅	Uranus	11° ♏	Scorpio 42
☿	Mercury	11° ♏	Scorpio 45
♆	Neptune	17° ♏	Scorpio 18
♄	Saturn	14° ♏	Scorpio 21

Chapter 2
The Fall of the Templars
Eris conjunct Pluto

On October 13, 1307, Eris was at 1 Pisces 05, and Pluto was nearby at 28 Aquarius 41. Both dwarf planets were retrograde. Mars was semi-sextile in late Capricorn. The Sun in Libra was trine Pluto and forming an out-of-sign trine with Eris. It was on this day that the King of France was supposed to meet with leaders of the Knights Templars to discuss certain matters regarding the organization. It was a meeting that would not take place, because at dawn the soldiers of France began arresting Templars, and by the end of the day the majority of Templars were in prison. One historian has commented on the amazing efficiency of such a raid, in which there was no warning given to the Templars, and they were captured completely unaware.

Who were the Templars? Where did they go? If you believe the novelists and the conspiracy theorists, they were a secret society that managed to survive persecution and go underground for centuries. Some have speculated that the Templars reached America before Columbus, and that their treasure is hidden somewhere on the East Coast. Others have speculated that their "treasure" was really a great secret about the origins of Christianity, and that knowledge has remained hidden until modern times. Whatever happened to the Templars, there is a historical record explaining their origin.

Shortly after the First Crusade, thousands of pilgrims started to visit Jerusalem, which had been restored to Christian rule. Although the city was militarized, the outside lands had no protection. Groups of pilgrims were attacked by bandits on the roads of the Holy Land. A solution was offered in 1120, when a French knight named Hugues de Payens offered to start a monastic order that would give military protection to pilgrims. Nine knights joined Hugues de Payens in establishing this order. They were given headquarters in the location of the former Temple of Solomon, and were given the name "Templars" because of that location.

The Templars had to swear vows of poverty and chastity like other monks, but the main difference between them and other monastic orders was that they were allowed to go out into the world and fight. They wore distinctive uniforms with a large red cross on the front. The symbol for the Templars was two knights riding a horse, as if to accentuate poverty shared by the Templars. This impoverished condition was only going to last for a short time, because the Templars were about to achieve a degree of prosperity.

According to the conspiracy theorists, the Templars found a treasure and/or secret in Solomon's temple, and they were quick to share it with the Papacy. Pope Innocent II was very impressed with the Templars, and in 1139 he issued a Papal Bull, which established the Templars as an official order in the church. Through the intercession of prominent supporters, the Templars began receiving donations of land and money, along with new recruits who had no qualms about killing for the sake of the church. For an order devoted to poverty, the Templars amassed great wealth throughout Europe. Much of it came through the sale of holy relics brought from Jerusalem, since it was believed that the presence of relics touched by saints would bring protection from sin and evil.

Part of the success of the Templars came from an early attempt at international banking. If a pilgrim was traveling from London to Jerusalem, he could deposit a sum of gold at the Templar lodge in London, and then he would receive a letter of credit. The pilgrim could take the letter of credit to any other Templar house in Europe or the Middle East, and he would be able to draw out funds based on the letter of credit. It could also be suggested that the Templars were the first international hotel chain, since their lodges offered shelter to all those traveling to the Holy Land.

The order began to lose popularity after 1187, when Muslim forces conquered the Kingdom of Jerusalem. The Templars were not able to operate in the Middle East, though they still had extensive holdings throughout Europe. They did try to drum up support for later Crusades, but there was a bit of an attitude that the Templars did not do all that they should have done to protect Jerusalem. Another element of contention was that the Templars were performing secret rituals, and some people started to wonder what was going on in the Templar lodges.

The crisis started in the early 14th Century with King Philip IV of France, known as "Philip the Fair." (This superlative was based on his good looks, not his moral character.) At the start of the century, King Philip had been involved with a conflict against the Papacy. Pope Boniface VIII insisted that the Papacy had power over kings and political authority. King Phillip insisted that kings had a right to control church property. The conflict was unresolved by the sudden violent death of Boniface VIII, and the short Papacy of Pope Benedict XI.

King Philip's power expanded in 1305 when the Archbishop of Bordeaux, Raymond Bertrand de Got, was elected as Pope Clement V. This was the beginning of the "Babylonian exile of the Papacy," in which the French took control of the Roman Catholic bureaucracy, and Avignon replaced Rome as the center of the Church. Clement V rescinded most of the policies of Boniface VIII, and for much of his reign seemed to be a puppet of King Philip. This lack of separation between church and state would become evident during the trials of the Templars.

King Philip was the sort of monarch who was always in debt, and who was always seeking out ways to reduce that debt. In 1306, he ordered that all Jews had to leave France, and he was able to seize all land and property left behind. That still was not enough to pay off the money he owed, particularly the money he had owed to the Knights Templar. However, events were to take place which would enable King Philip to write off the owed money in a different way.

A former Templar had been making wild charges against the members of the order, claiming that the knights had spit on the cross, practiced sodomy, and worshipped an idol called Baphomet. The charges were brought before Clement V, who asked King Philip to conduct an investigation. This was the pretext King Phillip needed for breaking the order. The leaders of the Templars, including the Grand Master Jacques De Molay, were requested to visit Paris by Clement V. There was to be a discussion about merging the Templars with another monastic order, the Knights Hospitaller. Neither order was pleased with the idea of a merger, but they agreed to discuss the matter for the sake of the Pope. It was because of this meeting that Templar leaders were completely surprised and arrested on the morning of October 13, 1307.

The Burning of DeMolay

In a short time, every Templar in France was under arrest, and taken away to dungeons for torture, until a confession of heresy was given. There were Templars outside of France, but they were not arrested. However, since their leaders had been arrested, there was no organized defense for the Order For the next three years, the people of Paris were shocked by the confessions of the Templars, who confessed to any crime under torture. When the Templars came to trial, some of them tried to recant their testimony given under torture. Because of this attempt, they were denounced as "lapsed heretics" and burned at the stake,

Pope Clement V found himself in a difficult position, not wanting to be a puppet of the French King, but not wanting to defend the Templars.. He refused to accept the heresy convictions made against the Templars. According to a document released by the Vatican in 2001, Pope Clement V absolved the Templars of heresy in 1308, and ordered that all Templars convicted of heresy should be restored to the Sacraments. King Phillip did not pay attention to this command, and continued the trials of the Templars.

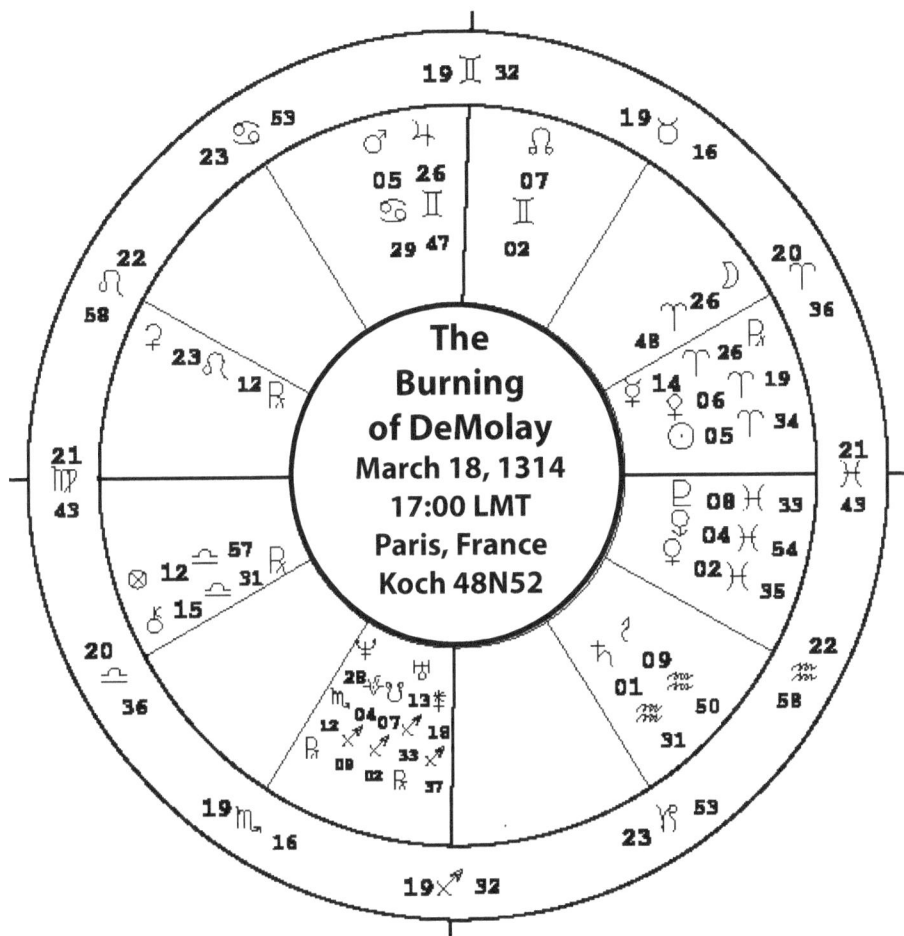

The Burning of DeMolay
March 18, 1314
17:00 LMT
Paris, France
Koch 48N52

In 1312, the Council of Vienne, declared that the Templar order was to be disbanded. The remaining Templars in Europe were given the chance to switch their allegiance to the Knights Hospitaller, and most of the property owned by the Templars was turned over to the Knights Hospitaller. In Portugal, the Templars changed their name to "Knights of Christ," and were able to maintain control of the Templar property, thanks to support by King Denis. Some Templars fled to Scotland or Switzerland, which did not follow Papal authority. The Scottish connection helped maintain the legend of the Templars, that they had gone underground as a secret society, only to appear 400 years later as Freemasons. (More on that, later!)

The climax of the Templar controversy came in 1314, with the burning of Grand Master Jacques De Molay. He had spent seven years in prison, being tortured and forced to sign confessions. When he dared to recant the confessions, he was declared to be a "lapsed heretic" and

21.

sentenced to be burned at the stake. According to legend, just before his death, he delivered a curse upon King Philip IV and Pope Clement V. The Pope died in April, 1314, and the King died in November, 1314, thereby cementing De Molay's reputation as a curser.

And what were Eris and Pluto doing during this time? From the arrests in 1307 to the death of De Molay in 1314, Eris and Pluto were conjunct in Pisces. It was after De Molay's death that they started to separate. King Philip was acting out the Eris role, inciting hatred against the Templars on religious grounds, though they had been a respected religious order for nearly 200 years. The King was also playing out the Pluto role, depriving the Templars of their wealth and power. Although the King tried to seize the Templar lands for the Crown, the Church awarded them to the Knights Hospitaller. However, the King was able to charge rent for the years when he had control of the lands.)

In the chart for the death (burning) of De Molay, Eris and Pluto are just less than four degrees apart, and they are both trine Mars. Pardon the pun, but it seemed that De Molay went out in a blaze of glory, becoming a martyr against royal and papal tyranny. The Sun and Pallas are square Mars. Perhaps cursing the king and pope was not the wisest act by De Molay, but it made his passing all the more memorable. Vesta and the South Node are square the Eris-Pluto conjunction.

Maybe the memory of De Molay's curse served as a deterrent to keep future kings from pillaging religious orders. Other kings did not attempt to acquire Templar property the way the late Phillip had done. Church and state relations remained stable until the coming of the Reformation. The sacking of English monasteries by King Henry VIII was directed at the Catholic Church as a whole rather than to a particular order, and as we will see in a later chapter, England experienced the upheavals of Eris as a result of that action. In the 18th century, the Jesuits were suppressed for a while, but they did not experience the martyrdom of the Templars.

Today, the official stance of the Roman Catholic Church is that the Knights Templar were not guilty of heresy, and the order was destroyed by the connivance of the King of France. It was a time of treachery and back-stabbing situations. Such betrayal would propel the Templar legacy into the realm of legend. Instead of being a simple land grab, greedy King Phillip created a mythology which persists to this day in tales of secret wealth and private gatherings. In another 450 years, France would pay dearly when Eris and Pluto joined again.

The years of the Eris-Pluto conjunction also marked the time when Dante Alighieri was writing his masterpiece, "The Comedy." (A later writer, Giovanni Boccaccio added the word "Divine" to the title.) Dante's epic poem is a description of the Christian afterlife, with graphic descriptions of Hell and Purgatory that would become fodder for future sermons. The work reveals a lot about Dante's prejudices, since the worst punishments of Hell are reserved for the politicians of Florence who exiled Dante, and the highest heavenly praise is reserved for Beatrice, a woman who is known only by the unrequited love that Dante had for her.

The numerological and allegorical elements of the poem would later inspire conspiracy novelist, Dan Brown, to write a gripping best seller, *Inferno,* just as the Templars had inspired him to write *The Da Vinci Code*. The Eris-Pluto conjunction may have inspired two of the most successful works in modern literature.

The Eris-Pluto conjunction also marked the timing of another literary legend who may or may not have existed. In the early 14th century, the Swiss canton of Uri began a resistance against control by the Austrians. A man named William Tell refused to bow before the hat of Austrian noble, Gessler. As punishment, William Tell was forced to shoot an apple off the head of his son. The deed was accomplished, and William Tell became a leader of the Swiss fight against the Austrians.

The earliest written account of William Tell did not appear until circa 1474, around the time of an Eris-Pluto quincunx, which usually marks the victory of an underdog against a stronger opponent. Afterwards it was spread and embellished by authors and song writers who were supporting freedom causes. No historical evidence proves the existence of William Tell, but it may be that the period of the Eris-Pluto conjunction contributed to more works of literature.

Another legend which is gathering publicity in modern times is that the fleeing Templars may have aided in the formation of Switzerland. During the early struggle for the Swiss Confederacy, there were stories of knights clad in white who rode into battle against the Austrians. There are suggestions that the Templar method of banking, as well as Templar symbols, were adopted by the Swiss. Of course, the Swiss Guards would later become the security force of the Vatican, to make sure that no king could dominate the Pope in the way that Philip the Fair had dominated Pope Clement V.

Bibliography - Chapter 2
Internet Sources

The Knights Templars

https://en.wikipedia.org/wiki/Knights_Templar

Jacques De Molay

https://en.wikipedia.org/wiki/Jacques_de_Molay

King Philip the Fair

https://en.wikipedia.org/wiki/Philip_IV_of_France

Pope Clement V

https://en.wikipedia.org/wiki/Pope_Clement_V

The DaVinci Code
  https://en.wikipedia.org/wiki/The_Da_Vinci_Code

The Knights Hospitaller
  https://en.wikipedia.org/wiki/Knights_Hospitaller

Baphomet
  https://en.wikipedia.org/wiki/Baphomet

King Denis of Portugal
  https://en.wikipedia.org/wiki/Denis_of_Portugal

Knights Templar in Scotland
  https://en.wikipedia.org/wiki/Knights_Templar_in_Scotland

Rosslyn Chapel
  https://en.wikipedia.org/wiki/Rosslyn_Chapel

Dante Alighieri
  https://en.wikipedia.org/wiki/Dante_Alighieri

The Divine Comedy
  https://en.wikipedia.org/wiki/Divine_Comedy

William Tell
  https://en.wikipedia.org/wiki/William_Tell

Templars and Switzerland
  http://blog.templarhistory.com/2010/03/did-the-templars-form-switzerland/

Book Sources

Barber, Malcolm, *The Trial of the Templars*, University Press, Cambridge, UK, 2000

Ridpath , John Clark. LL.D., *Cyclopedia of Universal History: Being an account of the Principal Events in the career of the Human Race from the beginning of Civilization to the Present Time. From Recent and Authentic Sources, Vol. II, Part I*, The Modern World, Cincinnati, Ohio, The Jones Publishing co, 1885

Simon, Edith, *Knights of the Maltese Cross*, Horizon, March 1961, American Horizon Inc., New York, NY, Pages 48 -71.

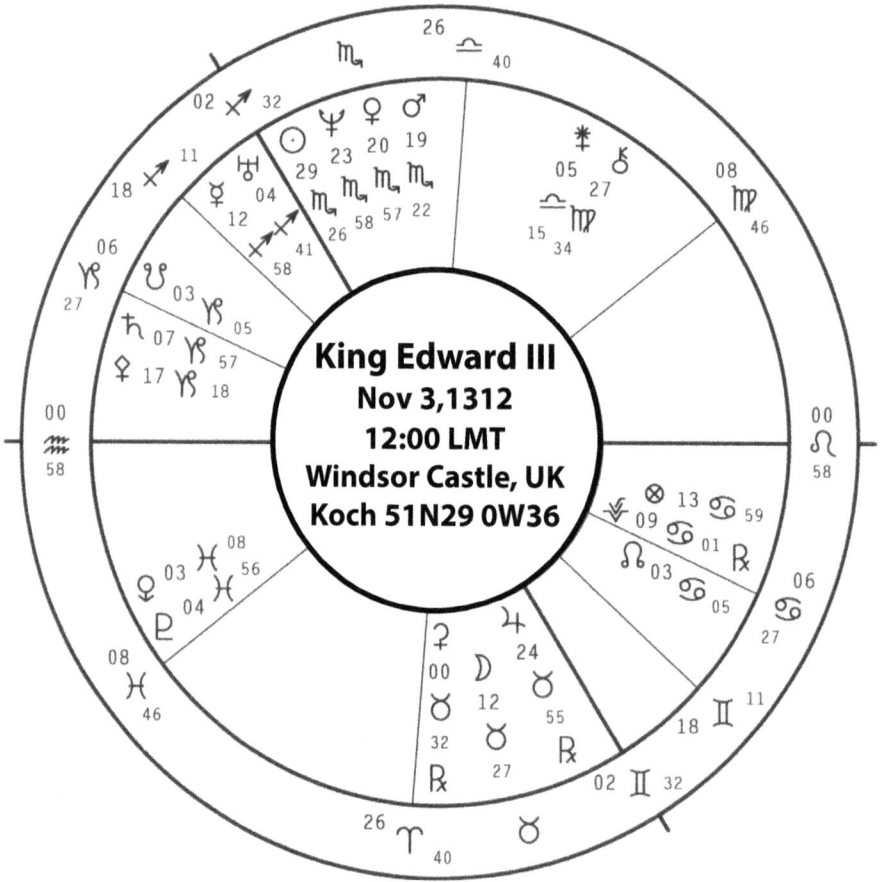

King Edward III
Nov 3, 1312
12:00 LMT
Windsor Castle, UK
Koch 51N29 0W36

Chapter 3

King Edward III and the Battle of Crecy (where warfare got messy.)
Eris semi-sextile Pluto

During the 13th Century, the English army was considered to be something of a joke. They were constantly being beaten by the Scots, under the leadership of William Wallace. (See the film "Braveheart" starring Mel Gibson.) The French were humiliating the English by conquering lands in France that the English King had titles to rule. In 1259, the English were forced to sign a demeaning treaty, which ceded all of the English claimed lands to the King of France. The English King was allowed to keep the Duchy of Aquitaine, but in doing so the English King had to declare himself a vassal of the King of France. It was a cruel wound to national pride, and it would make the English people eager for revenge.

Under the reigns of Edward I (who was portrayed as the evil "Longshanks" in Mel Gibson's movie) and the reign of Edward II (who was the subject of a play by Christopher Marlowe), it appears that not very much headway was made against France and the disrespect shown to the English. It was only with the coming of King Edward III that the tide changed in favor of the English. (Incidentally, Edward III was the English King supposedly spawned when William Wallace had a tryst with the French wife of Edward II. Unfortunately for Mel Gibson's history, Edward III was not born until seven years after William Wallace was executed by the English.)

Edward III was born during the Eris-Pluto conjunction in the early 14th Century. He represented the dynamic and powerful elements of Eris-Pluto. There was a certain amount of treachery when he came to the throne in 1327. His mother had instigated the overthrow of his father, who had turned out to be a pleasure-loving fool. Edward III was crowned at age 14, thanks to the help of his mother and her lover, Roger Mortimer, who became the real ruler. Three years later, Mortimer was deposed and executed by Edward III, who took complete command of his kingdom at age 17.

With Eris-Pluto squaring the Midheaven and Uranus, King Edward III was innovative and revolutionary in his planning. He began making improvements to the army, and within two decades the French would fear the English forces. Eris-Pluto were quincunx Juno, and King Edward III was fortunate in his marriage to Queen Philippa, fathering 14 children, nine of which lived to maturity. He did well in his alliances, making peace with Scotland so he could go after France. Eris-Pluto were also sextile Ceres, and for most of his reign the king was short of cash, and even heavy taxation could not help the financial burden caused by wars and the upkeep of the military.

In 1337, the King of France died without an established successor, and various candidates put their names in for the position. King Edward III recalled his own French heritage, and he submitted his name with the other claimants. The application of King Edward III was denied on the grounds of Salic law. This meant that succession could only come through male relatives, and Edward's attachments to the French court were on his mother's side. To add to the insult, the new King of France, Philip VI, seized the Duchy of Aquitaine. The response of Edward III was to bring his army to France and start a conflict which became known as "the Hundred Years War."

Technically, "The Hundred Years War" lasted 116 years from 1337 to 1453. There were several years of peace, particularly when the bubonic plague passed through the area. Nevertheless, historians decided that "The Hundred Years War" sounded better than "The Hundred and Sixteen Years War." So, they decided to round off the date, and kept the shorter title.

The lengthy war began in favor of the English. Rather than commit a large land army to the fight, the English King began sending in small groups. In effect, what Edward III was doing created the concept of the "commando raid." The English sent over small forces and landed them on the coast of France. These forces moved inland, and started pillaging

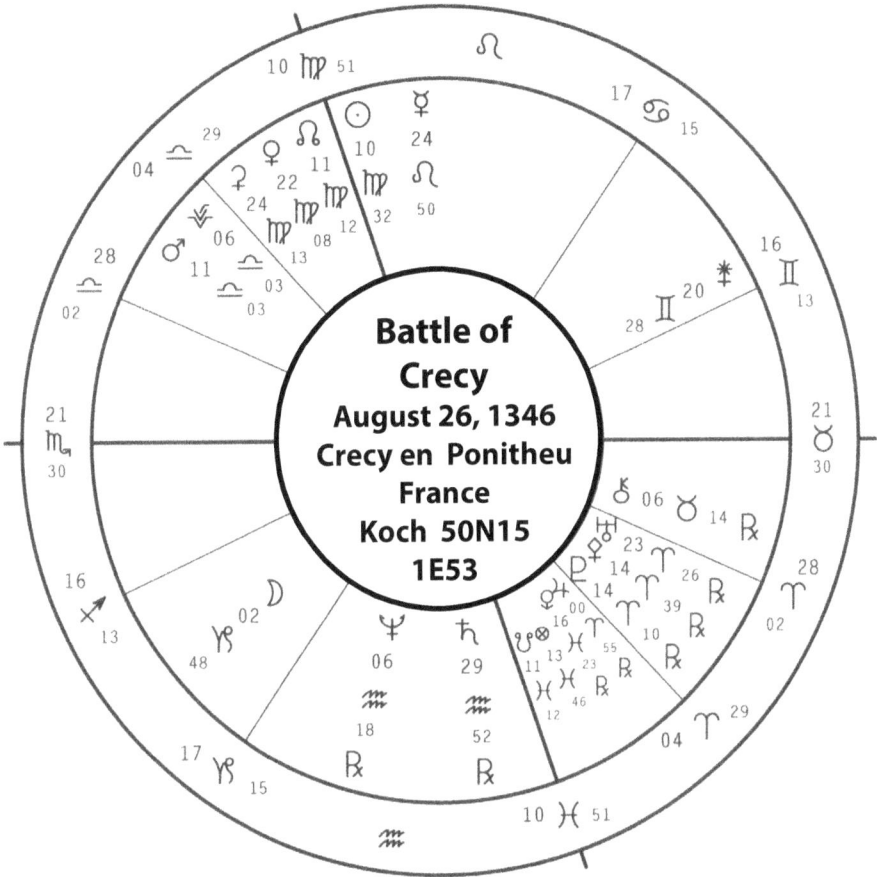

Battle of Crecy
August 26, 1346
Crecy en Ponitheu France
Koch 50N15 1E53

and burning any villages that were in their path. The English forces would go as far as the center of France and then turn around to march back to the coast. By the time that the French forces could be rallied, the English would be on the ships heading back to England.

In 1346, King Edward III personally commanded an attack upon France. However, by the time he was done pillaging, the French were able to rally their army. As the English forces were retreating to the sea, they were pursued by a French army which had twice as many men. Rather than take a chance of being trapped, King Edward III stopped in an area near the forest of Crecy to make a stand. He chose a large open area, which had hills on the sides to protect his flanks. In this way, he was able to use the topography for his advantage. There are questions about the sizes of the armies involved. Historians have estimated that the English army had 10,000-15,000 men, while the French had between 20,000-25,000 men. All accounts agreed that the English were outnumbered, and the French were overconfident in being able to beat them.

Yet, the French did not consider the calculations of King Edward III. By suddenly ending his retreat, the English King was able to give his troops a day of rest. In contrast, the French were hurrying to catch up to the English, and they charged into the battle straight from a long march. To complicate matters, the French had been marching in the rain, and many of their crossbows had wet strings. This meant it was very difficult to crank the bow strings so that they would be able to fire. The English had carefully protected the strings to their longbows, making sure they would be able to use them once the battle started.

To begin the battle, the French sent in mercenary troops, crossbowmen from Genoa. These bowmen tried to warn the French commanders that their weapons would not be effective because of the wet strings. Their complaints were met by curses and accusations of cowardice. The Genoese bowmen did attempt an attack but they could only fire about two bolts per minute. In contrast, the English bowmen, using the superior longbow, were able to fire six arrows per minute, and they had a greater range of 400 yards. The mercenary bowmen fell back to the French lines, where they were attacked by French troops for daring to retreat.

The French knights decided it was time for them to enter into the battle. In the past, armored cavalry had been a decisive factor in battles, and knights would spend most of their money in maintaining the best armor for man and horse. However, the French knights did not reckon with the fact that the English bowmen were using iron-tipped arrows. At close range, using the superior propulsion of the English longbows, these iron-tipped arrows were able to penetrate armor. Overconfident knights suddenly found themselves turned into metallic pin-cushions on the battlefield.

As if the iron-tipped arrows were not enough, the Battle of Crecy marked the first time that cannons were used on the battlefield. Cannons had been used by European armies as early as the 13th Century, but their main use had been for siege warfare, and battering down the walls of castles. At Crecy, King Edward III decided to turn the power of cannons on the French forces. Small iron balls were loaded into the cannons, and shot at the French army. Even if a French knight's shield and armor were able to block an iron-tipped arrow, they could not ward off iron balls flying at them.

It was estimated that about 4000 French knights were killed during the battle of Crecy. More than two thousand heraldic coats were taken off the field of battle. In contrast, the English lost about 300 knights. As for casualties for the lower classes, there was no final tally for either army, though most accounts agreed that the French had the worst of it. The French King, Philip VI, was wounded in the battle and forced to retreat. It was during the retreat that a number of the greatest French casualties took place.

In the chart for the battle of Crecy, Eris in Pisces is semi-sextile Pluto in Aries. Pluto is conjunct Pallas, asteroid of wisdom, and both are in opposition to Mars. This is appropriate because the battle of Crecy marked the death of conventional military wisdom. During the Middle Ages, knights were professional warriors (supposedly living by a chivalric code) who were much sought after by the nobility in times of war. Each knight would try to have the best armor, not just for protection, but as a mark of distinction to show who had the most wealth to buy the finest armor. Knights would be given the most glory for each victory, and those who survived battles would have the greatest reputations (and the greatest costs.)

Crecy changed the whole concept of military glory, because the armor worn by the knights was rendered useless by cannons and iron-tipped arrows. Courage and fortitude in knights were no longer helpful if the strongest warrior could be taken down by the weaponry of the weakest opponent. The glory of the battle went to the bowmen, who were of a lower social status than knights. As more cannons were developed, fewer knights appeared on the battlefield. Some armor would continue to be worn into the 17th Century, but it would often be seen as a relic of a by-gone day rather than a source of protection.

For England, Crecy was the first great victory of the Hundred Years War. However, King Edward III was not able to follow up on the victory because of circumstances unfolding in Europe. About the time of the battle of Crecy, the first wave of the bubonic plague was coming out of Central Asia and had arrived in the Crimea. By 1348, the plague had been carried to Italy via rats on the ships. By 1349, the plague had spread across France and England, causing a death toll that would wipe out more than half of the population of Europe.

During the years of the plague, Eris and Pluto were still semi-sextile each other, marking the pall of mass death which spread across the continent. The aspect did not start to separate until the mid-1350's. (Ironically, some 14th Century Astrologers attributed the Black Death to a conjunction of Mars, Jupiter, and Saturn in Aquarius, which took place in 1345.) It was in 1356, when Eris and Pluto were separating, that England scored the second great victory of the Hundred Years War, the battle of Poitiers. Glory for that battle went to the son of King Edward III, Edward the Black Prince (named because of his distinctive dark armor.) King John II of France was captured during that battle, leading to a substantial ransom to be paid for his release. The wealth obtained from this ransom would support the English treasury for the next 60 years.

King Edward III continued warfare against France until his death in 1377, after serving 50 years on the English throne. Unfortunately, Edward the Black Prince died shortly before King Edward III, and the throne went to the child king, Richard II. He is best remembered as the irresponsible king who started off William Shakespeare's cycle of history plays, which described English royal power through the 15th Century. The reign of King Richard II ended ignominiously in the Tower of London, at the time of the next Eris-Pluto aspect, when Eris in Aries was sextile Neptune and Pluto in Gemini.

Also during the Eris-Pluto semi-sextile, Giovanni Boccaccio (who was born under the Eris-Pluto conjunction) created his masterpiece work, "The Decameron." It is a collection of 100 short stories, told by a group of noble ladies and gentlemen, who have gone off to the countryside to escape the Black Death. As a contrast to the suffering of the times, most of the stories are quite erotic, and many show the foibles of the clergy. Because of the erotic nature, "The Decameron" was often banned over the centuries by over-eager censors.

Bibliography - Chapter 3
Internet Sources

King Edward III
   https://en.wikipedia.org/wiki/Edward_III_of_England
King Edward II
   https://en.wikipedia.org/wiki/Edward_II_of_England
King Edward I
   https://en.wikipedia.org/wiki/Edward_I_of_England
Braveheart
   https://en.wikipedia.org/wiki/Braveheart
Treaty of Paris 1259
   https://en.wikipedia.org/wiki/Treaty_of_Paris_(1259)

Roger Mortimer
 https://en.wikipedia.org/wiki/Roger_Mortimer,_1st_Earl_of_March

The Hundred Years War
 https://en.wikipedia.org/wiki/Hundred_Years%27_War

The Battle of Crecy
 https://en.wikipedia.org/wiki/Battle_of_Cr%C3%A9cy

Edward, the Black Prince
 https://en.wikipedia.org/wiki/Edward_the_Black_Prince

The Black Death
 https://en.wikipedia.org/wiki/Black_Death

Battle of Poitiers
 https://en.wikipedia.org/wiki/Battle_of_Poitiers

King Richard II
 https://en.wikipedia.org/wiki/Richard_II_of_England

The Decameron
 https://en.wikipedia.org/wiki/The_Decameron

Book Sources

Ridpath, John Clark, LL.D., *Cyclopedia of Universal History: Being an account of the Principal Events in the career of the Human Race from the Beginnings of Civilization to the Present Time. From Recent and Authentic Sources. Vol. II, Part I*, The Modern World. Cincinnati, OH, The Jones Brothers Publishing Co, 1885.

Robinson, Nugent, *History of the World with all its Great Sensations together with Mighty and Decisive Battles and the Rise and Fall of its Nations from the Earliest Times to the Present Day, Vol. I*, New York, NY, P.F.Collier, Publisher, 1891.

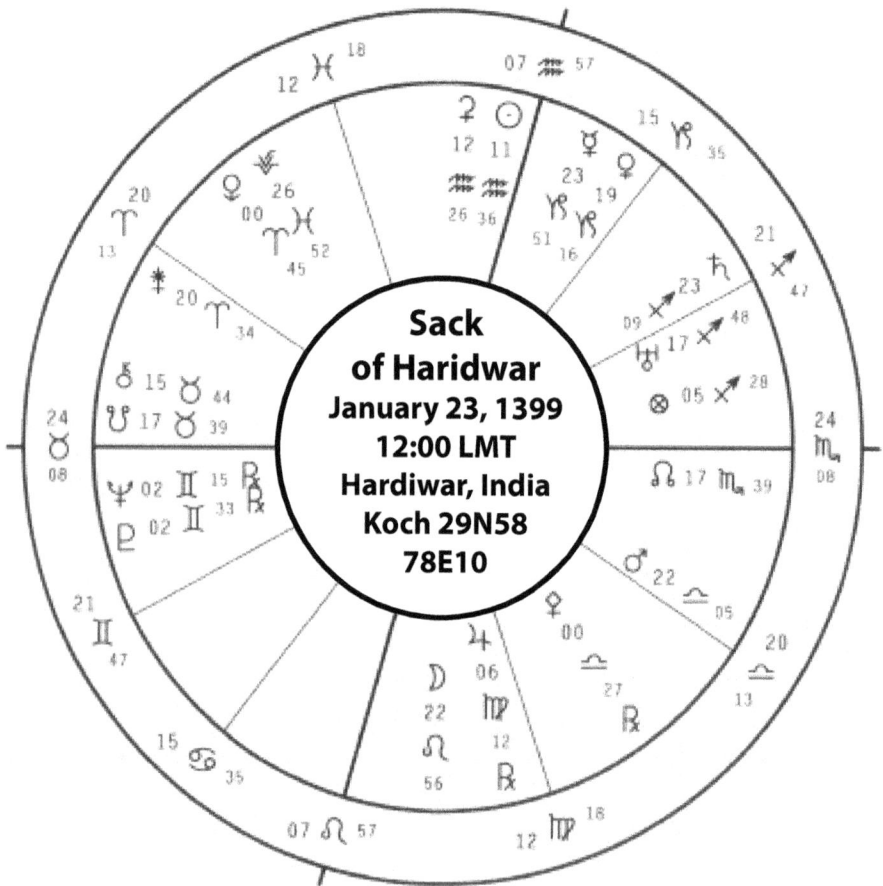

Sack
of Haridwar
January 23, 1399
12:00 LMT
Hardiwar, India
Koch 29N58
78E10

Chapter 4

The Battle of Delhi and the Sack of Haridwar
Eris sextile Pluto (1399)

If you were a ruler of a Central Asian kingdom at the end of the 14th century, and you were offered a choice of dealing either with the bubonic plague or an invasion by Tamerlane, chances are you would be better off dealing with the plague. Tamerlane was believed to be the first person in history responsible for the deaths of more than a million people during his lifetime, and some estimates claim that his decades of warfare may have killed up to 17 million people. Tamerlane combined the ruthless tactics of the Mongol horde with the violent passion of militant Islam. His army had a combination of blood lust and spiritual fervor, which became very difficult for non-believers.

From 1370 to his death in 1405, Tamerlane was the leader of the powerful army that swept across Central Asia. By 1380, he had defeated the Persian Empire, and if any Persian town dared to defy his will, he would massacre the population and leave a pyramid of skulls stacked outside of the city gates. His conquests took him through what we today call "the Stan nations", like Kazakhstan, Afghanistan, and Pakistan. His most vicious conquests came at the turn of the century, just as Eris in Aries was sextile Neptune and Pluto in Gemini.

In 1398, Tamerlane began an invasion of India. His primary goal was Delhi, which was ruled over by the tolerant Sultan of Delhi. Although the Sultan was a Muslim, he did not persecute the Hindu population. Tamerlane considered this to be an affront to Allah, and declared that the Sultan was not a real Muslim because he tolerated non-believers. With Pluto and Neptune conjunct, the blood lust may have been enhanced by religious fervor, and the sextile to Eris could have indicated the desire to set things right by warfare.

In December, 1398, the Sultan of Delhi assembled his army, and put his war elephants on the front lines. Wearing armor and having their tusks covered with points, the war elephants seemed to be an intimidating weapon, almost like the modern tank. However, Tamerlane was well aware that the elephants were just dumb animals, and could easily be frightened away. With that in mind, he ordered his men to dig a series of trenches around Delhi.

On December 18, 1398, Tamerlane ordered camels to be brought into the trenches. The camels were loaded with bales of hay and logs of firewood, which were strapped to their humps. When the war elephants of the Indian army were approaching the battlefield, Tamerlane ordered the bales of hay lighted by torches. The camels went running out of the trenches, screaming at a high pitch as bonfires erupted on their backs. The sights and sounds of the flaming camels were too shocking for the war elephants. They immediately turned to retreat, and ended up running over the troops of the Indian army.

Once Tamerlane had defeated the Indian army, his march into Delhi was not completely smooth. The residents of the city rose up and opposed the invaders. Tamerlane ordered the deaths of all those who resisted him and the streets of Delhi were soon littered with the bodies of 100,000 victims. It would take a century before the population of the city was able to return to its pre-Tamerlane level.

With Delhi defeated, Tamerlane marched on the holy city of Haridwar. This time 60,000 victims fell beneath the swords of his soldiers. The bodies were dumped into the Ganges River, and it was said that the holy river was the color of blood for months. Tamerlane ordered his men to pillage the city, and in particular they were to cut out the semi-precious stones that adorned the buildings. Tamerlane had the stones sent to his capital city of Samarkand as part of his spoils of war, and it took more than 100 elephants to carry the booty.

In the chart for the Sack of Haridwar, Eris has just entered Aries, and is in opposition to Pallas, asteroid of wisdom and military planning. The battles in India showed Tamerlane's skill as a tactician and in using unusual weapons. Pallas is also trine the Neptune-Pluto conjunction, again affirming the talent for mass destruction. The Neptune-Pluto conjunction takes place every 490 years, and the next conjunction in Gemini was to be in the 1890's. That conjunction marked the generation that saw the horrors of World War I, and those who survived that event would be even more horrified by World War II. On the positive side, it has been pointed out that Neptune-Pluto may have marked the beginning of the Renaissance in the 15th century, and the conjunction in the 1890's may have marked the advancement of the scientific age leading to greater discoveries by the 20th century, with such geniuses as Tesla, Marconi, Edison, and the Curies.

In 1401, while Eris and Pluto were still sextile, Tamerlane attacked Baghdad, and this time 20,000 victims fell beneath his swords. Tamerlane

Tamerlane

set quotas for his men, insisting that each soldier should bring back two severed heads as part of their conquest. From Baghdad, Tamerlane moved into the Turkish Empire, and his presence was so terrifying, the Turkish army sent requests for help to their enemies, the Venetians and Genoese. The Turks needed ships to evacuate their armies, and the Italian City states heard their call and dispatched the ships. Although some Europeans applauded Tamerlane for attacking the Turks, others realized that Europe could become his next victim.

Fortunately for Europe, Tamerlane turned his attention to attacking China. Early in 1405, he marched his army out of Samarkand, right into the blasts of a bitter cold winter. Although Tamerlane could conquer other armies, he could not conquer the weather. Many of his soldiers and horses ended up freezing to death. Tamerlane was able to make it back to Samarkand, but the experience undermined his health and he perished on Feb. 18, 1405.

There is some indication that the destructive power of Tamerlane may have continued after his death. In 1941, a Soviet archeologist named Mikhail Gerasimov was given permission to exhume the body of Tamerlane to study it. There was an inscription on Tamerlane's tomb that read, "When I rise from the dead, the world shall tremble." The tomb was opened on June 22, 1941, the same day that Germany started Operation Barbarossa, the invasion of Russia. Gerasimov was allowed to finish the study of Tamerlane's body, and then the body was reburied with an Islamic funeral in November, 1941, just before the Soviet victories began.

The Eris-Pluto sextile also marked the passing of the English author, Geoffrey Chaucer, who is best remembered for his "Canterbury Tales," written in vernacular style, as had been the works of Dante and Boccaccio. Like "The Decameron," Chaucer's work is a collection of stories, told by pilgrims on their way to Canterbury cathedral. Also like "The Decameron," some of the stories are bawdy and erotic, which have caused them to be banned by censors over the centuries.

The circumstances of Chaucer's death are surrounded in mystery. He was a supporter of King Richard II, and may have been regarded as an enemy by the usurping King Henry IV. The last official record of Chaucer was on June 5, 1400, when money owed to him was paid. The engraving on his tomb, erected more than a century later, marks his death as October 25, 1400, but no cause of death is given, leading some to suspect a political conspiracy.

Bibliography - Chapter 4

Internet Sources

Tamerlane
https://en.wikipedia.org/wiki/Timur

The attack on Delhi
http://www.ibiblio.org/britishraj/Jackson5/chapter09.html

Tamerlane the Scourge
http://militaryanalysis.blogspot.com/2013/04/tamerlane.html

Tamerlane: Mass Murderer or Patron of the Arts
http://ancientstandard.com/2011/01/24/timur-mass-murderer-or-patron-of-the-arts/

Mongol Conquests
http://war-history.blogspot.com/2008/12/mongol-conquests.html

Tamerlane conquest of Delhi and Haridwar
http://hinduism-proudtobeapartofvedicculture.blogspot.com/2012/06/timur.html

Geoffrey Chaucer
https://en.wikipedia.org/wiki/Geoffrey_Chaucer

Book Source

Robinson, Nugent, *History of the World with all its Great Sensations together with Mighty and Decisive Battles and the Rise and Fall of its Nations from the Earliest Times to the Present Day, Vol. I*, New York, NY, P.F.Collier, Publisher, 1891.

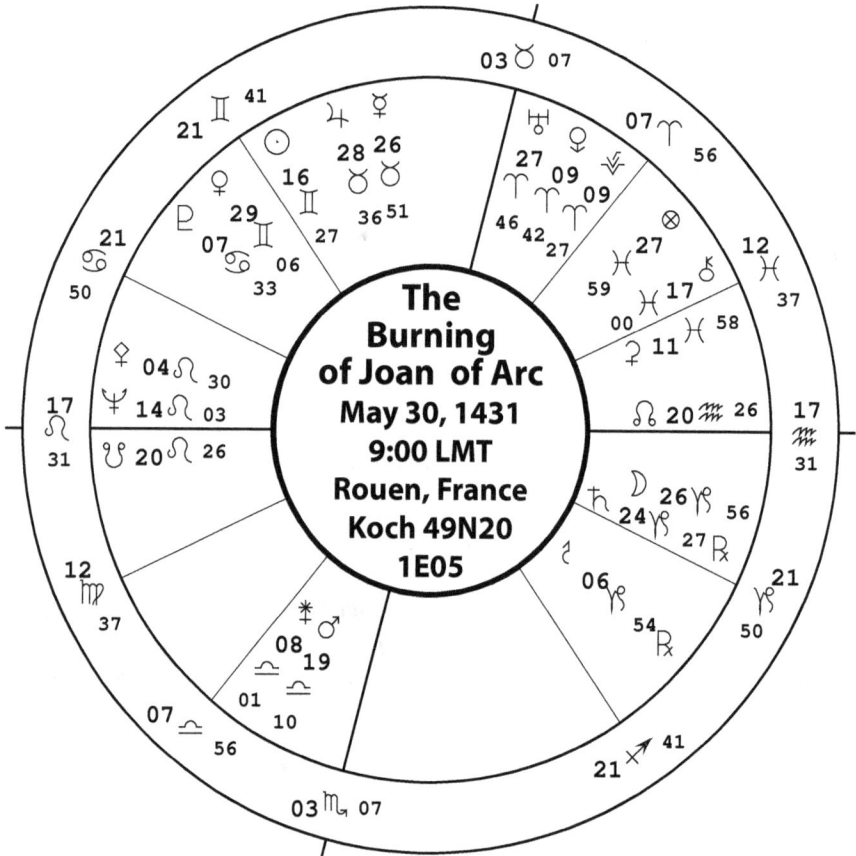

The
Burning
of Joan of Arc
May 30, 1431
9:00 LMT
Rouen, France
Koch 49N20
1E05

40. *Brother Pluto, Sister Eris*

Chapter 5

The Burning of Joan of Arc
Eris square Pluto

In 1429, the Hundred Years War was in its 92nd year, and France was experiencing its worst beating. The English had formed an alliance with the Duke of Burgundy, and were conquering large areas of France. The reigning monarch, King Charles VII, was a young man, and the leadership of the nation came from nobles, who had conflicting agendas. The English and Burgundians were laying siege to the city of Orleans, the location of which was pivotal for the conquest of the rest of France. It appeared that France was helpless and doomed to defeat, when a young woman showed up at the royal court, claiming that she had spoken with Saint Michael, Saint Margaret, and Saint Catherine about driving the English out of France.

King Charles VII was skeptical of this young woman, and he decided to test her. An impostor was placed on the throne while the King dressed as a courtier and joined the crowd in the throne room. When the maid Joan entered the throne room, she ignored the figure on the throne, and went straight to the real king and kneeled before him. This impressed King Charles VII so that he was willing to have a private conversation with Joan. He later admitted that she told him things that he had wished for in silent prayers. This convinced him that she did have a divine power behind her, and he was willing to go along with her requests.

Joan was given a suit of armor, and sent with the army to relieve the siege of Orleans. The commanders of the army did not think much of her visions, but they did listen to her at their war councils. There is some debate to this day about how much fighting she actually did. Most accounts claim that she appeared on the front lines, and was slightly wounded in the neck by an arrow. Her presence at the battle may have been a positive psychological inspiration for the French troops. (One could almost hear the French sergeants haranguing their troops, "You sissies! Are you going to let a little girl do all the fighting for you?")

Once the English retreated from Orleans, Joan was recognized as a national heroine. With the thought that God was on the side of France, the war against the English changed from political struggle to religious crusade. The influence of Joan was increased when she organized a military plan to recapture the city of Reims, the historical site of coronations for French kings. Although Charles VII was the rightful king, he was referred to as the "Dauphin" (French term for "Crown Prince") until he had been crowned at Reims. Joan and her forces were able to capture Reims on July 16, 1429, and the coronation was held the next day.

In September, 1429, Joan took part in an attack to recapture Paris, but the effort was unsuccessful, and Joan was wounded in the leg by a crossbow bolt. She was rescued by one of her commanders, and the French army withdrew from the attack. In October, she was with the army when they were able to capture Saint-Pierre-le-Moutier. However, in November and December, she and the army were unable to capture La-Charite-sur-Loire. In spite of this failure, King Charles VII rewarded Joan by conferring titles of nobility on her family.

Early in 1430, there was a truce with the English, and Joan was left with nothing to do. The truce ended in May, and Joan took part in the battle for Compiegne. On May 23, 1430, Joan was with a rear guard when there was a sudden attack by Burgundians. Joan was pulled from her horse and taken prisoner by the Burgundians. She was imprisoned in Beaurevoir Castle, from which she made a few escape attempts, one time leaping 70 feet from her tower, and landing in a soft, marshy moat. The English finally gained custody of her by paying the Duke of Burgundy 10, 000 livres, and the English quickly moved Joan to the city of Rouen.

Because Joan had used religious language to describe her mission, the English were eager to ruin her spiritual reputation by trying her as a witch and a heretic. The record of her trial still exists, and her responses to the court showed her to be a quick witted and intelligent young woman. The English had packed the court with English clergy, and would not listen to any French clergy who spoke on her behalf. There were efforts to refer the case to the Pope, but the English were not going to allow that to happen. There were also plans to attack Rouen in an attempt to rescue Joan, but those were beaten back by the English forces.

In the end, Joan was found not guilty of witchcraft, but convicted of being a "lapsed heretic." One of the charges against her was that she was guilty of wearing men's clothing, and upon her capture she was given women's clothing. During the trial, she stopped wearing the women's clothing and dressed as a man again. There are conflicting reasons given

for her dressing that way. One reason was that wearing men's clothing helped deter sexual assaults by men in the prison. Another reason given was that someone had stolen her women's clothing, and left the men's clothing in its place, leaving her no choice but to dress as a man.

For the court, it was the excuse needed to sentence her to death. The burning of Joan of Arc was on May 30, 1431. Actually, she had three burnings. The first burning killed her with heat and asphyxiation, leaving her charred body behind. The second burning removed her flesh and left the skeleton behind. The third burning reduced her skeleton to ashes, which were thrown into the river so that no relic would remain behind for her followers.

In the chart for the burning day, Eris in Aries is square Pluto in Cancer. There is a Grand Trine in Air with the Sun, Mars, and the North Node. This was a fiery event that would be talked about for ages, especially for its religious message. Uranus in Aries is square Saturn and the Moon in Capricorn. It was a revolutionary event, which appeared to signal victory for those in authority, but would mark the breaking of their power. Uranus was also sextile Venus, and the spirit of Joan would rise from the flames like a Phoenix to become a saintly figure.

Eris is also conjunct Vesta, the asteroid of hearth and home. Eris and Vesta are opposing Juno, the asteroid of marriage and social connections. Although she seemed abandoned by her family and friends, by her death, Joan was able to make more converts to her cause than ever before. Part of it may have been due to the shock and horror over the way the English treated a young French girl. The cruelty and unfairness of Joan's trial may have washed away apathy from the French public. There may have been a realization that if the English could do such a thing to one young woman, what would keep them from performing other outrages against other French women? People rallied to fight for hearth and home. King Charles VII was seen as a dynamic leader, using the example of Joan and uniting the nation behind his war efforts.

The English had hoped that the death of Joan would have broken the will of the French to resist. However, they totally misjudged the situation and found that the martyrdom of Joan brought about a strengthening of the national will. Instead of lighting Joan's funeral pyre, they had lit a fuse that would cause explosions in years to come.

By 1453, the French had rallied and kicked the English out of most of France, culminating with the Battle of Castillon in Gascony. Supposedly, news of this defeat drove the English king, Henry VI, into madness. This

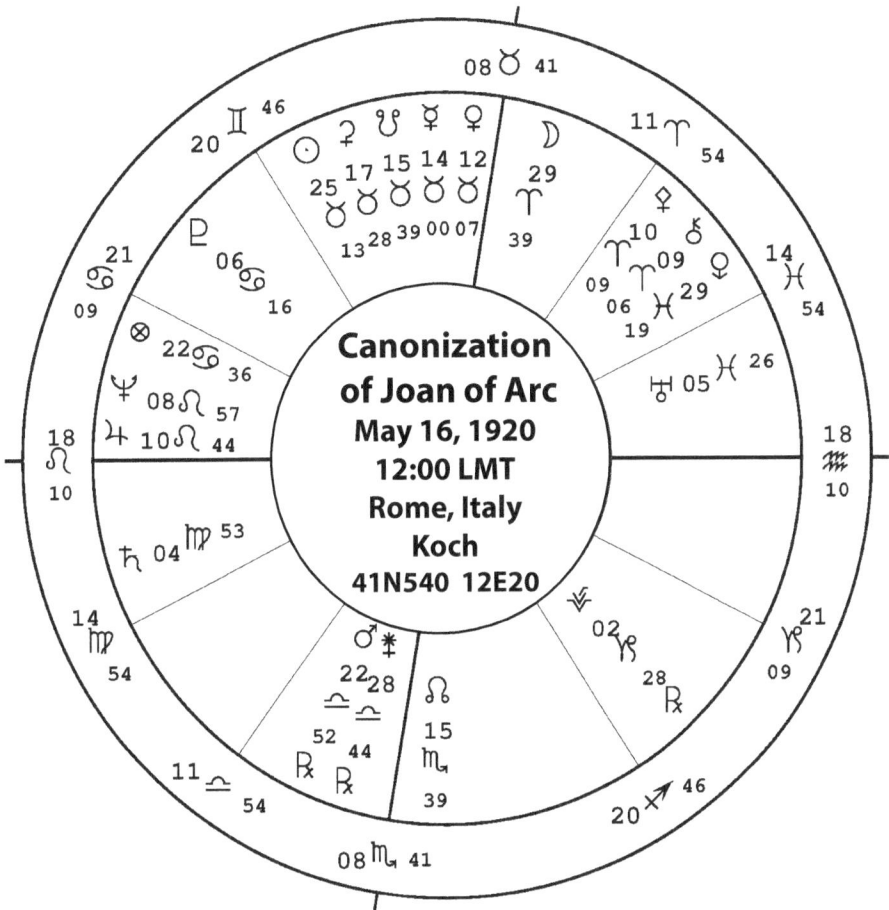

Canonization
of Joan of Arc
May 16, 1920
12:00 LMT
Rome, Italy
Koch
41N540 12E20

created a power vacuum, which the family of York tried to fill with the War of the Roses. This civil war prevented the English from fighting in France. After 116 years of fighting, the Hundred Years War finally came to an end.

By the 1450's, French nobles felt emboldened enough to ask for a reversal of Joan's conviction. Spurred on by Joan's family and French clergy, a retrial was held in Rome, and it was obvious that the English had manipulated the original trial to get a conviction. Pope Calixtus III reversed the findings of the court, allowing the memory of Joan to be promoted as a national heroine. On May 16, 1920, after years of campaigning by French nationalists, Joan was made an official saint of the Roman Catholic Church.

In a comparison between the chart of the burning and the canonization of Joan, there are some interesting Eris connections. On the day Joan became a saint, Jupiter and Neptune were conjunct in Leo. This conjunction was trine the Eris-Vesta conjunction in the chart for the martyrdom of Joan. For the first time, organized religion (represented by Jupiter-Neptune) had recognized the importance of a militant woman. Eris in the canonization chart is square the Venus of the burning chart, indicating a powerful female role model. Eris in the canonization chart is also sextile Jupiter in the burning chart, and may have marked a slap across the ages at the 15th century church that would be used for political purposes.

Pluto in the canonization chart is approaching a Pluto return to the position in the burning chart. It took two Pluto cycles, but Joan finally had the last laugh, with millions of Catholics offering prayers to her instead of cursing her. Once again, Pluto was square Eris in the burning chart, as well as trine Uranus in the canonization chart. Joan's fame as a saint may have been aided by mass media, with stage, movies and later television spreading her story around the world. However, with Pluto squaring Chiron and Pallas in the canonization chart, there may have been a darker motive for her saintly status for the French, adding to the militarism between the world wars. Since France was recovering from World War One, Chiron conjunct Pallas might have brought a healing to the national psyche. However, the Pluto square may have added an unhealthy desire for power. Would Joan have gone on to greater conquests if she had not been burned by English manipulation of the courts?

For centuries, the English maintained an attitude that Joan was a witch and had only succeeded because of her summoning of diabolical forces. This image is best displayed in Shakespeare's play King Henry VI, Part I, in which the demonic influence of "La Pucelle" is seen as responsible for England's decline. Rather than give Joan a dignified death scene, Shakespeare depicts her as a liar and a dissembler, with her claiming htat she is of royal blood, even though her own father contradicts this to her face. Shakespeare also makes her say she is a virgin, but when that plea does not prevent her executions, she pleads her belly, claiming she is pregnant by the King and various other nobles in a vain attempt to avoid the stake. Shakespear's play is a crude propaganda piece, which flies in the face of the images we have today of the stoical Joan resolved to experience her fate. This may be the reason why King Henry VI , Part I, is rarely performed in modern times.

The Eris-Pluto square also marked the births of two notorious figures who would play sinister roles later in the 15th century. First was the birth of Pope Alexander VI, the famous Borgia Pope, who spawned Cesare and Lucretia Borgia, and became legendary for his voluptuary excesses. Second was the birth of Vlad III of Wallachia, aka Vlad Tepes, aka Vlad the Impaler, and ultimately known as Count Dracula. Unfortunately, no set birth data is available for Vlad. The only references say he was born in November or December of 1431.

Bibliography - Chapter 5
Internet Sources

Joan of Arc

https://en.wikipedia.org/wiki/Joan_of_Arc

Siege of Orleans

https://en.wikipedia.org/wiki/Siege_of_Orl%C3%A9ans

King Charles VII

https://en.wikipedia.org/wiki/Charles_VII_of_France

The Trial of Joan of Arc

https://en.wikipedia.org/wiki/Trial_of_Joan_of_Arc

Retrial of Joan of Arc

https://*en.wikipedia.org/wiki/Retrial_of_Joan_of_Arc*

The Battle of Castillon

https://en.wikipedia.org/wiki/Battle_of_Castillon

Shakespeare's Play: "King Henry VI: Part One"

https://en.wikipedia.org/wiki/Henry_VI,_Part_1

Book Sources

Ridpath, John Clark, LL.D., *Cyclopedia of Universal History: Being an account of the Principal Events in the career of the Human Race from the Beginnings of Civilization to the Present Time. From Recent and Authentic Sources. Vol. II, Part I, The Modern World.* Cincinnati, OH, The Jones Brothers Publishing Co, 1885.

Robinson, Nugent, *History of the World with all its Great Sensations together with Mighty and Decisive Battles and the Rise and Fall of its Nations from the Earliest Times to the Present Day, Vol. I,* New York, NY, P.F.Collier, Publisher, 1891.

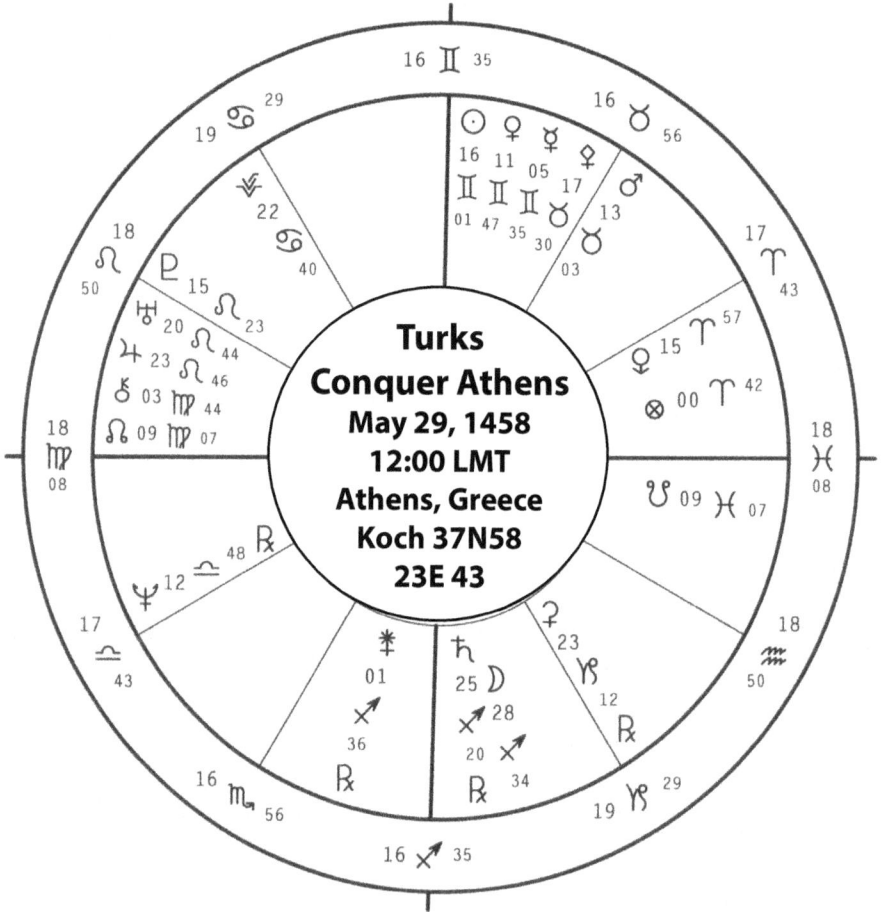

16 ♊ 35

19 ♋ 29

16 ♉ 56

☉ ♀ ☿ ♂ ♃
16 11 05 17
♊ ♊ ♊ ♉
01 47 35 30

♂ 13
♉ 03

♆ 22

♋ 40

18 ♉ 50

♇ 15 ♌

17 ♈ 43

♅ 20 ♌ 23
♃ 23 ♌ 44
♂ 03 ♍ 46
♌ 09 ♍ 44
♍ 07

**Turks
Conquer Athens**
May 29, 1458
12:00 LMT
Athens, Greece
Koch 37N58
23E 43

♀ 15 ♈ 57

⊗ 00 ♈ 42

18 ♍ 08

18 ♓ 08

☊ 09 ♓ 07

♆ 12 ♎ 48 ℞

17 ♎ 43

✶ 01 ♐ 36

♄ 25 ♐ 28 ♐ 20 ℞ 34

� 23 ♑
♑ 12 ℞

18 ♒ 50

16 ♏ 56

℞

☽ ♐

19 ♑ 29

16 ♐ 35

Chapter 6

The Turks Conquer Athens
Eris trine Pluto

In 1453, as the last English forces were being kicked out of France, the attention of Europe was distracted by an event taking place in the East. The great city of Constantinople, the last remnant of the Roman Empire, had been conquered by the Turks. Although the city was surrounded by gigantic walls, the Turks were determined to fulfill a promise made by the Prophet Muhammed that someday the city of Constantinople would fall to the Muslim world. The Turkish leader, Mehmed II, fulfilled that promise, and was rewarded with the title "Mehmed the Conqueror."

With a sobriquet like that, Mehmed was not one to sit around on his laurels, and he planned further military actions into Europe. Mehmed was very diplomatic when it served his purposes. After the fall of Constantinople, he spared the residents and allowed them to keep their property. He would show equal magnanimity when moving in to take other lands. In the mid-1450's, the Turkish army moved into Greece, and by 1458 they had captured the city of Athens.

At the time, Athens was a backwater town, not providing much in the way of commercial value. However, the symbolic value of the city was important due to the studies of ancient classics which were taking place during this period that is referred to as the Renaissance. Athens had been hailed as the cradle of Western Civilization and a major center of learning, even during the Roman Empire. During the Middle Ages, Athens had been taken by the Byzantines, the Franks, and the Venetians, until the Turks moved in for a 360 year occupation.

Regarding the chart for the conquest of Athens, understand that it is only a speculative date, based on the fifth anniversary of the fall of Constantinople. Oddly enough, one answer that cannot be found on Google is for the question, "what date did the Turks conquer Athens?" All that can be found is that the Turks conquered Athens sometime in the year 1458. There is no indication as to the month or the season. So, this speculative chart, set for about the middle of the year, is enough to show the Eris-Pluto trine taking place as the Turkish Empire expanded. This chart also shows Neptune in opposition to Eris, which is fitting because the religious factor did not cause much discord during this conquest.

When Mehmed the Conqueror entered Athens, he was amazed by the loveliness of the ancient architecture. He decided to protect the heritage of Athens, and he gave an order that the ancient buildings were not to be harmed. The famed Parthenon was made into a mosque. It had already been a church under the Byzantines after being a temple of Athena for more than 800 years. The religious rights of the Athenians were respected, and followers of the Orthodox Church were allowed to set up new monasteries. Athenians were allowed to keep their own judges, called "demogerontes", who mainly adjudicated cases between Christians. Larger cases involving the city laws were handled by a Muslim judge.

After the fall of Athens, the loudest protests in Europe came from the Greek scholars teaching at the universities. Perhaps the loudest protest came from an unlikely churchman (and writer of erotic verse) named Aeneas Silvius Piccolomini. In the summer of 1458, he was elevated to the Papacy as Pope Pius II. Once crowned, he began advocating a new crusade against the Muslims. This plan did not unify the major powers of Europe as in previous crusades. Most European powers were at odds with each other, and did not follow the Pope's plans for reconciliation. In particular, the Venetians had signed a trade treaty with the Turks, and were not too eager to have their finances upset.

In 1459, Pope Pius II called the Council of Mantua, asking for representatives of the different nations to meet so they could organize a crusade. In spite of all arguments, only one leader wanted to go to war against the Turks. This was Vlad III of Wallachia, also known as Vlad Tepes, also known as Vlad the Impaler, and ultimately known as Count Dracula. Mehmet the Conqueror had threatened to march against Vlad because he had not been paying tribute to the Turks. Without the support of other nations, Vlad had to deal with the Turks in his own repulsive way.

By the 1460's, Pope Pius II managed to convince the Venetians into going to war against the Turks. However, his health started to fail, and by 1464 he was dying. His final act was to visit the crusader army at Ancona in order to raise morale. However, even the presence of the Pope was not enough to inspire the crusader soldiers. Many of them got tired of waiting for the Venetian fleet to show up, and they deserted. Two days before his death, Pope Pius II was able to see the Venetian fleet on the horizon, and he died with the expectation that the crusade would go forward. Unfortunately, the Venetian attack against the Turks was ineffectual, and there were no more calls for a crusade.

The Eris-Pluto trine marked the beginning of European conquests by the Turks. For the next two decades, they would make advances into the Balkans, opposed only by minor nobles like Vlad Tepes. As for the people of Athens, the first years of their occupation were pleasant, but by the 16th century the circumstances changed. The Turks began referring to the Athenians as "rayah", which means "slaves." The young people were subjected to the "paedomazoma", which was a general round-up of children so that the boys could be trained for the Turkish army, and the girls could be sent to the Sultan's harem. It was not until the 19th century that the birthplace of democracy rose up against slavery to form the nation of Greece

Mehmed the Conquerer

Bibliography - Chapter 6
Internet Sources

Greece under the Ottomans
http://www.ahistoryofgreece.com/turkish.htm

Ottoman Greece
https://en.wikipedia.org/wiki/Ottoman_Greece

History of Athens
https://en.wikipedia.org/wiki/History_of_Athens

Mehmed the Conqueror
https://en.wikipedia.org/wiki/Mehmed_the_Conqueror

Pope Pius II
https://en.wikipedia.org/wiki/Pope_Pius_II

Vlad the Impaler
https://en.wikipedia.org/wiki/Vlad_the_Impaler

Book Source

Robinson, Nugent, *History of the World with all its Great Sensations together with Mighty and Decisive Battles and the Rise and Fall of its Nations from the Earliest Times to the Present Day, Vol. I,* New York, NY, P.F.Collier, Publisher, 1891.

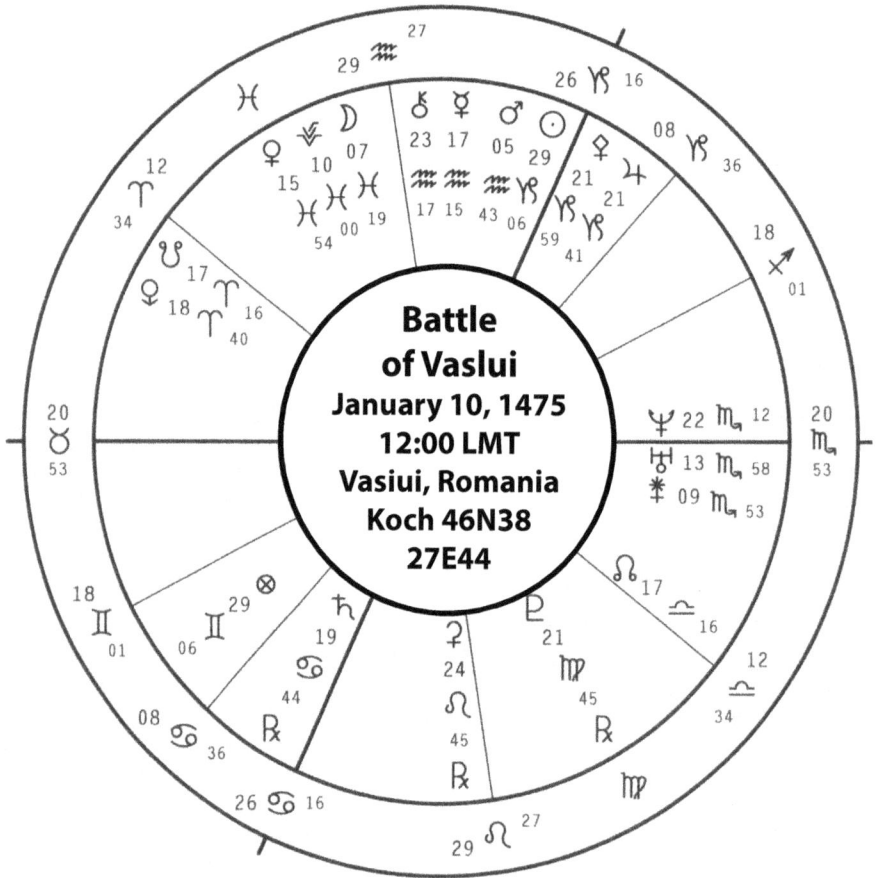

**Battle
of Vaslui**
January 10, 1475
12:00 LMT
Vasiui, Romania
Koch 46N38
27E44

Chapter 7

The Battle of Vaslui
Eris quincunx Pluto

After the fall of Athens and the collapse of the Crusade against the Turks, the foremost opponent of the Turks was Vlad the Impaler. In the 1460's, he took the lead in harassing the Turkish forces by his signature method of torture. Turkish prisoners were impaled upon wooden spikes, and Turkish soldiers were horrified to see rows of their comrades covering the countryside in a gory spectacle. Vlad used the terror tactic of disguising himself and his men as Turks, then infiltrating the camps so the Turks could be slaughtered unaware. For this tactic of dubious morality, Vlad was heralded as a hero throughout Europe.

However, Vlad himself became the victim of treachery. Stories started to spread about his cruelties, claiming that his own men were subjected to impaling, and that he enjoyed dining while listing to the groans of dying men (sounds like Eris walking the battlefield and enjoying the groans of dying men.) The Boyars (or Chiefs) of the local communities resisted his reforms, which helped the peasants and tried to create a stable economy through regulation of trade. The final blow came when his brother, Radu, and prominent Boyars went over to the Turks and began leading an army against Vlad.

King Stephen

For a while Vlad was able to resist the invaders, but then he went to Hungary to borrow funds to hire more mercenary soldiers. The King of Hungary, Matthias Corvinus, had received 40,000 gold coins from the Pope in order to raise an army against the Turks. The King had spent most of the money on personal expenses. When Vlad showed up at the palace, instead of being greeted, he was arrested. For more than ten years (the dates are imprecise) he was held prisoner in Hungary and was not able to stop the Turkish advance into Wallachia and Moldavia.

In 1474, Turkish general Suleiman Pasha was ordered to march on Moldavia. The orders came late in the year, and it was uncommon for European armies to fight in the winter. The Turkish strategy was to conquer Moldavia in the winter, and to have their forces in position to strike against Hungary in the spring. The size of the Turkish army has not been accurately established. The smallest number reported was 60,000 men, and the largest number reported was 120,000 men. The cavalry was supposed to have numbered 30,000 men. In addition, 20,000 Bulgarian peasants were sent as an advance force, to clear snow from the roads and to repair bridges.

The opposition to the Turks fell to King Stephen of Moldavia. Although not a Roman Catholic, he had sent requests for help to the Pope. The responses he got were rather meager. The Kingdom of Hungary sent only 1800 men, and the Kingdom of Poland sent just 2000 men on horseback. The Moldavian army only had about 40,000 men, and of those about 15,000 were professional soldiers. The rest were peasants with home-made weapons who were conscripted into the army.

When Turks arrived in Moldavia, December, 1474, King Stephen ordered a tactic that would be referred to in current times as a "scorched earth" policy. Civilians and their farm animals were evacuated to the hills. Wells were poisoned to sicken the invaders. No material was left behind that could help the Turks. Moldavian forces performed lightning commando raids against the Turks, breaking their fighting morale. The Turkish scouts finally reported that undamaged villages were to be found in the district of Vaslui, and Suleiman Pasha ordered his troops in that direction.

On January 10, 1475, the Turkish army arrived in Vaslui, and found themselves at the entrance to a valley. It had been a rough march for the Turks, with cold rain drenching the soldiers. When they arrived at Vaslui, the area was covered with a dense fog. This helped to hide the whereabouts of the Moldavian army. Suleiman Pasha was unsure of what direction to take, until he heard the sound of music coming out of the valley. King Stephen had ordered drummers and buglers into the valley, telling them to perform with sufficient loudness to convince the Turks that the Moldavian army was in the valley. With the thought of finally being able to do battle with a standing army, Suleiman Pasha ordered the Turkish army into the valley.

Vlad the Impaler

The Moldavian cavalry, now already in the valley, harassed the vanguard of the Turks. This convinced the Turks that a major battle was to be fought there, so they charged the bulk of their army into the valley. What they didn't know was that the Moldavian army was gathered on the ridges of both sides of the valley. Once Turks were in the valley, Moldavians began firing arrows and cannonballs from above. Even though the dense fog made aiming impossible, the Turks were so tightly pressed into the valley that every shot from above managed to hit someone. To further complicate matters, King Stephen ordered buglers to play from behind the Turkish lines, making it seem as though another army was coming in to surround the Turks.

Suleiman Pasha lost control of his army, and a disorderly retreat began as thousands of Turks ran out of the valley. For three days, the retreating Turks were pursued by the Moldavian and Polish cavalry, until they were finally able to regroup at the town of Oblucita. Back in Vaslui, the casualties were counted and it was estimated that the Turks had lost 40,000 men. King Stephen ordered that four captured commanders and thirty-six standards be sent to King Casmir of Lithuania, in the hope he would join with Moldavia against future Turkish attacks.

King Casmir pleaded poverty, but his own troops rebelled against him for his inaction. Prisoners and standards were sent to King Matthias of Hungary, but then he tried to take credit for the victory by writing to the Pope about it.

However, King Stephen had already sent prisoners and standards to the Pope, in his hope that the Papacy would be able to provide some financial assistance in the fight against the Turks. The Pope did not send any money, but he bestowed on King Stephen a title "Athleta Christi, which means "Champion of Christ." It was considered to be the greatest victory of Christian forces against Islamic forces.

King Stephen took a modest attitude towards the battle. He insisted that the victory belonged to God. After the battle, the King spent forty days in prayer and fasting in return for the victory. He was also then able to use his influence to get Vlad the Impaler, who was his cousin, released from prison. In 1476, Vlad's brother, Radu, had died, so Vlad was able to return to the throne of Wallachia. Vlad proved a valuable ally when Sultan Mehmed organized an army of 150,000 to attack Moldavia. This included 30,000 Tartars, who attacked from the North. They proved to be no match for the Moldavians, who caused the Tartars to retreat so quickly that they left behind most of their equipment.

King Stephen's forces killed 30,000 Turks in July, 1476, but he was forced to retreat. The Turks wasted time laying siege on two fortresses, and then they were forced to retreat when disease and famine started to afflict their army. During their retreat through Wallachia, Vlad was able to attack the Turks with an army of about 30,000 men.

Reports claim that Vlad died in battle with the Turks. The date of his death is uncertain, taking place either in late 1476 or early 1477. Although he would later become a Romanian national hero, his reputation for cruelty was remembered and he would be regarded as a figure of horror, even in the afterlife.

King Stephen lived until 1504, and had more battles with the Turks. He was the figure who received the glory for stopping the Turkish advance into central Europe. By doing this he managed to keep the Kingdom of Hungary safe until the mid-16th century when the Turks were on the march again. No figure that was comparable to either King Stephen (or Vlad the Impaler) was there to stop them.

In the chart for the Battle of Vaslui, Pluto was not only quincunx Eris, but was also quincunx Mercury, and Eris was sextile Mercury. Miscommunication was definitely a factor in winning the battle. Pluto was trine Pallas and Jupiter, and Eris was square Pallas and Jupiter. Military wisdom and religious fervor utilized by King Stephen (whether it was by divine inspiration or not) were also key points in the victory.

Pluto sextile Neptune and Eris quincunx Neptune further suggest that spiritual devotion was the driving force behind the victory. Pluto sextile Saturn, and Eris square Saturn indicate the military discipline in arranging such a battle.

Eris and Pluto were still quincunx each other in 1476 when King Stephen and Vlad the Impaler won follow-up victories against the Turks. As we will see in further chapters, Eris quincunx Pluto is the sort of aspect that marks a "David versus Goliath" type of victory and can make powerful forces pause before attacking again.

It is possible that the quincunx marks a sense of over-confidence in the "superior forces,"making them overlook the possibility that the other side has resources and ingenuity that can change the battle. As will be seen with later examples of the Eris-Pluto quincunx, sometimes a secret weapon or original tactics will change the course of a battle.

Bibliography - Chapter 7

Internet Sources

Battle of Vaslui
   https://en.wikipedia.org/wiki/Battle_of_Vaslui

King Stephen III
   https://en.wikipedia.org/wiki/Stephen_III_of_Moldavia

Matthias Corvinus, King of Hungary
   https://en.wikipedia.org/wiki/Matthias_Corvinus

Ottoman defeat at Vaslui
   http://staffblogs.le.ac.uk/crusading/2015/01/07/ottoman-defeat-in-the-eastern-balkans-the-battle-of-vaslui-1475/

Who was the Real Count Dracula
   http://history.howstuffworks.com/history-vs-myth/real-count-dracula.html

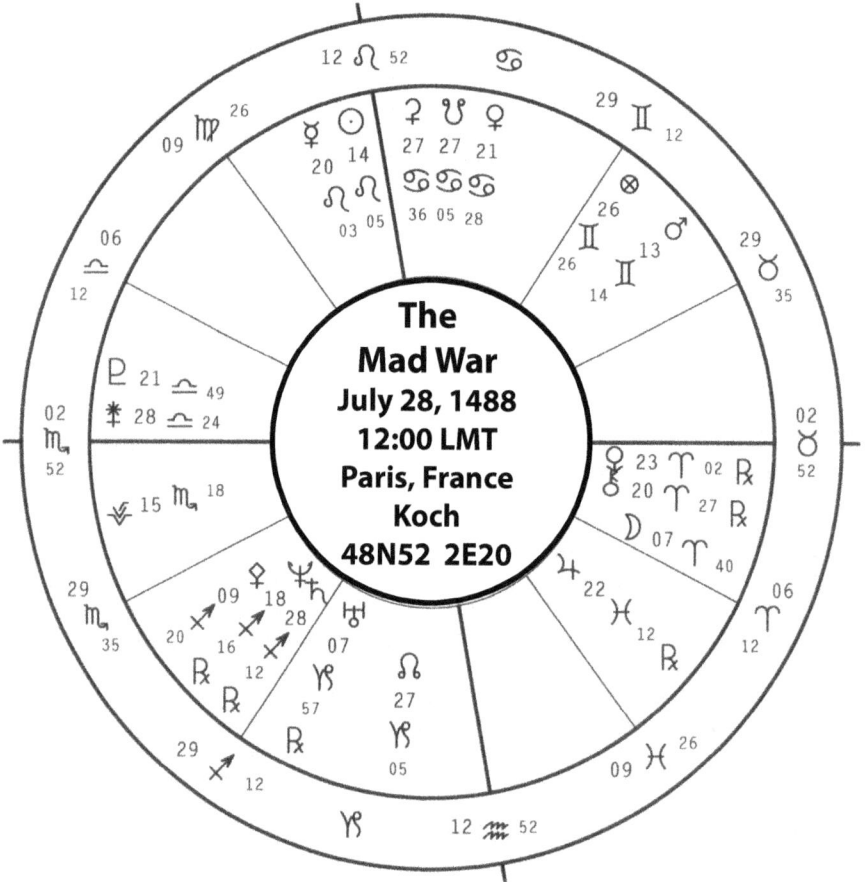

The
Mad War
July 28, 1488
12:00 LMT
Paris, France
Koch
48N52 2E20

Chapter 8

(WTF?) What the France?
Eris opposing Pluto

There is an old story (usually attributed to Abraham Lincoln) about two wrestlers who became hopelessly entangled with each other due to intricate wrestling holds. One wrestler decided he would break up the entanglement by biting his opponent's leg, which was only an inch from his mouth. After taking a sharp bite, the wrestler painfully discovered that he had in fact bitten his own leg!

This sort of entanglement and confusion fits in with the Eris-Pluto opposition. Eris demands new conquests and new struggles. Yet, if Pluto in opposition already has all the power or the potential for power, then what is all the fighting about? This question may have entered in the minds of thousands of French soldiers in 1480's, when the Eris-Pluto opposition took place at the time of a conflict known as "the Mad War." Actually, "the Mad War" was a series of civil wars that afflicted France, and the outcome would leave fighting men scratching their heads, wondering what it was all about.

The start of the conflict began with the rise of King Charles VIII to the French throne. Unfortunately, the King was underage, and a regency was proclaimed, which was ruled over by the King's elder sister, Anne de Beaujeau. The regency of Anne de Beaujeau was not universally popular, and she received stern opposition

Louis, Duke of Orleans

from the king's cousin, Louis, Duke of Orleans. Louis made an attempt to take control of the regency, but his efforts were blocked by the Estates-General, the parliamentary body of France, which ruled in favor of Anne de Beaujeau.

Louis then planned to take a more aggressive approach to gain power, and he formed an alliance with Francis, Duke of Brittany. Francis wanted Brittany to remain an independent duchy, separate from control by the French crown. As part of the alliance, Louis agreed to marry Anne, daughter of Francis. Unfortunately, Louis was already married to Joan, sister of King Charles VIII. Louis had to send an appeal to the Pope to get an annulment. While waiting for Papal bureaucracy to take its course, Louis decided upon more direct action. Returning to the royal court, he took charge of a troop of soldiers and attempted to kidnap King Charles VIII. The attempt was beaten back by nobles loyal to Anne de Beaujeau, and Louis was made a prisoner.

Louis was placed under house arrest, but he escaped, and fled to Alcenon. There he made a public repentance for his crime against the King, which may have saved him from the death penalty for treason when he was recaptured. As part of his punishment, Louis was locked up in Orleans. Royal troops were sent to Brittany to keep forces of Duke Francis from marching to Orleans. Realizing he could not win a battle against the royal army, Duke Francis signed a truce treaty, which lasted one year.

In 1486, when the truce expired, Duke Francis tried to make more trouble. This time he was assisted by Austrian emperor, Maximilian I, who sent thousands of troops to attack northern France. The Austrian emperor worked to weaken France by making an alliance with the Duke of Brittany and offering to marry his daughter, Anne of Brittany.

At the same time, Louis, Duke of Orleans, escaped, taking refuge in Brittany. He was not much help to the alliance, because all of his property had been confiscated by the crown. The romantic situation of Anne of Brittany was further confused by the arrival of Alain d'Abret, a rebellious nobleman who had received money from the court of Spain to aid the cause of Brittany. He sought to marry the daughter of Duke Francis.

French forces fought back the invading Austrian troops, and then blocked the forces of Alain d'Abret from joining the Austrians. The royal army was sent into Brittany to break the rebellion. Not everyone in Brittany sided with Duke Francis, because his regime had been notoriously corrupt. When the duke attempted to call the population to arms, he had a very poor turnout. The crown had hired corsairs from Normandy to block the ports of Brittany, preventing the arrival of supporters from England

and Austria by the sea. A few thousand foreign supporters did manage to reach Brittany, but they were still outnumbered by the royal army. To further complicate matters, the French commanders organized a rebellion in Flanders, which was under Austrian rule, and the Austrian emperor had to divert troops to put down the rebellion.

The forces of Duke Francis were finally defeated by the royal army at the battle of Saint-Aubin-du-Cormier on July 28, 1488 (The "Mad War"). Duke Francis was forced to sign a punitive treaty with the King of France, which stated that the Duke of Brittany was a vassal of the King of France, that foreign troops had to be removed from Brittany, and that only the King of France could decide upon the marriage arrangement for the daughter of the Duke of Brittany. Shortly after signing this treaty, Duke Francis died, and his daughter Anne became the Duchess of Brittany.

In the chart for the battle of Saint-Aubin-du-Cormier, Eris conjuncts Chiron, which might indicate contention and purging in the body politic. Eris and Chiron were square Venus, marking a "romantic" element to the struggle, with everyone trying to marry Anne of Brittany. However, Pluto was squaring Venus, so marriage was not the simple solution to the issue. Pluto was sextile Mercury and Neptune. There was cunning and planning going on behind the scenes, not to mention some unrealistic expectations, such as a Papal annulment. Pluto quincunx Jupiter, and Eris semi-sextile Jupiter may have suggested that the king would come out best in this conflict, but as it turned out it was a result with more confusion than resolution.

The battle may have seemed like a simple ending to a complex rebellion, but the events of the next decade were likely to cause a lot of head-scratching among the veterans of this battle. Louis, Duke of Orleans, was locked up in a fortress, but in 1491, when King Charles VIII reached his majority and took over the throne, he ordered Louis to be freed from prison. The Duke of Orleans was reinstated as a member of the royal court, and he became the best friend and chief advisor to King Charles VIII. There may have been a lot of soldiers who were puzzled over the fact that a man they opposed for so many years should suddenly have been restored to royal favor.

The Austrian emperor still tried to make trouble, and pressed his suit for the hand of Anne, Duchess of Brittany. In 1490, supporters of the Austrian emperor promoted marriage by proxy for Anne to Maximilian. This was a violation of the peace treaty which said only the King of France could determine who could marry the Duchess of Brittany.

The French army was sent into Brittany again, but the Austrian emperor did not send any troops to Brittany. Once Brittany was under royal control, King Charles VIII declared that he would marry Anne. Again, this must have caused so much head-scratching, that the leader of the rebellious duchy should become the Queen of France. (Incidentally, Anne was only fifteen years old when her marriage to the King was validated by the Pope. This meant she had not even gone through puberty when she had three political lovers attempting to marry her.)

Though it was a marriage of political necessity, King Charles VIII fathered four children by Anne, but none of them survived childhood. The situation was complicated by the marriage contract, which stipulated that the spouse who outlived the other would inherit Brittany. If Queen Anne outlived the King, and there were no heirs, she was obligated to marry the next King so that he could inherit control of Brittany. This odd arrangement came to pass in 1498, when King Charles VIII died without heirs, and his successor was his cousin, Louis, Duke of Orleans. This situation must have really dismayed the veterans of "the Mad War" who had spent years of fighting to keep Louis from power.

The reign of King Louis XII was complicated by the fact that he was still married to Joan, the sister of the late King. Once again, Louis appealed to the Pope for an annulment so that he could marry Queen Anne. This time, Anne gave him a deadline of one year for the annulment to come through. To everyone's surprise, King Louis XII was given an annulment by Pope Alexander VI, the notorious Borgia Pope. King Louis had argued that his wife Joan was so ugly, he had not been able to consummate the marriage. Joan brought in witnesses who had heard the boasts of Louis that he had consummated the marriage. Since the Pope wanted to remain on the good side of Louis, he ruled in favor of the King. The case was called "one of the seamiest lawsuits of the age." Joan was forced to retire to a convent, and in 1950 she was canonized as a Roman Catholic saint because of her piety.

King Louis XII took Queen Anne as his reluctant bride, which was another puzzlement for the veterans of "the Mad War," since they had spent so many years in an attempt to keep them apart. After 15 years of marriage, Louis and Anne produced only two daughters who survived to maturity. Queen Anne died of a kidney ailment in 1514. King Louis immediately contracted a marriage to Mary Tudor, the sister of King Henry VIII of England. It was said that Louis wore himself out by his frequent copulation with Mary in his attempts to father a male heir. After his death in 1515, he was succeeded by his cousin Francis, who married the eldest daughter of Louis and Anne, thus making himself the King's son-in-law.

As follow up to the marital happenings of King Louis XII, regarding the Papal annulment, the brother-in-law of King Louis, King Henry VIII of England, may have thought it was quite an easy thing to get a marriage annulled. As we will see in a later chapter, the circumstances of a Papal Annulment were not as easy as King Henry VIII expected, and the situation he faced would have a major impact on the course of religion in European history, as well as the development of a new empire.

While the "Mad War" was going on in France, another civil war was taking place in Scotland. King James III of Scotland was notoriously unpopular, mainly because he would not keep his word after making an agreement. Nobles started deserting his cause, and gave their support to Prince James, heir to the throne, who was only 15-years-old at the time. This "shadow government" alarmed King James III, but he promised he would negotiate with his son rather than start a war. However, the king broke this promise by riding out of his stronghold with a large army. This act caused more nobles to desert his cause. On June 11, 1488, King James III rousted rebels out of the town of Stirling, but the next day the rebels returned for a fight.

The battle of Saint Aubin du Cormier

According to the chronicles of Lindsay of Piscottie, on the day of battle the king rode a grey horse, given to him by one of his subjects who promised the horse would carry him into battle or out of battle faster than any other horse. However, the horse proved to be treacherous, because it rose up in the middle of battle and threw the king to the ground. There are conflicting reports as to whether the king died from the fall, or whether enemy soldiers killed him.

Prince James was then crowned as King James IV of Scotland. For the rest of his life, he wore an iron chain around his neck as repentance for the way he came to the throne by rebelling against his father. Saturn was opposing the Sun at the time of the victory, and Saturn could have stood for the defeat of the old king, while the Sun was the rising of the new king. Yet, Saturn stands for connections to the past, and wearing an iron chain could have been a remembrance for King James IV not to be like his father.

Bibliography - Chapter 8
Internet Sources

The Mad War
https://en.wikipedia.org/wiki/Mad_War

King Charles VIII
https://en.wikipedia.org/wiki/Charles_VIII_of_France

Louis, Duke of Orleans (and later King Louis XII)
https://en.wikipedia.org/wiki/Louis_XII_of_France

Anne of Brittany (later Queen Anne)
https://en.wikipedia.org/wiki/Anne_of_Brittany

Maximilian I (Emperor of Austria)
https://en.wikipedia.org/wiki/Maximilian_I,_Holy_Roman_Emperor

Joan of France (wife of Louis, Duke of Orleans)
https://en.wikipedia.org/wiki/Joan_of_France,_Duchess_of_Berry

Scottish Civil War
https://en.wikipedia.org/wiki/Battle_of_Sauchieburn

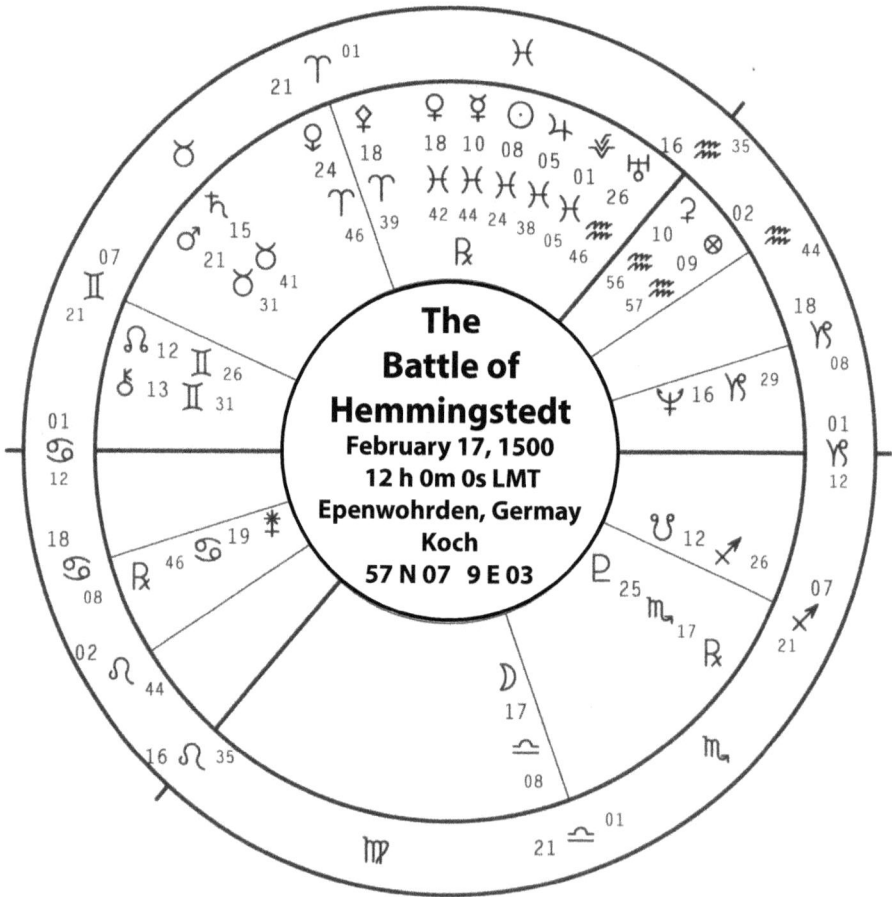

The
Battle of
Hemmingstedt
February 17, 1500
12 h 0m 0s LMT
Epenwohrden, Germay
Koch
57 N 07 9 E 03

Chapter 9

The Battle of Hemmingstedt
Eris quincunx Pluto

In the year 1500, when Eris was quincunx Pluto, there took place perhaps the oddest battle in the history of warfare. The setting (believe it or not) was in a peasant's republic called Dithmarschen, located in the Schleswig-Holstein region of what is now Northern Germany. For centuries, this area had been fought over by Danish kings and German nobles, until finally the residents of Dithmarschen had enough of the feudal warfare. They declared themselves an independent republic, not ruled by any nobility, and the management of the land was done by a council of 48 representatives chosen from the peasant population.

Since the fall of the Roman Empire, the word "republic" was rarely used in medieval Europe. The only republics of note were Venice, Switzerland and the distant island of Iceland. For more than a century, the Dithmarsians were able to maintain their autonomy, mainly through shrewd negotiations which pitted one warlord against a rival warlord. By means of these shifting alliances, the Dithmarsians resisted domination by any noble, while providing troops to assist other nobles who were fighting against a noble who had designs on the peasant republic.

To the modern view, the story appears to be a melodrama, with heroic freemen standing against the tyranny of nobles. By the year 1500, the main villain of the story was Duke John V of Saxe-Lauenberg. For years he had tried to dominate the Dithmarsians, but they had been able to find allies to stand against him. By 1499, Duke John V, with the help of his son, Magnus had constructed a series of alliances, which left the Dithmarsians politically isolated. All that was needed was a ruthless army to descend upon the peasants.

Magnus hired the services of the Black Guard, a nefarious force of mercenaries from the Netherlands. The terms of the agreement were that the Black Guard could pillage all they wanted from Dithmarschen, and

Magnus

70.   *Brother Pluto, Sister Eris*

then the land would belong to Duke John V. When they were on their way to Dithmarschen the Black Guard showed their violent skills by sacking monasteries and nunneries in their path. The number of the Black Guard was about 4000 men. In addition, John V managed to get another 3000 men from various duchies. The King of Denmark contributed 5000 men. The peasant's republic was only able to muster about 1000 men for combat, meaning that they were outnumbered 12 to 1.

At this point, it seemed more than likely that massacre was going to take place, so the Black Guard then approached Dithmarschen with an attitude of overconfidence. The peasants, who were outnumbered, had the good fortune to have a strong leader, with the dramatic name of Wulf Isenbrand, (iron sword) who set out the battle plan ahead of time. Rather than march out to face the invaders, the Dithsmarsians took to the high ground, setting up their artillery on every hilltop. This made it necessary for the Black Guard to march the extra distance for the battle, and placed them at the disadvantage of being fired upon from above.

On February 17, 1500, as the Black Guard approached the Dithmarsian positions, Wulf Isenbrand had one more weapon to unleash, which was the topography of the battlefield. The members of the Black Guard were so intent on the battle, they did not notice that the lay of the land was like that of the Netherlands. The area was below sea level, and required dikes to hold back the sea. When the Black Guard approached, Wulf Isenberg ordered that one of the dikes be knocked down, allowing the sea to flood the battlefield.

At once, cavalry became ineffective, as the horses lost their footing on the marshy ground. The infantry was not doing much better, since the mercenaries were weighted down by armor and supplies, and they had no firm ground to march upon. It was later said that most casualties of the battle were from drowning, rather than from the weapons of the Dithmarsians firing from the hilltops. The invaders lost about 7000 men, with another 1500 wounded or injured. No account remains about any Dithmarsian casualties.

After the battle, the surviving members of the Black Guard marched to the castle of John V and surrounded it. They delivered the ultimatum that unless John V paid them off with proper wages, they would attack and pillage the castle. John V, having lost so many of his own men, had no choice but to use his remaining funds to pay off the Black Guard. The decisive battle marked the end of attempts by John V and Magnus to attack Dithmarschen.

Before the battle, the Dithmarsians had prayed to the Virgin Mary for victory, and then they celebrated the victory by building a Franciscan Friary. They had also captured a large number of battle flags, which they put on display at a church for many years to remind the public of the victory. Unfortunately, the peasant republic of Dithmarschen lasted only 60 more years before the area was dominated by King Frederick II of Denmark, when Eris was sextile Pluto. The whole area of Schleswig-Holstein was finally seized by the Prussians in 1864, during another Eris-Pluto sextile, and to this day that area remains a part of Germany.

The significance of this battle of Hemmingstedt (named for a nearby town) was that it contributed to the legends that a virtuous, small force of men could defeat a larger, less virtuous army. It became the sort of tale that could be told in times of adversity. Even the Nazis, as the Third Reich declined, used the story of Hemmingstedt as an encouragement to fight back, though they were outnumbered on two fronts. Of course, the real secret of success was the topography of the land, combined with the overconfidence of the attackers. Had the Black Guard been more prudent, or had Dithmarschen been a little higher than sea level, the outcome would have been different.

In the chart of the battle, apart from the Eris-Pluto quincunx, Neptune is square the Moon and Pallas, asteroid of military wisdom. Neptune represents the sea, and how the land battle became a sea battle. Neptune opposing Juno may have stood for the fact that the power of the sea broke the coalition organized against the Dithmarsians. Moon opposing Pallas might stand for overconfidence and lack of judgment by the invaders. Neptune trine Saturn and sextile Venus marked the good fortune of the Dithmarsians in standing still and receiving the help from the sea, as well as a female presence. One of the legendary figures of the battle was a "virgin" named Telse, who acted like Joan of Arc by waving a battle flag to inspire the Dithmarsians to repel the invaders. Mars was in opposition to Pluto, semi-sextile Eris and square Uranus. Also, Uranus was square Pluto and sextile Eris, marking the unexpected victory. It was a battle which sent a message that any weapon was permissible in times of war, even the power of the sea. The Black Guard ended up getting scrubbed by the sea, thanks to ingenuity of the Dithmarsians. All was fair in love and war, and that included topography.

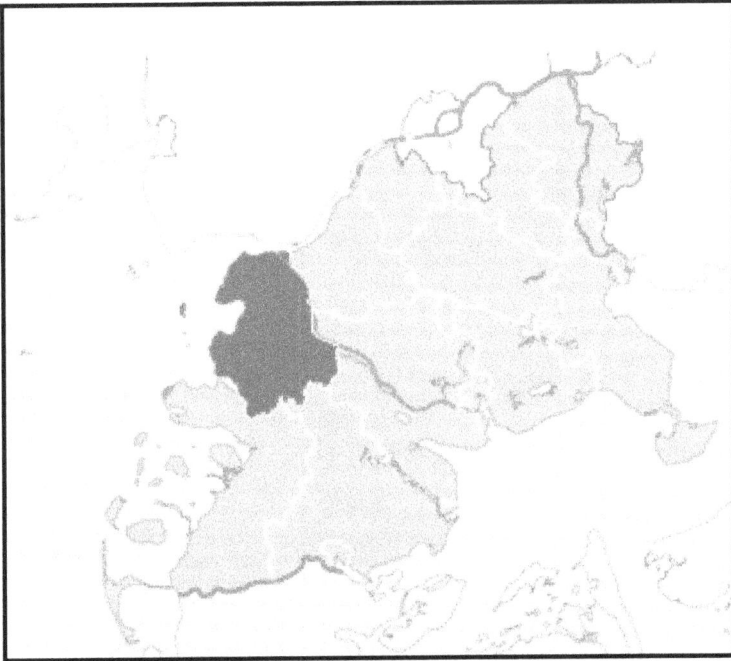

Location of the peasants republic

Castle of Duke John V

The Black Guard being overwhelmed by the sea

Painting of the battle done in 1910

Bibliography - Chapter 9
Internet Sources

Battle of Hemmingstedt
https://en.wikipedia.org/wiki/Battle_of_Hemmingstedt

Peasant Militia defeats Danish army
http://burnpit.us/2018/02/battle-hemmingstedt-peasant-militia-defeats-danish-army-opening-dikes-and-drowning-them

Dithmarschen
https://en.wikipedia.org/wiki/Dithmarschen

John V of Saxe-Lauenburg
https://en.wikipedia.org/wiki/John_V,_Duke_of_Saxe-Lauenburg

Magnus of Saxe-Lauenburg
https://en.wikipedia.org/wiki/Magnus_I,_Duke_of_Saxe-Lauenburg

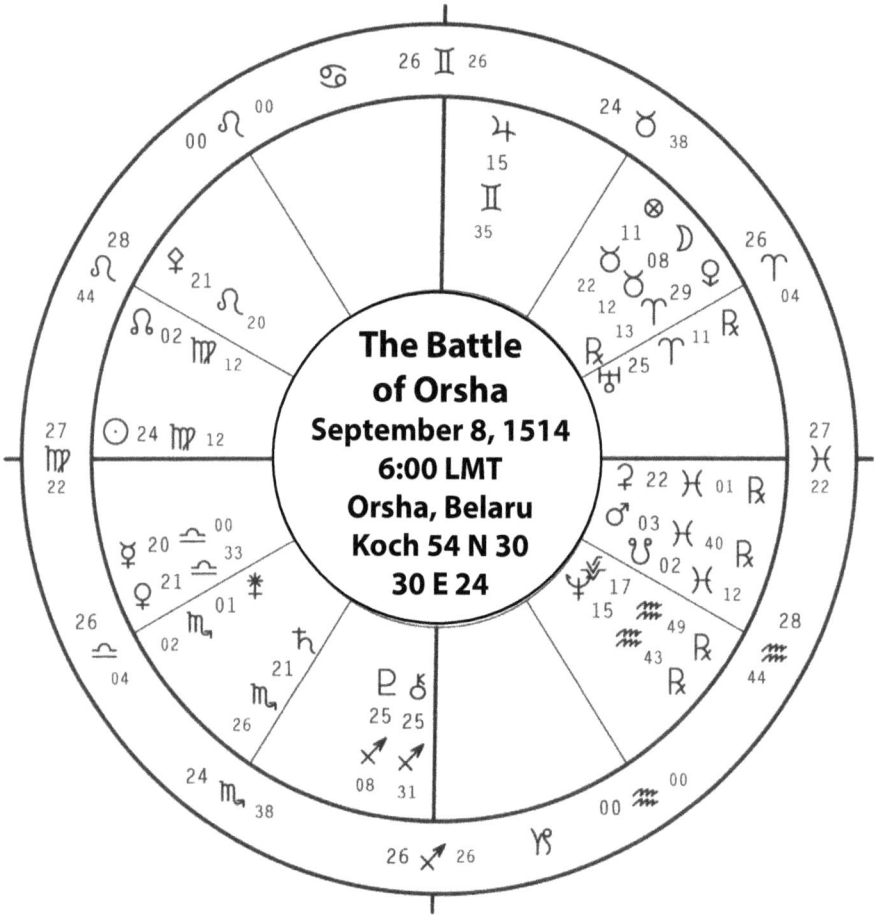

The Battle
of Orsha
September 8, 1514
6:00 LMT
Orsha, Belaru
Koch 54 N 30
30 E 24

Chapter 10

The Battle of Orsha
Eris trine Pluto

In the late 15th Century, Grand Duke Ivan of Moscow (also known as "Ivan the Great") began consolidating the lands around Moscow, and managed to create the nation- state that we now call Russia. The area had been filled with different city-states and scattered duchies, which were often in conflict with invading Tartars. With the collapse of the Tartar threat in the 15th Century, the Grand Duchy of Moscow became the leading power in the area. Previously, the Grand Duke of Moscow had been a vassal leader under the Byzantine Empire. However, with the collapse of Constantinople in 1453, Moscow gained greater autonomy and influence.

Ivan the Great began a series of wars with Lithuania and Poland, which were carried on by his son, Vasili. Today we do not think of Lithuania and Poland as powerful nations, but during the Middle Ages they were the leading military powers in Northern Europe. The border of Lithuania extended from the Baltic Sea to the Black Sea, covering the areas of the Ukraine, Belarus, and Ruthenia. As the Russian state began to grow, it was inevitable that conflict with the two powers would take place. By the year 1514, the Russians were on their fourth war with Poland and Lithuania. It was the beginning of an Eris-Pluto trine, which would be marked by the major bloodshed of the Battle of Orsha.

Wars during this time were usually conducted by small armies with about 10, 000 men. Only large empires (like Turkey) could manage to raise armies of more than 50,000 men. For this 4th effort against Poland and Lithuania, Grand Duke Vasili raised an army of 80,000 men. There has been debate about the exact size of the Russian army. Most historical accounts came from Poland, and there is a question as to whether the size of the Russian force was exaggerated. There are suggestions that the Russian army may have only been 50,000 or 40,000 men. Nevertheless, the one thing agreed upon was that the Russians outnumbered the armies of Poland and Lithuania, which only had about 30,000 men.

The great advantage of the armies of Poland and Lithuania was that they were made up mainly by cavalry. This gave their forces needed speed for rapid attacks and swift communication. Lack of communication became the source of the Russian defeat at the battle of Orsha.

Because the Russian army was so large, there was no uniform system for passing down orders. The result was that the army was divided into sections spread out across a large landscape. Because of the separation of the units, there was no overall plan of marching and movement during battle. The cavalry of Poland and Lithuania took advantage of this by attacking small sections of the Russian army, and finishing them off before reinforcements could arrive.

By this method of "divide-and-conquer," the King of Poland claimed that 30,000 Russians fell in battle, and hundreds of nobles were captured for ransom. It is possible that the King of Poland was exaggerating to impress others with the glory of his army.

However, his account of the battle went to the Pope in Rome, and it is not likely he would have tried to "humbug" the Vicar of Christ. Very few Russian accounts of the battle remain, probably because it was a humiliating defeat for them, and they likely did not want to talk about it.

In spite of defeating the larger Russian army, the armies of Poland and Lithuania did not understand the important message of the Russian psyche, which would later turn the tides of battle against Napoleon and Hitler. The Russians viewed suffering as a way of life, and the loss of a large army was seen as a temporary setback rather than a major defeat. For the next few years, as Eris was trine Pluto, the Russians continued their war with Poland and Lithuania. It was not until 1520 that a truce was finally arranged, and a final peace was signed in 1522.

In the chart for the battle of Orsha, Pluto is conjunct Chiron, and this would fit in with the philosophy later expressed by Frederick Nietzsche,

That which does not kill me makes me stronger.

For centuries this would be a guiding principle of the Russian state, because no matter how many defeats they suffered, the Russians would always spring back. There would be later wars against Poland and Lithuania, and little by little the Russians would impose upon the geography of their neighbors, until essentially nothing was left.

Also in the chart of the battle, Juno (asteroid of marriage) is in opposition to Eris. The saving grace for the Russians may have been the successful alliances made by Grand Duke Vasili. He had acquired the autonomous provinces of Pskov and Novgorod, and the final result of the war against Poland and Lithuania was the capture of the city of Smolensk, which greatly weakened Lithuania. The successes of the Russian army

Grand Duke Vasili

may have been due to a rebellious Lithuanian prince, Mikhail Glinski, who helped the Russians get artillery and engineers. As a result, after the battle of Orsha, the Russians went on to real victories.

In the 1520's, Grand Duke Vasili had marital problems to deal with, since his wife of 20 years proved to be barren, and no heir to the crown had been born. Against the will of the church, Vasili wed a Serbian princess, and tried again to father an heir. At first, it seemed he was going to be unsuccessful, but then in 1530 he finally got a son, Ivan IV, who is best remembered in history books by the sobriquet, "Ivan the Terrible." Grand

Duke Vasili's problem was historically ironic, because another ruler was having a similar problem at that time, and his conflict over the religious nature of his marriage is to be found in the next chapter.

Another change marked by this Eris-Pluto trine was the beginning of the collapse of a religious empire that had dominated Europe for a thousand years. On October 31, 1517, Pluto had entered Capricorn and was in an out-of-sign trine with Eris at 29 Aries. This date is regarded as the birth of the Protestant Reformation, and the beginning of the end for Papal control of Europe. This was supposed to be the date when Martin Luther nailed his 95 Theses to the door of All Saints Church in Wittenberg. Some historians consider this to be a fanciful event, comparable to George Washington cutting down the cherry tree. However, on this date, it is a fact that Luther sent his 95 Theses to the bishop of Mainz, and that action could still be considered a birth moment for the Reformation.

The Eris-Pluto trine also marked the rise of another empire, as Portuguese ships created havoc in the Far East with colonial expansion. Since the time of the previous Eris-Pluto trine in the 1450's, the Portuguese had been gradually sailing down the coast of Africa. They finally rounded the tip of Africa in 1488, in time for the Eris-Pluto opposition. By the time of the Eris-Pluto trine, they had set up a colony in Goa, India, arrived at the spice islands of Malacca, discovered New Guinea, attacked states in the Persian Gulf, and sent diplomats to China and Japan to open up trade. Unfortunately, the Portuguese ended up resorting to piracy, as well as kidnapping to send Asian slaves back to Portugal. It was the start of international exploitation which would make Portugal one of the wealthiest nations in the world.

Meanwhile, on the other side of the world, the Spanish expanded their wealthy empire with gradual settlement of the Caribbean. However, the great wealth they were seeking would not be found until Eris entered into Taurus, marking the historic encounter between Hernando Cortez and the Aztec civilization. The Conquistadors found the Native American people to be easily conquered, thanks to their fear of horses, their lack of immunity to smallpox, and an eschatological mythology about the second coming of their Messiah. With all opposition swept away, the wealth of the Aztecs became a major boost for the Spanish treasury.

Bibliography - Chapter 10
Internet Sources

The Battle of Orsha

https://en.wikipedia.org/wiki/Battle_of_Orsha

Russian Nationalism

https://en.wikipedia.org/wiki/Russian_nationalism

Grand Duke Vasili III

https://en.wikipedia.org/wiki/Vasili_III_of_Russia

Russian Soul

https://en.wikipedia.org/wiki/Russian_soul

Muscovite-Lithuanian Wars

https://en.wikipedia.org/wiki/Muscovite%E2%80%93Lithuanian_Wars

Martin Luther

https://en.wikipedia.org/wiki/Martin_Luther

Portuguese Empire

https://en.wikipedia.org/wiki/Portuguese_Empire

Spanish Empire

https://en.wikipedia.org/wiki/Spanish_Empire

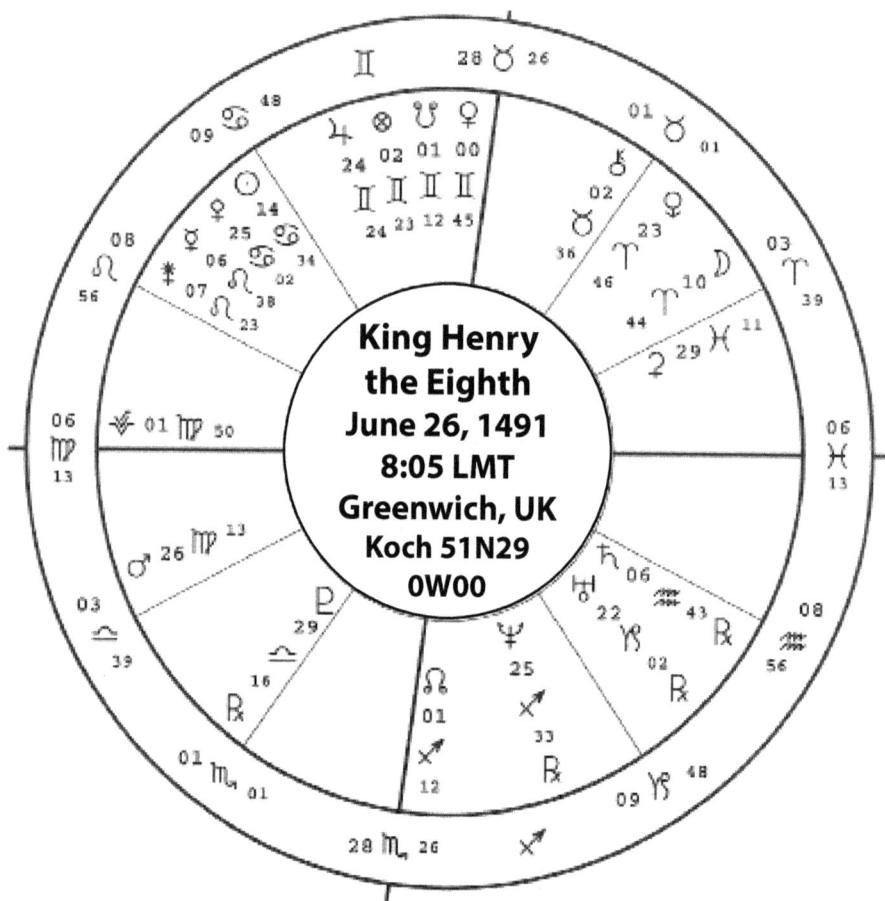

King Henry
the Eighth
June 26, 1491
8:05 LMT
Greenwich, UK
Koch 51N29
0W00

Chapter 11

The Pilgrimage of Grace
Eris square Pluto

In the 1520's, King Henry VIII of England was suffering from the same marital problems as Grand Duke Vasili of Moscow. After being wed to Catherine of Aragon for nearly 20 years, the king had only produced one child who lived beyond infancy, which was his daughter, Mary. It was believed that the nation needed a male heir to the throne to prevent uprisings, such as the "War of the Roses," which had afflicted England in the previous century. In order to procure a male heir, King Henry VIII believed it was necessary for him to end his royal marriage and seek a new wife. As a devout Roman Catholic, he thought that the Pope would annul his marriage and leave him free to marry a more fertile woman.

Henry was born with Eris squaring Uranus and sextile Jupiter. He was definitely on top of the major political discord of his times, and he was quite a spendthrift in maintaining his rule. It was by a twist of history that Henry ended up as England's most married king. Originally, his elder brother, Arthur, was expected to be king, and Henry was to end up as Archbishop of Canterbury or in some other religious post requiring a vow of celibacy. However, in 1502, when transiting Eris was trine Henry's Neptune and square his Pallas, his expectations for a religious life came to an end with the death of his brother. Henry became the new heir to the throne.

King Henry VIII

Henry took his brother's widow as his bride, and it seemed that Catherine would provide him with an heir. Unfortunately, the children born (except for Mary) died in infancy.

By the 1520's, transiting Eris was conjunct Henry's natal Chiron, trine his Vesta, and semi-sextile his Venus. Henry decided that the lack of a male heir was because he had sinned in taking his brother's widow as his wife. He prepared a case to be presented to the Pope as an argument for an annulment.

Unfortunately for the timing of King Henry VIII, the Pope was not likely to help him. In 1527, Spanish troops were invading Italy, resulting in the sacking of Rome, and the loss of Vatican property. The Spanish King, Charles V, was the nephew of Catherine of Aragon, and he was not likely to support an annulment that would embarrass his aunt before the royal world. The Pope was made to understand that if he wished to remain on the good side of Charles V, he would not allow an annulment.

The result of this religious-political deadlock was that King Henry VIII started taking an interest in the Protestant doctrines that were just appearing in Europe. He began to listen to anti-Vatican politicians and churchmen, who thought the church in England should be under the control of the king. The result was that the king declared himself to be the head of the Church of England, and the control of the Vatican was considered to be at an end.

The king took Anne Boleyn (mother of Queen Elizabeth I) as his second wife. Catholic supporters, such as Sir Thomas More, were declared to be traitors and imprisoned or beheaded. Ironically, by 1536, Anne Boleyn and her supporters were imprisoned and beheaded, since she had failed in the task of giving the king a male heir.

In 1536, as Eris was square Pluto, King Henry VIII made his boldest move by seizing all the church property in England, and closing down the monasteries and convents. During the Middle Ages, a monastery was more than a place where monks lived a life of contemplation. A monastery also served as a relief center in times of economic hardship. If food was needed during time of famine, the local monastery would provide the needs of the hungry. If a poor person needed a new garment, clothing could

The Pilgramage of Grace

be found at the local monastery. To close the monasteries not only sent a religious shock throughout the land, but threatened the economic security of the lower classes.

In the autumn of 1536, religious discontent caused rebellions to take place over the closing of the monasteries. A rebellion broke out in Lincolnshire in early October, with the rebels occupying the local cathedral, and demanding a return to Roman Catholic worship. The rebels quickly dispersed when the King sent word that unless they gave up their protest, they would be attacked by military forces lead by the Duke of Suffolk. The crowds left the area, and the leaders of the rebellion were captured and executed for treason.

On Oct. 13, 1536, a larger rebellion broke out in Yorkshire, and this one attracted 40,000 people to the cause. This caused an urgent crisis for King Henry VIII, since the rebels outnumbered his standing army. It would take weeks to raise enough troops to be able to smash the rebellion. The rebels decided to take advantage of the King's weakness by marching to London. They called themselves "The Pilgrimage of Grace,"and though there were other political issues brought forth as grievances, such as taxation, the main impetus of the protest was religious.

The leadership of the Pilgrimage of Grace was given to Robert Aske, a London barrister and war veteran, who was noted for his piety. Aske lead a force of 9000 followers through Yorkshire, seizing the old monasteries and kicking out all the new tenants. When the royal commissioners came for negotiation, they met with Aske. Arrangements were made for Aske and other leaders to meet with the King under a flag of truce, and they accepted the offer for negotiation.

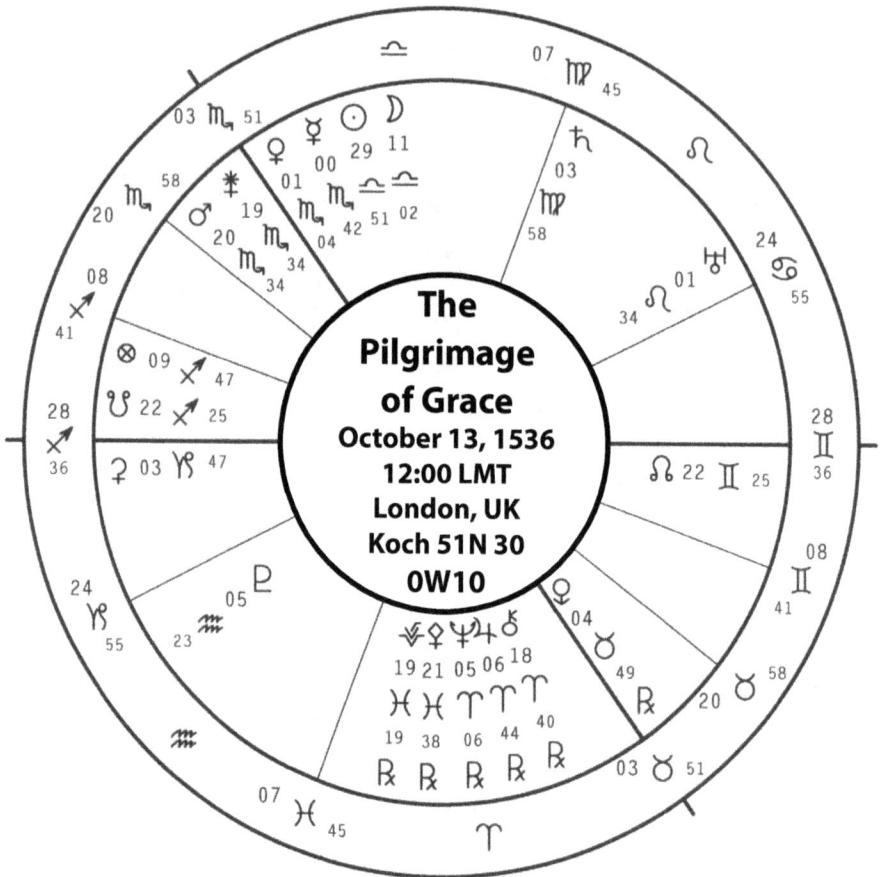

The Pilgrimage of Grace
October 13, 1536
12:00 LMT
London, UK
Koch 51N30
0W10

In the meantime, King Henry VIII had quickly dismissed his Protestant advisors and ministers. When the King met with the leaders of the Pilgrimage of Grace, he declared he was shocked, SHOCKED, to find that Protestant nobles had closed down the monasteries. The King announced that the monasteries would be reopened and that Catholic services would be restored. With that assurance, the leaders dispersed the Pilgrimage of Grace, and advised their followers to return home.

However, the good intentions of King Henry VIII only lasted long enough for him to assemble his army to strike back at areas that dared to rebel. Another rebellion was in February, 1537. King Henry VIII used that event as an excuse to arrest Aske and other leaders of the Pilgrimage of Grace, even though they were not involved with the rebellion. When others tried to protest, they found the army already on the scene, watching over the sacking of the monasteries. After leaders of the rebellion were executed, no one was ever again able to organize another Catholic rebellion in challenge to the power of King Henry VIII.

In the chart for the Pilgrimage of Grace, Pluto is sextile Neptune and Jupiter in Aries, while Eris is semi-sextile Neptune and Jupiter. Eris is also trine Saturn in Capricorn and Ceres in Virgo. It was a time when the old religious structure of the land was toppled, and great property losses for the Church ended any Roman Catholic economic influence. The king was set as the religious master of the kingdom, and, except for a brief resurgence during the reign of Queen Mary, Roman Catholicism has not controlled England.

As for Henry, in spite of getting a male heir in 1537, he still had marriage troubles. His queen, Jane Seymour, died after giving birth. Henry's Protestant advisors pushed for more reforms in the Church of England, and arranged for the king to marry a German noblewoman, Anne of Cleves. Unfortunately, her looks were not to Henry's liking, and the king retaliated by killing off some of his Protestant advisors. Henry eased out of that marriage by claiming non-consummation.

At that time, transiting Eris was square his Saturn and his Mercury, and trine his Ascendant. King Henry VIII tried to be sensible about marriage by marrying a young and attractive woman whom he hoped could provide him with another son.

Unfortunately, his wife, whose maiden name was Catherine Howard, was notorious for sleeping around, which was bad news for pro-Catholic nobles who had supported her. The Protestant nobles found out about her peccadilloes and exposed her affairs to the king, thereby bringing about her visit to the chopping block.

By the mid-1540's, Eris was in square to Henry's Juno, and he finally settled upon a practical marriage to Catherine Parr, who became a good stepmother to his children. She was fortunate in being able to outlive King Henry VIII before more courtly infighting did her in, like her predecessors.

It is an interesting speculation on what might have happened if King Henry VIII had really given in to the Pilgrimage of Grace and restored Roman Catholicism to England. Would the British Empire have developed at all if there had not been religious conflict with Spain? England helped the Netherlands separate from Spanish control because of the Spanish suppression of Protestants. Would the Netherlands have developed into a seafaring power under Spanish domination?

The reason for English colonies in America was to disrupt Spanish shipping, and provide a dumping ground for non-conformist Protestants. With a Roman Catholic England, there may have been no American colonies, no American Revolution, and no reason for a British Navy, with Sun never setting on the Union Jack. Theorists of political science can decide whether that would be a better world, particularly for Roman Catholics.

However, the result of the Pilgrimage of Grace was paranoia towards Catholics that persisted even into modern times. Catholics were seen as spies, subversives, and possible revolutionaries. This would be confirmed by the Gunpowder plot of 1605, when Guy Fawkes was immortalized as the archetypal Catholic terrorist.

After that came the Puritan revolution, the fear-mongering of Titus Oates, and finally the Glorious Rebellion of 1688, when another Eris-Pluto aspect marked the removal of all vestiges of Catholicism from British royalty, as will be explained in Chapter 14.

King Henry VIII

Bibliography - Chapter 11
Internet Sources

King Henry VIII
https://en.wikipedia.org/wiki/Henry_VIII_of_England

Catherine of Aragon
https://en.wikipedia.org/wiki/Catherine_of_Aragon

Suppression of the Monasteries
https://en.wikipedia.org/wiki/Dissolution_of_the_Monasteries

Pilgrimage of Grace
https://en.wikipedia.org/wiki/Pilgrimage_of_Grace

Monastery
https://en.wikipedia.org/wiki/Monastery

Book Sources

De Lisle, Leandra, *Tudor: Passion, Manipulation, Murder, The story of England's Most Notorious Royal Family,* New York, NY, Public Affairs, 2013.

Hoak, Dale, Ph.D, *The Age of Henry VIII,* Chantilly, VA, The Teaching Company, 2003

Ridpath, John Clark, LL.D., *Cyclopedia of Universal History: Being an account of the Principal Events in the career of the Human Race from the Beginnings of Civilization to the Present Time. From Recent and Authentic Sources. Vol. II, Part I, The Modern World.* Cincinnati, OH, The Jones Brothers Publishing Co, 1885.

Robinson, Nugent, *History of the World with all its Great Sensations together with Mighty and Decisive Battles and the Rise and Fall of its Nations from the Earliest Times to the Present Day, Vol. I,* New York, NY, P.F.Collier, Publisher, 1891.

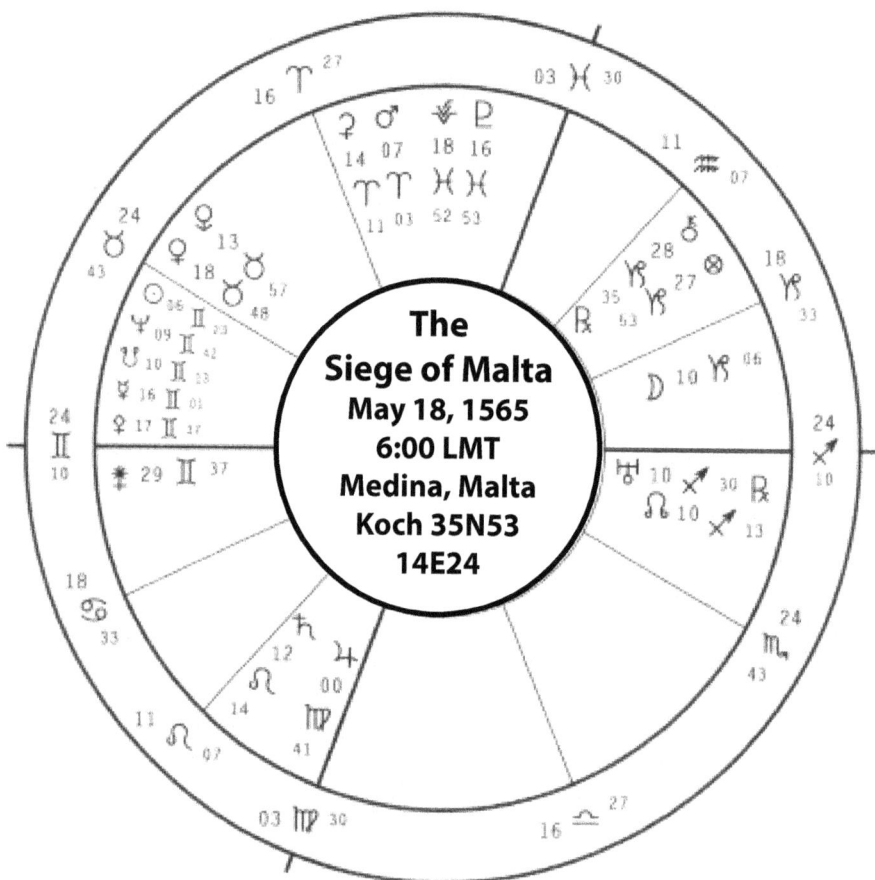

The
Siege of Malta
May 18, 1565
6:00 LMT
Medina, Malta
Koch 35N53
14E24

Chapter 12

The Siege of Malta
Eris sextile Pluto

During the 16th Century, the Ottoman Empire developed its naval power to threaten the forces of Christian Europe. One of their most significant victories, in 1522, was the capture of the island of Rhodes, which had been under the control of the Knights Hospitaller. The Knights had been a distinguished religious order since the days of the Crusades, and they suddenly found themselves without a home. To help their situation, Holy Roman Emperor Charles V gave them the island of Malta, and in 1530 the Knights of Malta were formed to manage the small island near Sicily.

Because of Malta's proximity to North Africa, the Ottoman Empire began to take interest in the island as a naval base, from which attacks could be launched against nations of Western Europe. Barbary corsairs, in the pay of the Turks, made surprise raids against Malta, and attempts were made with small military expeditions to capture the island. Each time, the attacks were foiled by defenses set up by the Knights of Malta.

The rulers of Western Europe, particularly King Philip II of Spain, recognized the strategic significance of Malta, and that retaliation needed to be made against the North African corsairs. In 1560, a fleet of more than 50 ships was sent out for an expedition to Tripoli in North Africa. When they arrived in Tripoli, the invading soldiers suffered from a lack of water, and a sudden storm hampered their advance. The Christian troops retreated to the island of Djerba, where they defeated the locals and set up a fortress. However, a Turkish fleet of 86 ships had sailed from Turkey, and attacked on May 11, 1560. About half the European ships ended up getting smashed by the superior forces of the Turkish fleet, and about 10,000 sailors were killed. The soldiers in the fortress were under siege for three months before they finally surrendered, and were carried off to Turkey as slaves. The battle of Djerba marked the high-water mark of Turkish naval achievements in the Mediterranean Sea.

At the battle of Djerba, Pluto was sextile Eris, and Eris was conjunct Pallas, asteroid of military wisdom. Pluto was square Saturn and Chiron. There was poor planning and a lack of organization by the Christian soldiers and the fleet. Although the Turkish fleet had the strategic advantage after the battle, they unwisely wasted the momentum by not following up with conquests. If the Turkish fleet had sailed for an attack on Malta, it might have been successful because the Knights of Malta had not completed their fortifications. The Turks ended up delaying the attack on Malta, and the Knights of Malta had the time to improve their defenses.

The Grand Master of the Knights of Malta was Jean Parisot de Valette. He was far-seeing when it came to strategy. He was the one who kept improving the fortifications of Malta. He warned the Western European powers that the island was under threat from the Turks. De Valette also organized a spy network to let him know if the Turks were making plans to assemble a fleet bound for Malta. It took the Turks five years to prepare a fleet, and De Valette received word of it before the ships sailed.

In March, 1565, as forecast by De Valette's spies, a Turkish fleet sailed from Constantinople to Malta. The fleet had 193 ships, and approximately 48, 000 men were going to take part in the attack. In contrast, the Knights of Malta and local defenders could only muster a force of about 6000 fighters. When De Valette received word that Turkish forces were on the way, he ordered an immediate spring harvest, bringing in all the fruits and grains to keep them from falling into the hands of the enemy. Wells that were outside the fortress walls were poisoned by throwing dead animals into them. The idea was to present a "scorched earth" landscape to the Turks so they would not be able to use any resources after the invasion.

The Turkish fleet arrived at Malta on May 18, but then made a tactical blunder. Rather than start the invasion, the fleet spent a few days sailing around Malta. The purpose was to show the defenders that they were hopelessly outnumbered which would demoralize them and make them surrender without any resistance. This strategy backfired, because it allowed the Knights of Malta plenty of time to get everyone into the fortresses. By the time the Turks did arrive on the shore, the Knights of Malta were safe and secure, and ready for a lengthy siege.

DeValette's spies warned him that the first attack would come on the Fortress of Saint Elmo. He had spent much time reinforcing the fortress, and loading the most powerful cannons into the building. When

The Battle of Djerba
May 11, 1560
12:00 LMT
Koch 32N53
10E52

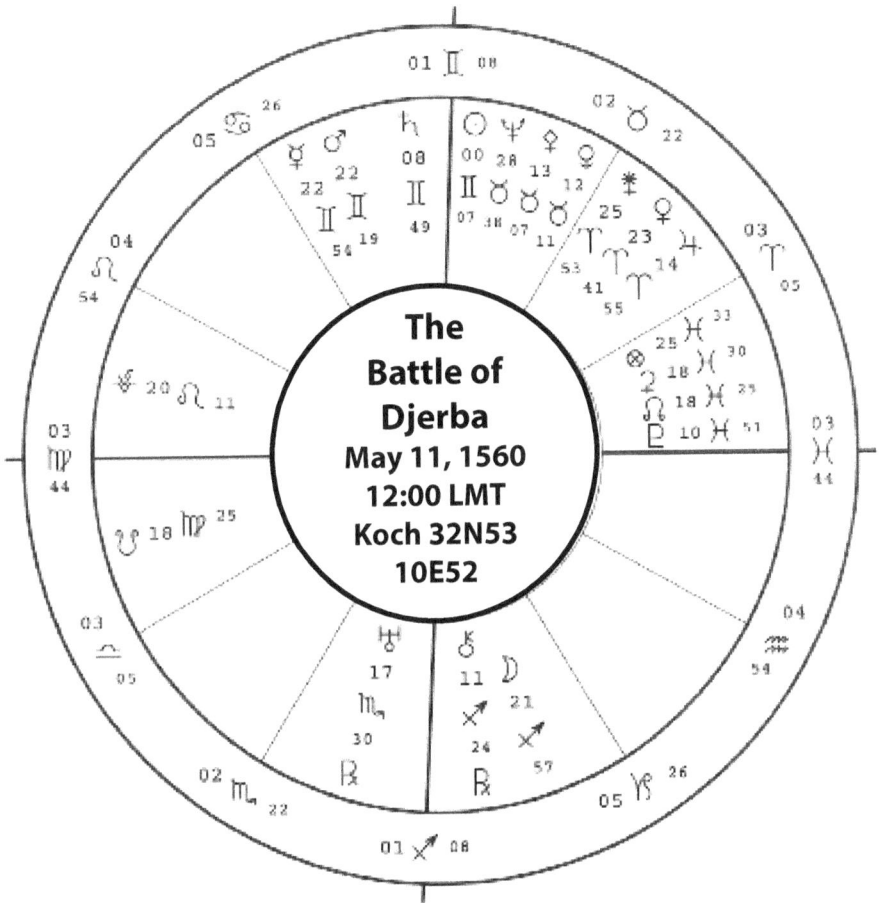

the Turks began their attack, they were massacred by the increased fire power from the fort. Saint Elmo was connected to the sea, and each night small boats would arrive from the main fortress, bringing more men and supplies, and taking away the wounded men.

DeValette hoped Saint Elmo would hold out until troops arrived from Europe. The news from Malta had frightened most European nations. Even Protestant Queen Elizabeth I of England saw the danger of the Turkish threat. However, the European powers were very slow in raising a relief party for Malta. One exception was a force of 600 Italian soldiers who sailed to Malta, managed to get around the Turkish fleet, and made a landing on the island to join the defenders. Their arrival was not strategically valuable, but they helped raise the morale of the defenders.

Saint Elmo fell on June 23, and the 1500 defenders were killed and decapitated by the Turks. In retaliation, DeValette ordered Turkish

The Fortress of Saint Elmo with a tower of skulls.

prisoners to be decapitated, and the heads of the prisoners were shot out of cannons to intimidate the Turkish army. The Turks were further demoralized by the conditions they found on the island. The main camp had been set up on a swamp, and the swarming mosquitoes infected the troops with malaria. In the end, disease would kill as many Turks as battle casualties.

In the chart for the Siege of Malta, Pluto is conjunct Vesta, the asteroid of hearth and home. For the residents of Malta, this was going to be a fight to the death for the sake of their homes. In previous raids by corsairs, those who surrendered were taken away and sold into slavery. This struggle would have a "Liberty or Death" spirit behind it.

Eris was trine the Moon, semi-sextile Mercury, Pallas, and Ceres, and square Saturn. Eris trine the Moon could represent the power of the sea, and how this battle was to play a part in the domination of the Mediterranean Sea. Mercury, ruler of Gemini, was conjunct Pallas, but with the semi-sextile to Eris and the square to Pluto, there is an indication of the confused planning for the battle. The corsair Turgut Reis was nominally in charge, but there were differences of opinion between the commanders of the land forces and the naval forces. The leadership became more muddled after Turgut Reis was killed about the time of the fall of Saint Elmo.

Eris semi-sextile Ceres might represent the loss of supplies that the Turks experienced once the Knights of Malta had all the crops brought inside the fortifications. Eris square Saturn could stand for the discipline and organization of the Knights of Malta in preparation for the siege, and for the intense resistance to the Turkish invasion. Heroic accounts described DeValette personally leading an attack against Turkish soldiers who had managed to break a hole in the walls. His leadership became legendary for rousing the besieged soldiers.

The siege went through the summer, and there was no sign of relief from the European powers. Finally, King Philip II of Spain ordered his vassal prince, Don Garcia, Viceroy of Sicily, to lead a relief expedition to Malta. Don Garcia had spent most of the summer raising troops, and he ended up with only 8000 soldiers. In spite of all the losses by the Turks, they still had twice as many men as Don Garcia. However, Don Garcia was able to trick the Turks with an act of daring. Rather than send a few ships as a vanguard, Don Garcia had his entire naval force arrive at once. The Turks were under the impression that these 8000 men were just the vanguard of a much larger force. On Sept. 11, 1565, the Turks boarded their ships and gave up on taking Malta. Accounts of Turkish casualties vary from 10,000 to 35,000, while the defenders of Malta lost one-third of their forces. The Turks got the worst of the siege and never attempted to invade Malta again.

Jean Parisot de Valette

In the aftermath of the battle, DeValette became an international hero, and the kings of Europe were more willing to listen to his plans for defense against the Turkish navy. The lesson learned from the Siege of Malta was that international cooperation was necessary to defeat a common enemy. By 1571, an alliance had been created called the Holy League, which brought together the naval forces of Spain, Naples, Sicily, Genoa, Venice, Tuscany, Parma, Urbina, and (last, but not least) Malta. This fleet destroyed the Turkish fleet at the battle of Lepanto, off the coast of Greece, on Oct. 7, 1571. The breaking of Turkish naval power meant that the Ottoman Empire was no longer a threat to Western Europe.

Aside from the humiliation of the Ottoman Empire, the story of the Siege of Malta added to the mythology of warfare that a righteous small force could hold out against a more sinister larger force. It was also the last victory won by Christian Knights, marking the passing of the spirit of chivalry.

Two hundred years after the battle, the French author Voltaire declared, "Nothing is so well known as the Siege of Malta." Yet, the downside of the siege was that it brought about greater dominance by Spain, with King Philip II as the model of an efficient tyrant. There was greater hegemony between Roman Catholic nations, which would lead to the next major conflict when Eris and Pluto aspected each other.

The Eris-Pluto sextile also marked the rise of a powerful Asian kingdom. In 1563, Prince Bayinnong came to the throne of Ayutthaya, which European explorers had designated as "Siam." King Bayinnong began a policy of expansion, which would increase the size of his kingdom with lands seized from Burma, Cambodia, and Malaysia. Economic growth came to Siam through trade agreements with the French and Portuguese traders. Ayutthaya remained a powerful kingdom until the mid-18th century, when provincial governors turned against the rulers, which was about the time of the next Eris-Pluto conjunction.

Bibliography - Chapter 12
Internet Sources

Knights Hospitaller
https://en.wikipedia.org/wiki/Knights_Hospitaller

History of Malta under the order of St. John
https://en.wikipedia.org/wiki/History_of_Malta_under_the_Order_of_Saint_John

Great Siege of Malta
https://en.wikipedia.org/wiki/Great_Siege_of_Malta

Turgut Reis
https://en.wikipedia.org/wiki/Dragut

Battle of Djerba
https://en.wikipedia.org/wiki/Battle_of_Djerba

Jean Parisot De Valette
https://en.wikipedia.org/wiki/Jean_Parisot_de_Valette

King Philip II of Spain
https://en.wikipedia.org/wiki/Philip_II_of_Spain

Battle of Lepanto
https://en.wikipedia.org/wiki/Battle_of_Lepanto

Ayutthaya Kingdom: The rise of "Siam"
https://en.wikipedia.org/wiki/Ayutthaya_Kingdom

Book Sources

Simon, Edith, **Knights of the Maltese Cross**, Horizon, New York, NY, March 1961, American Horizon Inc., Pages 48 -71.

Robinson, Nugent, **History of the World with all its Great Sensations together with Mighty and Decisive Battles and the Rise and Fall of its Nations from the Earliest Times to the Present Day**, Vol. I, New York, NY, P.F.Collier, Publisher, 1891

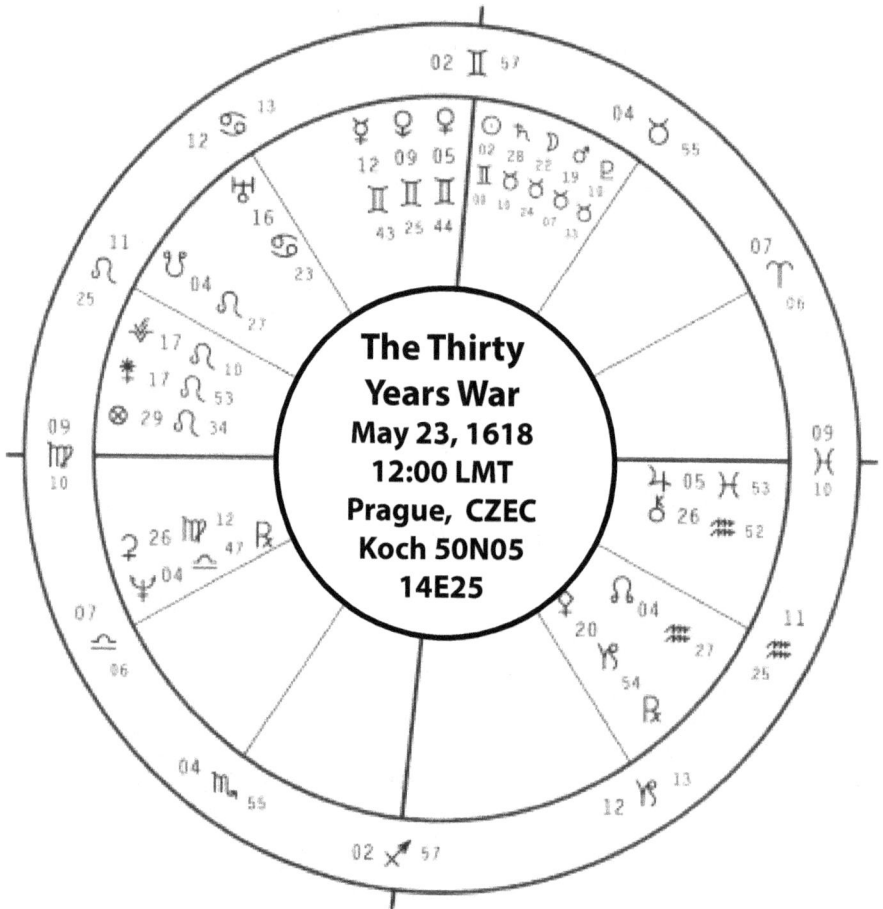

The Thirty
Years War
May 23, 1618
12:00 LMT
Prague, CZEC
Koch 50N05
14E25

Chapter 13

Eris Steps on the Gas,
or the Race of the Thirty Years War
Eris semi-sextile Pluto

Looking at the orbits of Eris and Pluto, it can be seen that Eris sometimes goes inside the orbit of Pluto. This was what happened during the 17th century, when Eris made its closest approach to the Sun, and started speeding up so that it was moving faster than Pluto. What was particularly interesting was that for a 30-year period (1618-1648), Eris and Pluto were moving at the same speed and were in a constant semi-sextile position with each other. In mundane matters, this semi-sextile corresponded with an event labeled by historians as the Thirty Years War.

Actually, it was not a single war, but a collection of wars in Northern Europe, which centered on the issue of religion. The Thirty Years War was considered to be the last great religious struggle in Europe, pitting the Roman Catholic kingdoms of Southern Europe against the Protestant kingdoms of Northern Europe. The main result was the weakening of the Holy Roman Empire, which Voltaire later declared, "Was not Holy, nor Roman, nor an Empire."

The seed for the Thirty Years War was planted in 1555, with a treaty known as the Peace of Augsburg. For years, there had been intermittent warfare between the Roman Catholic Holy Roman Empire and various German kingdoms and duchies which had embraced the teachings of Martin Luther. After much conflict, the Peace of Augsburg codified the principle of *Cuius regio, eius religio*, which meant that Lutherans could practice their religion freely in a land where the prince or duke was a Lutheran. The treaty did not address Calvinism, or any other new Protestant sect that might rise up.

The weaknesses became apparent in 1618 when Ferdinand II became the new Holy Roman Emperor. Trained by Jesuits, Ferdinand II had little tolerance for Protestants. One of his first decrees was to stop the construction of Protestant churches on what was considered "royal ground." This stirred up opposition in the Kingdom of Bohemia, which was ruled by the Holy Roman Emperor, but had been given a great deal of political and religious tolerance in the early 17th century. Emperor Ferdinand II sent four Catholic counselors to Prague to see that his will

Defenestration of Prague

was enforced, and when they met with Protestant lords of the Bohemian assembly, the meeting did not go well.

The meeting took place on the upper floor of the Bohemian Chancellery on May 23, 1618.

The Protestant lords began arguing as to whether the Catholic counselors intended to stop the construction of Protestant churches. The Catholic counselors dithered and equivocated, claiming they had to consult one of their colleagues before making a statement. Two Catholic nobles were permitted to leave the room. The remaining two, and their secretary, were accused of having drafted the letter ordering the end of Protestant church construction. The Protestant lords seized the two Catholic nobles, and their secretary, and tossed them out the window, which was 70 feet above the ground.

Miraculously, all three men survived the fall. Catholic reporters claimed that angels had saved them. Protestant reporters pointed out that there was a very large dung heap at the bottom of the tower. Whatever the result, this event became known as the "Defenestration of Prague", and for the Holy Roman Emperor it became a declaration of war. It took two years for Ferdinand II to get revenge, but by 1620 his troops had occupied Prague, 27 Protestant nobles were executed, and 12 nobles had their heads impaled on spikes as a warning to the population against defying the will of the emperor.

In the chart for the "Defenestration of Prague," Eris is conjunct Venus in House 10, and both are trine Neptune, in House 1 and retrograde. This would become a war of strange political bedfellows, though mainly focused on religion. Eris and Venus were square Jupiter, and the leaders in the war were willing to fight for religious beliefs, just as long as this did not interfere with their ability to rule.

Eris was also widely conjunct Mercury in Gemini, and in this war common sense strategies would be dominated by power politics and long-term plans by scheming leaders. The short term goals of victory on the battlefield were not as important as major rearrangements of alliances and boundaries.

The war between the Holy Roman Empire and Bohemia may have remained an isolated conflict except for the fact that other powers began to see it as an opportunity to take down the Holy Roman Empire. Lutheran kingdoms had formed themselves into a Protestant League, and began to rally and arm against the Holy Roman Emperor. In Hungary, a revolt broke out under the leadership of the Prince of Transylvania, Gabriel Bethien. With support from the Ottoman Empire, it was the wish of Gabriel Bethien to remove Hungary from the control of the Austrian empire. However, within a decade Gabriel Bethien switched sides, married a Hapsburg princess, and joined the Holy Roman Empire against the Ottoman Empire.

The Ottoman Empire also had a war on the side, with an attack against Poland, which was successful in crippling the Polish army. Poland had been an ally of the Holy Roman Empire, but was unable to send any military assistance. On the other side of Europe, Spain, which was also ruled by Hapsburgs, sent an army to assist the Austrian army. The Spaniards formed an alliance with the Protestant kingdom of Saxony, and their combined forces were able to defeat Protestant armies that were attempting to defend Bohemia.

It looked like Catholic forces might dominate central Europe, until the Kingdom of Denmark entered the war and began rallying the Protestant states. King Christian IV suffered several defeats and finally signed a peace with the Holy Roman Empire in 1629, which guaranteed his throne if he gave up his support of the Protestant states.

Gustavus Adolphus
Dec. 19, 1594
7:30 LMT
Stockholm,
Sweden
Koch 59N20
18E03

The first half of the war was particularly brutal, with little mercy being shown by the Catholic forces. The most horrific battle was the sack of Magdeburg in 1631, which was organized by the Count of Tilly. After a siege of two months, 25,000 citizens out of a population of 30,000 were put to death, including a column of children singing Lutheran hymns. The Count of Tilly considered himself to be the greatest conqueror since Ulysses defeated Troy, though he would be struck down the following year. Another Catholic leader who made a fortune for himself during the war was Albrecht Von Wallenstein, who seized the abandoned estates of fleeing Protestants. His greed and ambition became so notorious that even the Holy Roman Emperor turned against him, and Von Wallenstein was assassinated while fleeing from a charge of treason.

In 1630 Sweden entered the war. The most powerful military power in Northern Europe at the time was not going to stand by and allow the other Protestant nations to be destroyed. King Gustavus Adolphus proved

This illustration depicts the 1632 battle during which Gustavus Adolphus was killed.

to be a dynamic military figure that the Protestants could rally behind, and soon his army was winning major victories against the Holy Roman Empire. Previously, Gustavus Adolphus had been bogged down in a war against Poland and Lithuania, and had been unable to send help to the Protestant states. He got out of that war by convincing the Russian Czar, Michael I, to attack Poland and Lithuania in order to regain the Smolensk region. Czar Michael had been a supporter of the Hapsburgs, but the temptation to regain Smolensk was too great to resist. The Smolensk War became a sideshow in the Thirty Years War, with the Russians failing in their effort, but it freed up Sweden for the attack on Austria.

The natal chart of Gustavus Adolphus shows an Eris connection that may have enhanced his reputation. He had Jupiter opposing Saturn, and both were being squared by Eris. The square between Eris and Jupiter may have made him take his role as king very seriously. The square between Eris and Saturn may have made him seem stern, but

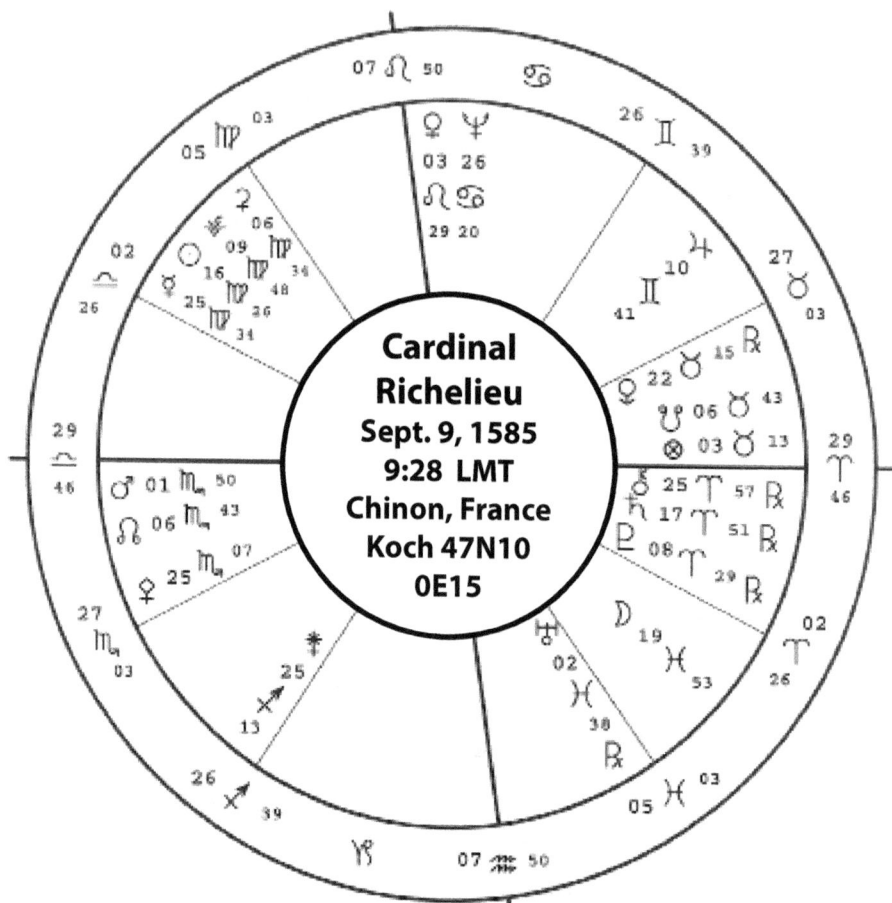

Cardinal Richelieu
Sept. 9, 1585
9:28 LMT
Chinon, France
Koch 47N10
0E15

fair in his dealings. He was the sort of blood-and-guts leader who was on the battlefield with his men, while other monarchs were hiding behind their armies. Pluto trine his Sun and Pallas may have contributed to this love of glory, and with Neptune making it a Grand Trine, there may have been elements of religious fanaticism to spur on his military ability.

In 1632, Gustavus Adolphus was killed in battle. His young daughter, Christina, (later to be immortalized by Greta Garbo in the film "Queen Christina") came to the throne. The

Armand Cardinal Richelieu

war continued under the regency of Count Oxenstierna, with the help of generous subsidies from France. At the time, the ruler of France was King Louis XIII. He had turned political matters over to his chief minister, Armand Cardinal Richelieu (best remembered as the villain in all of "The Three Musketeers" movies). Cardinal Richelieu arranged for payments to Sweden so they could hire German and Scottish mercenaries to continue the war. Although a Roman Catholic Cardinal, Richelieu was scheming against the Holy Roman Empire because he thought the Hapsburg dynasty was getting too powerful.

In the natal chart for Richelieu, Eris was trine Mercury, which was appropriate for this political mastermind who was always spinning plots and schemes. With his Eris opposing Pallas, he had the right amount of wisdom for determining which plots were best.

At the time when the Thirty Years War first began, transiting Eris was conjunct Jupiter in Richelieu's natal chart. Religious repercussions occurred because Richelieu was hiring Protestant mercenaries to attack the Austrian Catholics. According to legend, Richelieu responded that he was doing this only to keep Catholics from fighting Catholics.

The war started to turn against Sweden, and the Swedish army was expelled from the lands of the Holy Roman Empire. A temporary peace was signed in 1635, but a peace settlement was not in the interests of Armand Cardinal Richelieu. It was at that point Richelieu brought France into the Thirty Years War, fighting on two fronts against Spain and Austria. When the French war began, transiting Eris was semi-sextile Richelieu's natal Eris, and transiting Pluto was conjunct Richelieu's natal Eris. Richelieu maintained his discordant plots so well that the war would continue even after his death in 1642.

Spain was distracted from the war in 1640 when a war with Portugal began, and then increased attacks on Spanish holdings in the Netherlands, as well as a rebellion in Catalonia, further reduced Spanish military power so that no more aid could be given to the Holy Roman Empire. It was during this time of trouble for Spain that Eris and Pluto changed signs, with Eris moving into Cancer, and Pluto moving into Gemini. For the previous 60 years, Spain had control of Portugal, and the Portuguese royal family was in exile. On December 1, 1640, with Eris and Pluto having changed signs, King John IV of Portugal was restored to the throne, breaking the hold of Spain, and preventing Spanish troops from attacking the Protestant forces.

The only major power that was not involved with the war was England, which was having its own internal difficulties. Their last war was a brief one with France in 1627-1629 that was a minor sideshow to the larger conflict. Later attempts at war were blocked by the Puritans in Parliament, much to the fury of King Charles I, who was seen as too sympathetic toward Catholics.

As the Thirty Years War approached its climax, England was involved in its own civil war, leading to the beheading of King Charles I and the establishing of a Puritan commonwealth.

Although many German states had made peace with the Holy Roman Empire, Sweden was still eager for revenge, and hostilities were quickly resumed after a short peace. Their military efforts proved valuable in 1643, when Denmark threatened to enter the war again, but this time on the side of the Holy Roman Empire. The Swedish navy quickly destroyed the Danish navy, and the Swedish army seized Jutland in order to prevent the Danish army from joining the army of the Holy Roman Empire.

Negotiations to end the war dragged on for years, but the need for peace became apparent for the Hapsburgs after the French and Swedish armies started to link up. The final battle of the war was the conquest of Prague, which brought the war home to the place where it had begun thirty years earlier. Emperor Ferdinand II died in 1647, and his successor, Ferdinand III, was interested in ending the war and making a lasting peace. By this time, the fighting was widespread and involved numerous political quarrels besides the conflict between Catholics and Protestants. The result of the conquests was to spur on the diplomats who had been meeting in Westphalia. Just as the war had been a many-sided conflict, so too was the peace a many-sided array of treaties, with separate treaties for each nation and duchy. The last treaty was signed in October, 1648, and (guess what!) Eris and Pluto were still only semi-sextile from each other.

The peace that came out of the Thirty Years War would have an important effect on the concept of a nation-state. The German principalities were no longer considered vassals of the Holy Roman Empire. Ferdinand III had to make numerous concessions to the German states, including the issue of religious control. Princes and dukes would decide what religion would be practiced in their lands, and there was even a tolerance towards Calvinism. France and Sweden came out of the war with increased territorial gains, as well as financial rewards.

In the treaty chart, with Eris trine Venus and sextile Ceres, Spain and the Holy Roman Empire came out the worst for the conflict, having lost prestige and territory. Although the Austrian Emperor still called himself the "Holy Roman Emperor," it was a hollow title with little authority. Eris quincunx Neptune brought an acceptance of religious differences, and with Neptune opposing Pluto religious conflicts would be kept out of the public eye. Still, with Ceres square Mars and Chiron, there were divisions left by this war which would encourage resistance to other religious ideas.

The Eris-Pluto semi-sextile lasted for another three years after the Peace of Westphalia, but there was plenty of discord to be found in England, where shock waves were sent through the paradigm of the Divine Right of Kings with the execution of King Charles I. There were counter plots, with King Charles II attempting to rally the Scots against the Puritan commonwealth, but then being forced to sneak off to France after defeat by Oliver Cromwell. As Eris and Pluto separated, England settled down into being a dull, dreary country with no merriment, no monarchy, and no theater.

Perhaps Portugal came out the best of the European nations involved in the war, having the monarchy restored after 60 years of exile. However, this event, taking place just after Eris-Pluto changed signs, would have a major impact on English history. The daughter of King John IV of Portugal, Catherine of Braganza, married King Charles II of England. (According to legend, she was the one who introduced tea into England.)

Unfortunately, Queen Catherine was barren, which left King Charles II without an heir. The throne was taken over by his brother, James, who was a Roman Catholic. This Catholic King saw major discord at the time of the next Eris-Pluto aspect, which is described in the next chapter.

During the Eris-Pluto semi-sextile, there was another discordant theme running through central Europe, and that was an increase of Witchcraft trials. In the areas of the devastated German states, Catholic witch-hunters moved into the lands and started blaming supernatural forces for the failure of crops, famine, and plague. Numerous citizens, including high officials, were accused of Witchcraft, then tortured, tried, and executed. Of course, the property of accused witches would be up for grabs. Some historians think this period marked the peak of the European Witchcraft hysteria.

Europe was not the only area facing religious warfare during the Eris-Pluto semi-sextile. In Japan, there was a peasant revolt called the Shimabara Rebellion. Initially, it started over taxes when a new castle was built at Shimabara in 1637. It became a religious struggle when it was supported by thousands of peasants who had converted to Roman Catholicism. The shogunate had to send an army of 125,000 troops to suppress the rebel army of 27,000 men.

Once their stronghold was conquered in 1638, the rebels were beheaded, and the Roman Catholics were blamed for having caused the rebellion. Trade was banned with Spain and Portugal, and then Christianity became an outlawed religion. Japan had limited contact with Europe only by trading with Dutch ships at designated ports. This period of isolation would last for 216 years until the policy was changed. The event occured during another Eris-Pluto aspect.

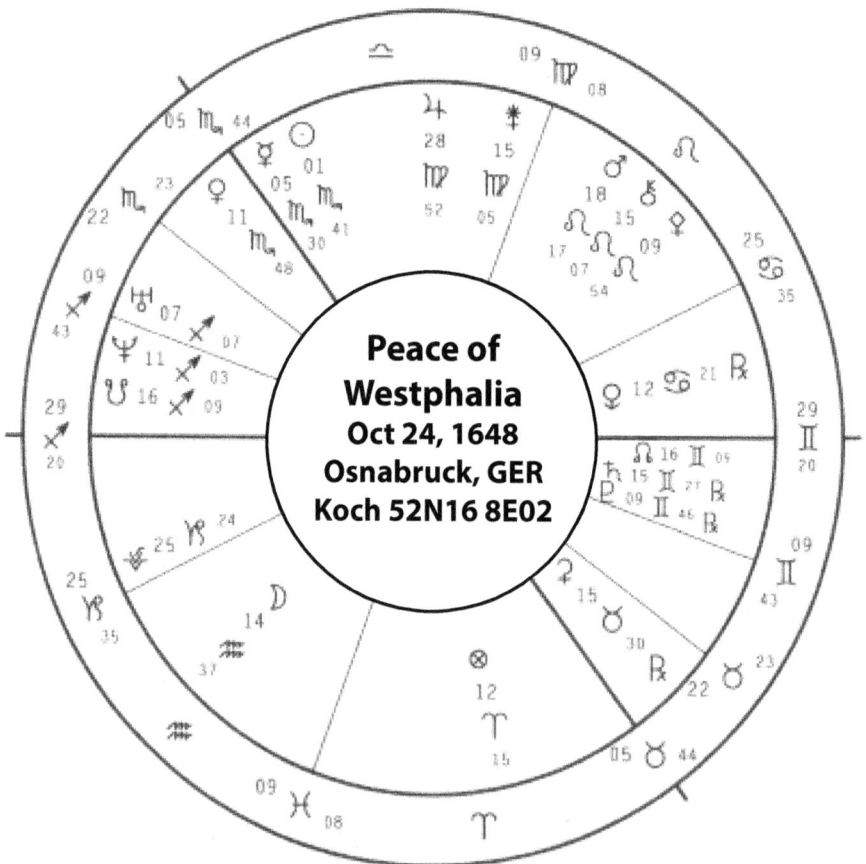

Peace of Westphalia
Oct 24, 1648
Osnabruck, GER
Koch 52N16 8E02

Bibliography for Chapter 13
Internet Sources

Thirty Years War
https://en.wikipedia.org/wiki/Thirty_Years%27_War

Count of Tilly
https://en.wikipedia.org/wiki/Johann_Tserclaes,_Count_of_Tilly

Sack of Magdeburg
https://en.wikipedia.org/wiki/Sack_of_Magdeburg

Albrecht von Wallenstein
https://en.wikipedia.org/wiki/Albrecht_von_Wallenstein

King Gustavus Adolphus
https://en.wikipedia.org/wiki/Gustavus_Adolphus_of_Sweden

Cardinal Richelieu
https://en.wikipedia.org/wiki/Cardinal_Richelieu

Peace of Westphalia
https://en.wikipedia.org/wiki/Peace_of_Westphalia

Wurzburg Witch Trials
https://en.wikipedia.org/wiki/W%C3%BCrzburg_witch_trial

Shimabara Rebellion
https://en.wikipedia.org/wiki/Shimabara_Rebellion

Book Sources

Ridpath, John Clark, LL.D., *Cyclopedia of Universal History: Being an account of the Principal Events in the career of the Human Race from the Beginnings of Civilization to the Present Time. From Recent and Authentic Sources. Vol. II, Part I*, The Modern World. Cincinnati, OH, The Jones Brothers Publishing Co, 1885.

Robinson, Nugent, *History of the World with all its Great Sensations together with Mighty and Decisive Battles and the Rise and Fall of its Nations from the Earliest Times to the Present Day, Vol. I*, New York, NY, P.F.Collier, Publisher, 1891.

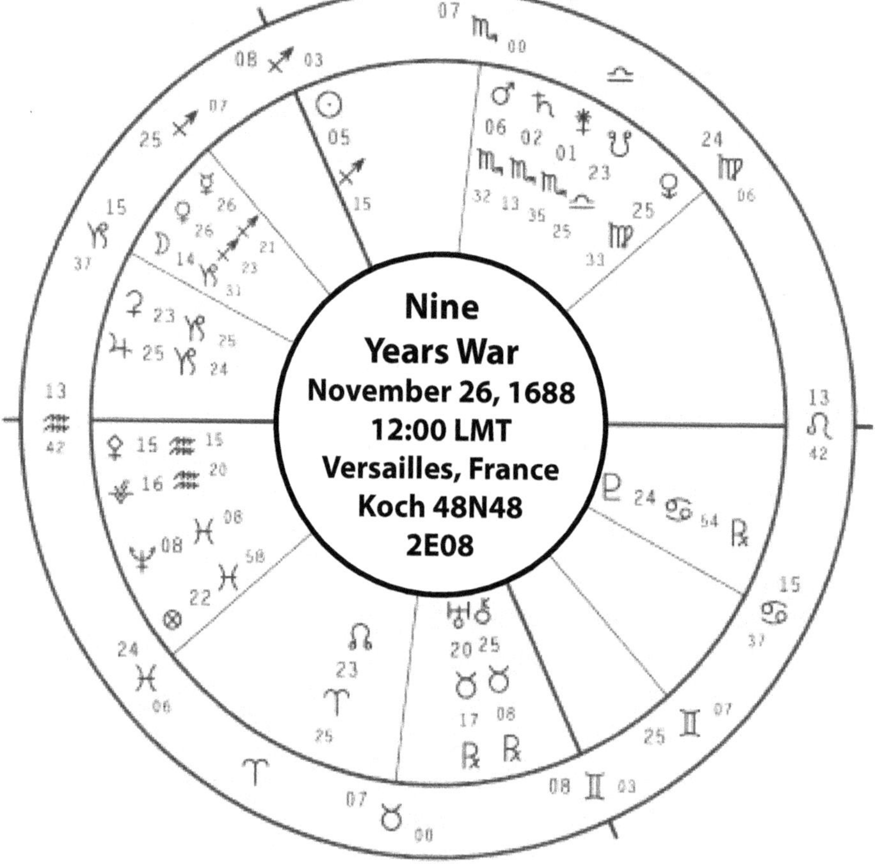

Nine
Years War
November 26, 1688
12:00 LMT
Versailles, France
Koch 48N48
2E08

Chapter 14

Eris in the Lead
The Glorious Revolution and
Queen Anne's War
Eris sextile Pluto

After 1648, Eris began speeding up as she was approaching the point in her orbit closest to the Sun. If astronomers at the time had more powerful telescopes, they might have been treated to a sight of two dwarf planets racing through the zodiac. Eris spent only 16 years in the sign of Leo, and then another 16 years in Virgo before starting to slow down. By 1688, Eris was far enough ahead of Pluto to form a sextile, and by the time Eris entered Libra, her speed had reduced so that it was synchronized with Pluto, resulting in a sextile that lasted about 25 years.

It was at the beginning of this sextile that an event took place, which could be seen as an inversion of the Eris-Pluto square of 1536. At that time, a Protestant King of England destroyed the power of his Roman Catholic subjects, establishing England as a Protestant nation, and reducing Roman Catholics to second-class citizens. In 1688, a Roman Catholic King of England was ousted by his Protestant subjects, confirming that England would remain a Protestant kingdom, and causing Roman Catholics to remain second-class citizens for nearly 140 years.

The "villain" of the story was King James II, who had openly flaunted his conversion to Roman Catholicism. King Charles II had allowed a certain tolerance of Catholics, especially since he was married to a Portuguese princess. Unfortunately, although King Charles II was notorious for fathering illegitimate children, he was unable to father a child with his own wife. This meant that his brother James would be heir to the throne, and this fact sent waves of fear through the Protestant population. From 1678 to 1681, there was an anti-Catholic hysteria, promoted by a writer named Titus Oates, who wrote a manuscript claiming that Catholics were going to assassinate King Charles II so that his Catholic brother could come to the throne as King James II, and make Roman Catholicism the religion of the land.

In the natal chart of King James II, there is a T-square with the Sun, Ceres, and Chiron. Such a square would suggest ego-issues and problems with nurturing and education. Certainly, being a prince on the run during the Puritan rebellion was not helpful for his development. To add to matters, Eris was aspecting the bodies in the T-square. Natal Eris was sextile Chiron, the wounded healer, and the role of James as a Catholic heir was quite divisive to the body politic. With Eris quincunx Ceres, he was noted for fathering several children, but only three survived past infancy. He also had Eris squaring the Moon, and by some accounts he was a devoted family man, and won the hearts of the public with his leadership skills, particularly when leading the effort to extinguish the Great Fire of London. However, he had Eris trine his Sun, and he did believe in the Divine Right of Kings, which made people worry that he would be as demanding and uncompromising as King Charles I.

To be fair to King James, when he came to the throne in 1685, he did not bring in the Inquisition as had Bloody Mary Tudor. His path was one of "tolerance", resulting in a "Declaration of Indulgence". This edict stated that all religions would be tolerated, and it would no longer be necessary to swear an oath to the Church of England to serve in the government. The edict was particularly popular in Ireland, since the Irish had been excluded from political participation because of their religion. Even non-conformist preachers like William Penn supported the "Declaration of Indulgence." However, the edict aroused the disfavor of the members of the Church of England, since it diminished their privilege in maintaining control over the government. Another act which brought discontent was the forming of a standing army that had Roman Catholic officers, which created a fear that Protestants would be attacked.

King James II

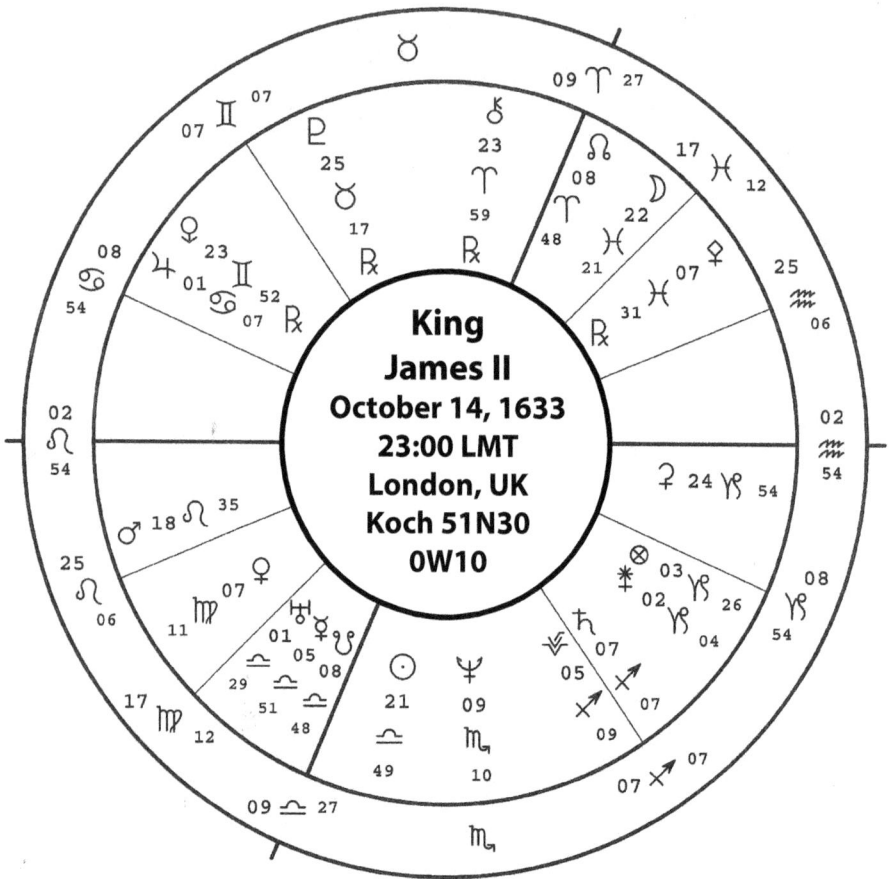

King
James II
October 14, 1633
23:00 LMT
London, UK
Koch 51N30
0W10

King James II aroused further discontent in the American colonies when he decided to do away with individual colonial charters and promoted a single colonial governor to rule over the "Dominion of New England." Sir Edmund Andros was given this task, and the colonists of New England regarded him as a tyrant. A game of hide-and-seek ensued, in which colonists would hide the royal charters so that Andros could not confiscate them, and the colonial legislatures would raise all manner of legal obstacles against Andros.

The English accepted the whims of King James because they believed his reign would not last long, since he was in his mid-fifties at the time. His daughters, Mary and Anne, who were likely to succeed him, were well-known Protestants. They could be persuaded to undo the "tolerance" that James had espoused. For members of the Church of England, it was a matter of sitting and waiting. However, that policy changed on June 10, 1688, when James' wife, Queen Mary, gave birth to a son. This prince was seen as a possible progenitor of a Roman Catholic dynasty. The birth aroused the Protestant population and created a sentiment that James had to go, and that he should be replaced by his daughter Mary.

In the chart for Princess Mary, Eris is conjunct Mars, which can indicate a stubborn determination to get things done. Mary may have expected to be Queen of England, and that the future of the Stuart dynasty would continue through her. Yet, her Eris-Mars conjunction was trine Saturn, and her sense of accomplishment may have been dominated by a stronger male figure. For Mary, this would have been her husband, William of Orange. Her Eris-Mars was also square Venus, and this might have brought a devotion to her spouse which made her willing to share everything, even political power.

William of Orange, Stadtholder of Holland, Utrecht, and Zeeland, was also a descendant of King Charles I of England, and had claims to the English crown. A conspiracy was formed to ask William and Mary to "invade" England and to take control of the monarchy. William was hesitant, but agreed to the request only after an official "invitation" was sent to him by seven leading nobles, acknowledging that this was the will of the English people. During the summer of 1688, William assembled a naval force of more than 400 ships (larger than the Spanish Armada) and 40,000 men. The fleet set sail towards the end of October, which was a surprise for the forces of King James, since autumn was considered to be a time of bad weather and not fit for naval expeditions.

In the natal chart of William, Eris is conjunct Saturn at the bottom of the chart. Eris-Saturn conjunctions can mark peaceful upheavals which shake the established authority. (The most recent Eris-Saturn conjunction, as of this writing, was in September, 1997. This was during the funeral of Princess Diana, when mountains of flowers were left outside of Buckingham Palace.) Other indicators of William upsetting authority are Eris sextile Mars, Chiron, and Vesta, and Eris trine Ceres. Eris aspects such as these can indicate losses, particularly property losses. Yet, Saturn joining Eris in these aspects may have added security to the proposition. This may have been the reason why William was reluctant to take the throne until he was "invited", thereby making sure that he had enough public support for the effort. William may also have been helped with Eris square his natal Neptune/Uranus conjunction, setting him up as one who changes the times and creates a new order. It is interesting to note that this conjunction took place during the reign of Oliver Cromwell and the dominance of the Puritans, and it was part of their Anti-Catholic mentality which helped propel William to greater power.

In 1688, transiting Eris was square William's natal Pallas, which was good for planning, and sextile his Sun, establishing him as a figure of discord. Transiting Pluto was trine his natal Sun and Jupiter, which was indicating a time for greatness and transformation. For the first time in 600 years, a foreign prince was able to cross the channel and take the English throne. Yet, William was greeted in England more as a liberator than an invader. There were some minor battles between William's troops and royalist troops, but the support for King James quickly dissolved.

King Louis XIV of France tried to help James by issuing a declaration of war against William on November 26, 1688, and this was the beginning of the Nine Year's War. In the chart for the declaration of war, Pluto is in opposition to Jupiter and Ceres, and Eris is part of an Earth grand trine with Jupiter, Ceres, and Chiron. The body politic of Great Britain would be wounded for centuries by the divisions made at this time. It was a costly affair, not just for the European powers, but for their American colonies as well. It was also a time of general insecurity, and fertile ground for mass hysteria, which may have contributed to the Salem Witch Trials in 1692. Pluto opposing Jupiter and Ceres may have added to the dark fears and panic.

Conversely, Eris was square Venus and Mercury, and apart from the military matters, it was also a time of intellectual advancement, aided by men such as Isaac Newton, Edmond Halley, and Gottfried Leibniz. It was the beginning of the enlightenment that would fully bloom in the 18th Century. Pluto was sextile Uranus and Chiron, and it may have been the origin of some helpful changes, particularly in the field of science.

In December, 1688, King James, his wife, and child had to flee from England to France. In the chart of King James, transiting Eris was trine his natal Pluto and his natal Ceres, indicating a transformation and a loss of property. Eris was square his natal Eris, and the Glorious Revolution may have ended the upheaval in the life of James. Though there were some unsuccessful attempts to regain the throne, he was relegated to the role of an exiled king. Transiting Pluto was sextile his natal Pluto, squaring natal Chiron and his Sun, as well as opposing natal Ceres. It marked a time when he was cast down, and the course of history changed with him being kicked to the side.

As a final act of petulance, King James tossed the Royal Seal into the River Thames. This action actually helped William to come

Queen Mary II
April 30, 1662
2:22 LMT
London, UK
Koch 51N30
0W10

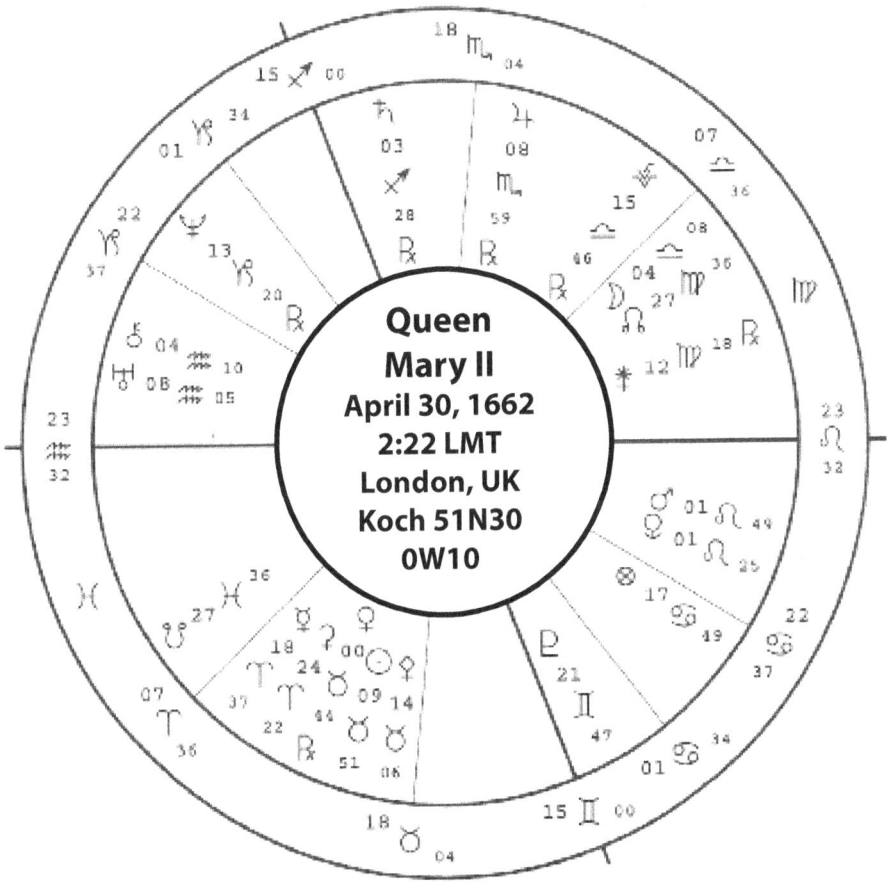

to the throne, because when Parliament debated the matter of William becoming king, it could not decide on whether King James had been deposed or conquered. It was finally decided that because he had tossed away the Royal Seal, King James had abdicated. His daughter, Mary was proclaimed as his successor, and William was made co-ruler with Mary. In her willingness to share with her husband, Mary had her sister, Anne, sign an agreement that

William would be able to rule even if Mary died. William's claim to the throne was maintained even after the death of Mary in 1694, and Anne was not able to claim the throne until William died in 1702.

Before he arrived in France, King James had been captured by Dutch troops, but King William ordered that he should be allowed to escape, since he did not want to make a martyr out of James. Upon his arrival in France, James was supported by King Louis XIV, and began a series of military expeditions to reclaim his kingdom. King William was distracted by a rebellion in Scotland, which enabled James to lead a military expedition to Ireland in 1689. James rallied the Irish to his cause, and hoped to win enough support to take back his crown. In 1690, King William and his army arrived in Ireland, and defeated the forces of James at the Battle of the Boyne. As military defeats went, it was only a minor setback, and James could have regrouped his troops by retreating to Dublin. Instead, he and his officers left the army and returned to France, ostensibly to bring back more military aid. The Irish forces were quickly defeated by King William, and the Irish long resented the abandonment by James, forever referring to him as "James the Shit!"

In the American colonies, Andros was removed as royal governor, and new royal governors were appointed, and new charters were given to the colonies. In the early 1690's, the French colonies in Canada formed alliances with Native American tribes to attack English settlements in Maine and New Hampshire. The English colonies made alliances with other Native American tribes to retaliate against the French. These battles in the colonies lasted until 1697, when France and England signed the Treaty of Ryswick, thereby ending the Nine Year's War. France agreed to no longer support James as the rightful king of England.

In spite of the period of peace, King Louis XIV remained as a threat to England. Louis was born with Eris trine his Ceres, and he was infamous for his extravagance, which was constantly bankrupting France. His Eris was sextile his Midheaven, and the main theme of his reign was the centralization of power, in which all of the nobles of France would be gathered at the King's court in Versailles so that the king could keep watch over them. The result of this was to remove the nobles from connections with the people they ruled, thereby making it impossible for nobles to help solve problems in their regions of France. The growing extravagance and centralization would help bring about the French Revolution in the 18th Century.

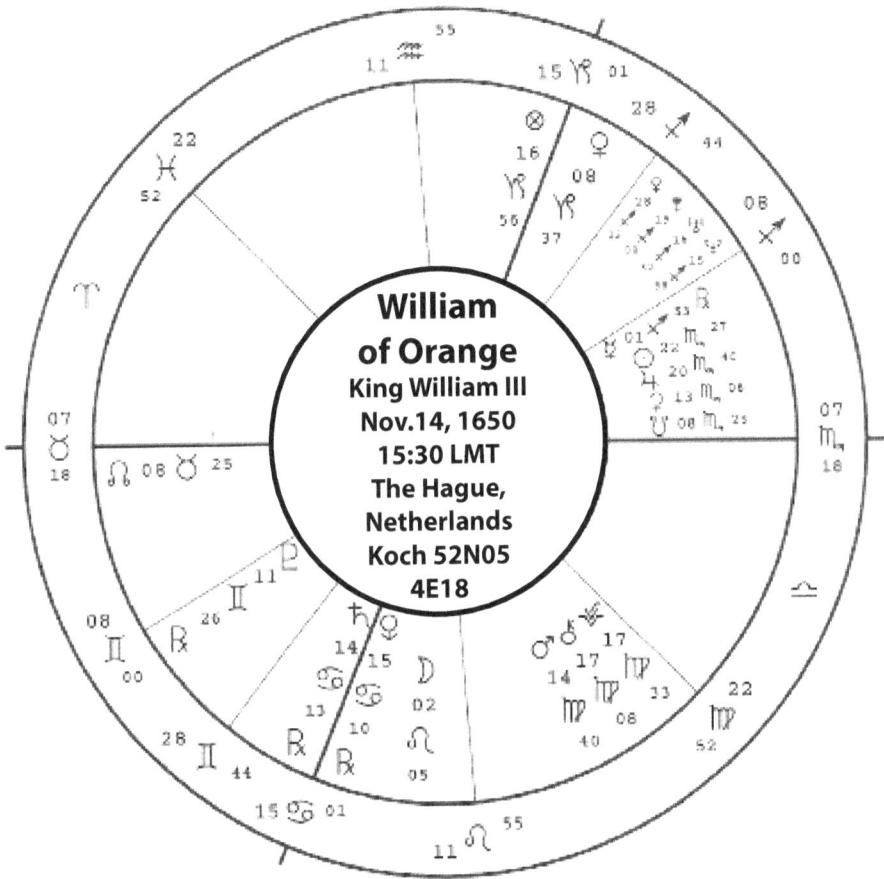

William
of Orange
King William III
Nov.14, 1650
15:30 LMT
The Hague,
Netherlands
Koch 52N05
4E18

The peace between England and France barely lasted four years when another bloody conflict broke out between the two countries. In Europe, the war was known as "The War of Spanish Succession," but in America it would later be designated as "Queen Anne's War." For years, there had been diplomatic arguments over who would become the next king of Spain, since the Spanish King Charles II had no direct heirs. Before he died in 1700, King Charles II bequeathed the Spanish crown to Philip of Anjou, the

nephew of King Louis XIV of France. The major European powers realized this would lead to a joining of the French and Spanish empires, and upset the balance of power between nations. The result was that England, Austria, Prussia, Portugal, the Dutch Republic, and various small kingdoms ganged up against France, which was aided by two small countries, Bavaria and the Duchy of Mantua. Spain was subjected to a civil war between "pro-Philip" factions and "anti-Philip factions."

The fighting in the "War of Spanish Succession" lasted more than ten years. In Great Britain, it made a national hero out of the Duke of Marlborough, the "dux bellorum" of the military forces, who commanded an English army into a European war for the first time in more than a century. His victory at the Battle of Blenheim insured that France would not have an easy victory, and the Kingdom of Bavaria dropped out of the war. However, there was no chance that the Grand Alliance against France would have an easy victory, and the war dragged on for years with a series of battles that ended inconclusively. After a while, the Duke of Marlborough fell out of favor, and more diplomatic solutions were proposed.

The Battle of the Boyne

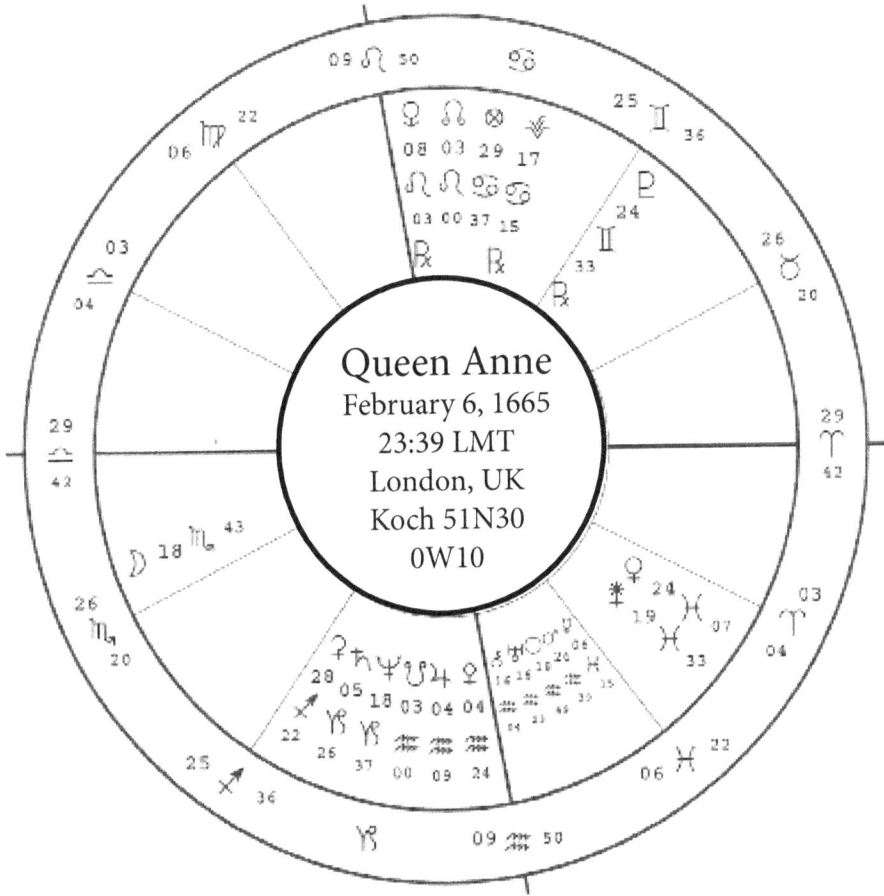

Queen Anne
February 6, 1665
23:39 LMT
London, UK
Koch 51N30
0W10

The war had begun under the reign of King William III, and it continued when Queen Anne came to the throne. In Anne's natal chart, Eris is conjunct the Midheaven. It had not been expected that this second daughter of King James II would become queen. King James or his daughter, Mary, were expected to continue the Stuart line. Yet, the twisting turns of political events put Anne in the line of succession. Unfortunately, she was not able to continue the Stuart line, as her children were stillborn or died in infancy due to drinking infected milk.

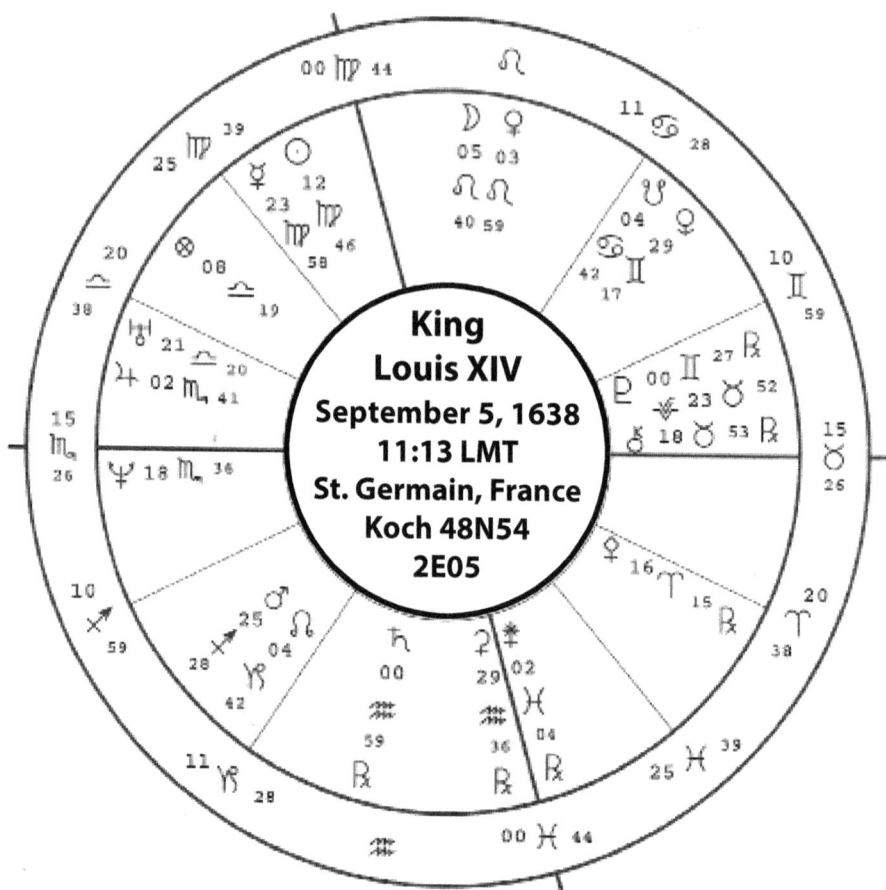

King
Louis XIV
September 5, 1638
11:13 LMT
St. Germain, France
Koch 48N54
2E05

Pluto square Venus would suggest problems in sexual matters. After 17 pregnancies, Anne's health was wrecked, and she began suffering from gout and became terribly obese. Her friend, Sarah Churchill wrote of her, "There was something of majesty in her look, but mixed with a gloominess of soul." Pluto trine her Mars might represent the conflict associated with most of her reign.

With Eris opposing her Jupiter and Pallas, her reign did become noteworthy with matters of style,

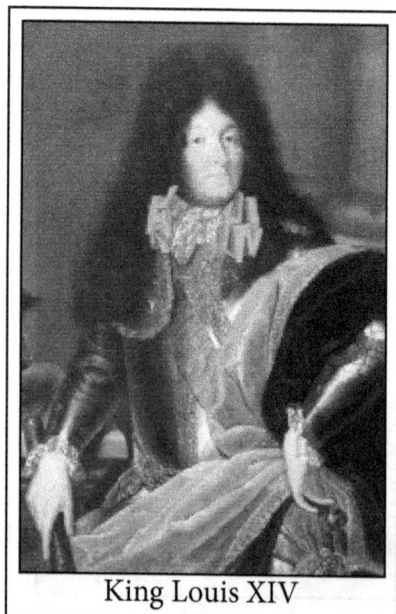

King Louis XIV

particularly with baroque architecture and distinctive curving furniture that was popular at the time. Eris was at the point of a Yod with Saturn and Mercury, and there was a somber seriousness to the times that would later appeal to some Victorians. In the 1880's, W.S. Gilbert would quip:

"Be eloquent in praise
Of the very dull old days
That have long since passed away,
And convince them, if you can,
That the reign of good Queen Anne
Was culture's palmiest day."

In the American colonies, far away from European political intrigue, Queen Anne's War was fought with determination by men defending their homes as opposed to royal honor. Once again, French and English colonies were embroiled in war, with Native American tribes choosing up sides. Adding to the warfare were attacks made

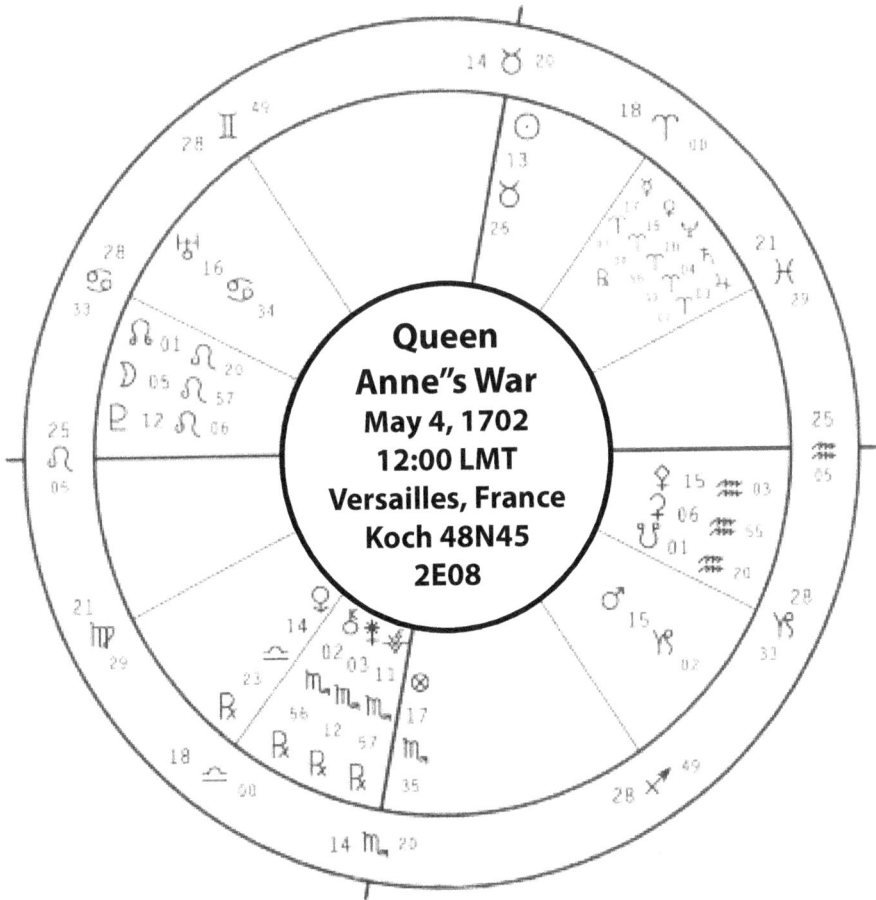

Queen
Anne"s War
May 4, 1702
12:00 LMT
Versailles, France
Koch 48N45
2E08

against French and Spanish colonies in the Caribbean, along the coast of Florida, and on the mouth of the Mississippi River. Major English victories took place in Maine and on the coast of Canada, disrupting communication between France and her colonies.

In the chart for "Queen Anne's War", Eris was square Mars and Uranus, opposing Mercury, and trine Pallas, asteroid of military wisdom. It was during this period that a new kind of warfare made its appearance. While European armies massed large forces and relied on strategies with cavalry and artillery, in America a simpler form of battle was taking place. Benjamin Church had served in King Philip's war in the 1670's, and he learned the warfare techniques of the Native Americans. Church formed a new fighting group called the "Rangers" which used these methods in the war against the French. A "Ranger" had to live off the land, be skilled in camouflage, and make rapid infantry marches. Benjamin Church wrote down all these techniques, and the lessons of his experiences provided training for future soldiers through the 18th century into the 20th century.

It was also during this period that famous pirates received their training for what was called "The Golden Age of Piracy." Historians have marked the Golden Age as starting around 1650, but the period after Queen Anne's War brought the most notorious pirates such as Edward Teach (Blackbeard), John Rackham (Calico Jack) and Bartholomew Roberts (Black Bart.) The post-war resurgence of piracy was populated by the most dangerous characters that would fight to the death rather than surrender. Though they were eventually vanquished, their exploits spawned a new genre of legends and adventure literature.

Another outgrowth of the war was the creation of the kingdom of Prussia. Originally, Prussia had been a duchy in the Holy Roman Empire, controlled by the Hohenzollern family. As the "War of Spanish Succession" was starting, the Holy Roman Emperor wanted Prussia to join in the fight against France. As an inducement, he declared that Prussia was no longer a duchy, and the Hohenzollerns could rule over it as kings. Through the 18th century, Prussia would grow in size and power to play a major role in the politics of Northern Europe. In the 19th century, Prussia was beaten by Napoleon, but was able to revive and finally defeat Napoleon at Waterloo. Later in the 19th century, Prussia took the lead in German Unification, with the Hohenzollerns becoming emperors, which would have a nasty result on European history.

"Queen Anne's War" dragged on until 1713, when issues were finally resolved by the Treaty of Utrecht. England came out the best

Treaty of Utecht
April 11, 1713
12:00 LMT
Utrecht, NETH
Koch 52N05 5E08

in the treaty, gaining control of Nova Scotia, Newfoundland, and the Hudson Bay area. However, the descriptions of the boundaries of the territories were unclear and eventually brought about later conflict. Philip of Anjou was allowed to become the King of Spain, but he had to renounce his connections to the French crown. Queen Anne was not able to enjoy the time of peace at the end of the war, since her health was declining and she died in 1714, the last Stuart monarch on the English throne. The Stuarts were replaced by the German House of Hanover, leading to complaints about German kings on an English throne. It was at this time that Eris started slowing down, though still sextile Pluto. As Eris entered Scorpio, Pluto began speeding up, and in 20 years there would be another semi-sextile aspect, and another upset to the balance of power in Europe.

Apart from the international struggle of Queen Anne's War, during the Eris-Pluto sextile there was a local struggle in Northern Europe, which lasted from 1700 to 1721. The Great Northern War was a series of wars between Czar Peter the Great of Russia and King Charles XII of Sweden, with shifting alliances of various states entering and leaving the war, such as Denmark, Poland, Saxony, Lithuania, and Finland.

Although King Charles XII was a dynamic leader, he did not have the resources of Peter the Great, and within twenty years Sweden lost most of its overseas lands in the Baltic region. This war would mark the rise of Russia in dominating the region, which will be shown in the next chapter.

Bibliography - Chapter 14
Internet Sources

King Charles II
https://en.wikipedia.org/wiki/Charles_II_of_England

Catherine of Braganza
https://en.wikipedia.org/wiki/Catherine_of_Braganza

King James II of England
https://en.wikipedia.org/wiki/James_II_of_England

Mary, daughter of James
https://en.wikipedia.org/wiki/Mary_II_of_England

William of Orange
https://en.wikipedia.org/wiki/William_III_of_England

Sir Edmund Andros
https://en.wikipedia.org/wiki/Edmund_Andros

Queen Anne
https://en.wikipedia.org/wiki/Anne,_Queen_of_Great_Britain

Queen Anne Style
https://en.wikipedia.org/wiki/Queen_Anne_style_architecture

King Louis XIV
https://en.wikipedia.org/wiki/Louis_XIV_of_France

Nine Years War
https://en.wikipedia.org/wiki/Nine_Years%27_War

War of Spanish Succession
https://en.wikipedia.org/wiki/War_of_the_Spanish_Succession

Benjamin Church
https://en.wikipedia.org/wiki/Benjamin_Church_(ranger)

Golden Age of Piracy
https://en.wikipedia.org/wiki/Golden_Age_of_Piracy

Kingdom of Prussia
https://en.wikipedia.org/wiki/Kingdom_of_Prussia

W.S. Gilbert—Patience
http://diamond.boisestate.edu/gas/patience/webop/pat06.html
https://en.wikipedia.org/wiki/Great_Northern_War

Book Sources

Ridpath, John Clark, LL.D., Cyclopedia of Universal History: Being an Account of the Principal events in the career of the Human Race from the beginnings of Civilization to the Present Time. From Recent and Authentic Sources. Vol. II, Part II, Cincinnati, OH, The Jones Brothers Publishing Co, 1885

Robinson, Nugent, History of the World with all its Great Sensations together with Mighty and Decisive Battles and the Rise and Fall of its Nations from the Earliest Times to the Present Day, Vol. I, New York, NY, P.F.Collier, Publisher, 1891.

The War of
Polish Succession
October 10, 1733
12:00 LMT
Versailles, France
Koch 48N48
2E08

The tiny
glyphs in
houses 11-12,
top down are:

- ♵ Ceres
- ♃ Jupiter
- ☽ Moon
- ♀ Venus
- ⚴ Pallas
- ☊ North Node
- ⚸ Eris
- ⚵ Juno

128.   *Brother Pluto, Sister Eris*

Chapter 15

The War of Polish Succession
Eris semi-sextile Pluto

In a way, "The War of Polish Succession" sounds like a joke. Very little of the war was fought in Poland. A main activity was land-grabbing by other countries, with some major duchies switching rulers. Right at the end of the war, two countries (Russia and Austria) decided to go to war against Turkey. The war was the beginning of the end for Poland, and by 1772 the nation was partitioned between Russia, Prussia, and Austria, leaving a legacy of incompetent leadership.

Since 1572, Poland did not have a hereditary monarchy. The king was chosen by a gathering of nobles, called a "sejm" (pronounced "same"), which served like a parliament. It helped to make the laws for the nation and kept the king from becoming an absolute monarch. However, the "sejm" was not very effective due to a regulation known as the "Liberum Veto." All decisions had to be unanimous, and if one cranky nobleman got up and declared, "I forbid it" then months of negotiation, debate, argument, and outright bribery could all be undone. With this kind of legislative gridlock, Poland became a weakening power.

The origins of the War of Polish Succession could be dated back to the Eris-Pluto sextile at the start of the 18th century. In 1704, King Charles XII of Sweden had invaded Poland, and decided to set up a "puppet" king who would form an alliance with Sweden. King Charles chose Stanislaw Lesczynski (henceforth known as "Stan"), a handsome young man of 26 who came from a respectable family. Through bribery and military threats, King Charles was able to organize a small "sejm" which declared Stan to be the king, followed by an opulent coronation in 1706. Stan repaid King Charles by forming an alliance with Sweden and Lithuania, and sending troops to fight against Russia.

In Stan's natal chart, Eris was sextile Pallas, asteroid of wisdom. Certainly, becoming a puppet of the King of Sweden was not a wise choice for Stan. His natal Pluto was trine natal Mars, and he did show promise

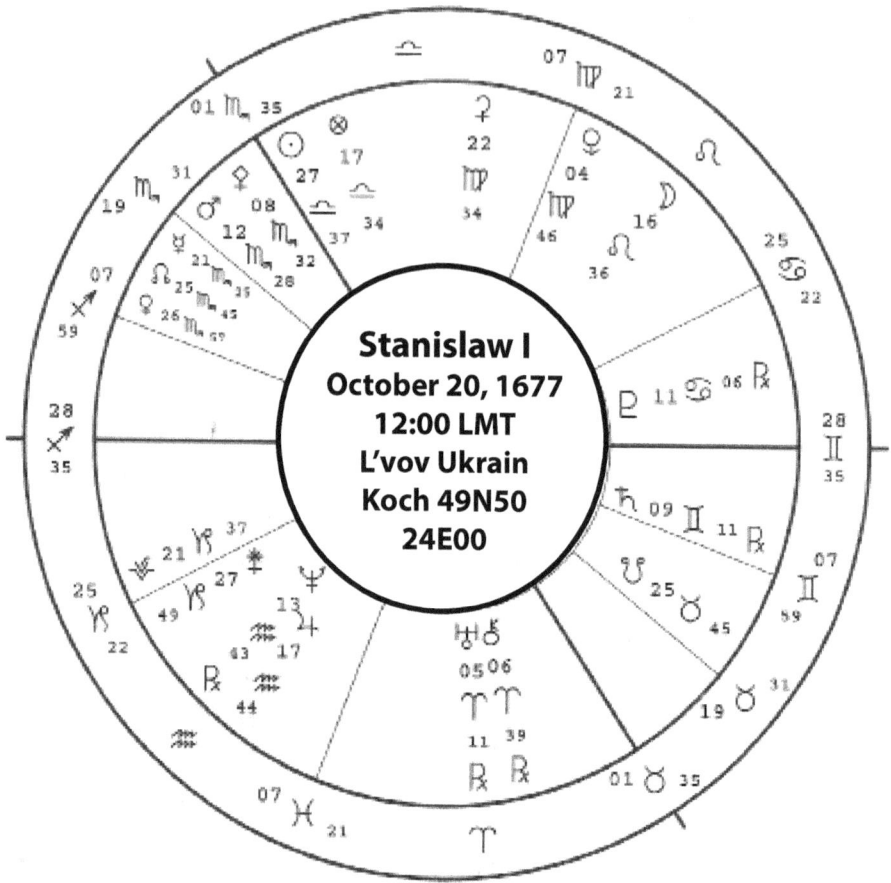

Stanislaw I
October 20, 1677
12:00 LMT
L'vov Ukrain
Koch 49N50
24E00

Stanislaw I

as a military leader. However, with his Mars squaring Neptune and Jupiter, his military success appeared to be all show and no action, since Sweden did most of the fighting to keep Stan on the throne.

The rightful king of Poland, Augustus II (aka Augustus the Strong) was forced into exile and had to deal with Czar Peter of Russia (aka Peter the Great). When Peter the Great overcame the Swedish forces in 1709, Augustus the Strong was returned to the throne of Poland. Stan was forced to leave the throne, and went into exile in Swedish Pomerania. For more than 20 years, he wandered around Europe, a king in exile. His greatest accomplishment came in 1725, when he watched his daughter marry King Louis XV of France, thereby enabling Stan to live in comfort as the royal father-in-law at the fashionable Chateau de Chambord.

In the meantime, arguments were still taking place over the rulership of Poland, due to the impending death of "Augustus the Strong." The leading candidate was Augustus, Prince-Elector of Saxony, who was the son of "Augustus the Strong." Prince Augustus (henceforth known as "Gus") was not very popular in Poland since he had lived most of his life in Saxony. However, he converted from Protestantism to Catholicism in the hopes of becoming the Polish king. In spite of this, the policies of "Augustus the Strong" alienated the nations that might have supported Gus. Rather than have Gus become king, Russia, Prussia, and Austria signed a treaty agreeing to support Prince Manuel of Portugal as the next king of Poland.

In 1733, "Augustus the Strong" died, and a sejm was assembled to determine who would be the next king of Poland. The one thing that the sejm agreed upon was that they did not want any foreign princes to become king of Poland. This eliminated Prince Manuel of Portugal, and it also eliminated Gus, who was Prince of Saxony. There was growing support in the sejm for bringing back Stan as king. Meanwhile, Gus was busy negotiating with Russia and Austria, and making all kinds of territorial and dynastic compromises to win their support.

In August, 1733, the Russians sent 30,000 troops across the Polish border to influence the voting of the sejm. However, the sejm was not intimidated, and 12,000 votes were cast for declaring Stan to be the king. This was not the end of the matter, though, because a group of disgruntled nobles crossed over to Russian lines, and on Oct. 5, 1733, a minority sejm of 3,000 declared Gus to be king of Poland.

In the natal chart of Gus, Eris was conjunct Jupiter, which suggests he had the ambition and authority to be a king, but he had to go about it through devious means. Eris was semi-sextile Venus, and he had a talent for winning friends and influencing people. Gus was born during the previous Eris-Pluto sextile, with Pluto conjunct Chiron, and Eris sextile Chiron. Although he may have seen himself as healing his country, instead he ended up causing further problems.

On October 10, France declared war on Austria and Saxony, but instead of aiding Poland, the French army crossed the Rhine and acquired the Duchy of Lorraine. The chief minister of France, Andre-Hercule Cardinal Fleury, was 80-years-old, and did not want to start a major European war, but he did want to weaken the influence of Austria, which controlled the not-Holy not-Roman not-Empire (as Voltaire called it.) To assist in this, France convinced Spain and the Kingdom of Sardinia to join in the war, and to attack Austrian holdings in Italy.

In the chart for the declaration of war, Eris is conjunct the North Node and Pallas, as well as sextile Mars. There might have been a lot of hoopla and ballyhoo about going to war, correcting an injustice, and fighting for glory. Yet, the plans turned out to be a muddle, and the war did not achieve its main purpose, which was to put Stan on the throne of Poland. Eris quincunx Neptune brought in loftier goals, such as reapportionment of the various powers, though Mars square Neptune may have added to the confusion about what all the fighting was about. The Sun and Pluto trine Neptune may have added a feel-good attitude, in spite of the fact that the end result was not very clear.

Austria had hopes that Great Britain and the Netherlands would join in the war against France, Spain, and Sardinia, but the two great maritime powers decided to remain neutral. Great Britain and the Netherlands did make offers of mediation in the crisis. King George II of Great Britain, though neutral, did manage to send some aid to Austria through his other title as Elector of Hanover. Austria was hampered by awkward dealings with Prussia, and Bavaria (one of the provinces of the Holy Roman Empire) signed a secret treaty with France with the promise of getting other provinces to not send troops to aid Austria.

As for Poland, although Stan was supported by the people as their king, Gus had the support of the Russian army, which captured Warsaw. Stan was forced to flee to Danzig (now Gdansk) where he was besieged by a Russian-Saxon army. A French attempt to break the siege was a dismal failure. At the time, transiting Eris was passing over Stan's Mercury, and he might not have had much mental clarity. Stan was able to escape and take refuge in France. In the meantime, Gus was busy fighting against Stan's supporters in Poland. Whatever military support Stan had was vanquished by the Russian army. Finally, by 1736 a "pacification sejm" was held which confirmed Gus as king of Poland for the sake of making peace.

Although Poland was the cause of the war, most of the fighting seems to have been done in Italy. Again, it sounds like a joke, because to aid Poland, France and her allies invaded Italy. The Austrians were forced to divert troops to repel the invasion. The allied armies had success in southern Italy against Naples and Sicily. In Northern Italy, there were political divisions since the Spanish troops tried to claim Mantua and Milan as spoils of war. The King of Sardinia refused to allow the Spanish the use of his siege equipment, and the armies could only blockade the cities, which was not very effective.

Then the whole war suddenly ended. Stan signed an official abdication document in 1736. Gus offered amnesty to followers of Stan, and ended the political problems in Poland. Stan was given the new title of Duke of Lorraine, where he settled down to an opulent life in exile, living long enough to see his great-great grandchildren. Francis Stephen, the actual Duke of Lorraine, was made Duke of Tuscany, but he had to wait a year until the reigning duke finally died. Charles of Parma (heir to the Spanish throne) lost his duchy to the Austrians, but was compensated by being made King of Naples and Sicily.

A war for Poland was not enough for the combatants, and as the campaign in Poland was winding down, Russia declared war against Turkey. Russia had signed a treaty with Persia, which was having a border dispute with Turkey. In 1737, with the Polish war barely ended, Austria declared war on Turkey as well. Turkey was better prepared for war than Poland was, and a campaign in the Crimea caused 30,000 casualties in the Russian army before they retreated to the Ukraine. The Austrians ended up losing Balkan territory all the way up to Belgrade. By 1739, Russia and Austria were depleted by the war, and they ended up signing separate peace treaties with Turkey.

As for Gus, he came out of the war with transiting Eris trine his Neptune. It would be nice to say that he settled down to being a serious king, but the truth of the matter was that he was a bit of a hedonist. He was the sort of king who could be found at an opera, or a party, or a fashionable spa. He did not notice that Poland was losing power to the growing strength of the Prussians and the expansion of Russia.

By 1772, Poland ceased to exist as a political entity, until Napoleon Bonaparte created the Duchy of Warsaw in the early 19th century. Russia and Prussia increased their roles as the dominant powers of Northern Europe during the rest of the 18th century.

While this confused struggle was going on in Europe, in America a legal struggle was taking place, which would have ramifications for the cause of freedom in the coming decades. In 1735, John Peter Zenger had written newspaper articles, attacking New York Governor William Cosby for his corruption. Governor Cosby's response was to arrest John Peter

Augustus III
October 17, 1696
12:00 LMT
Dresden, Germany
Koch 51N03
12E44

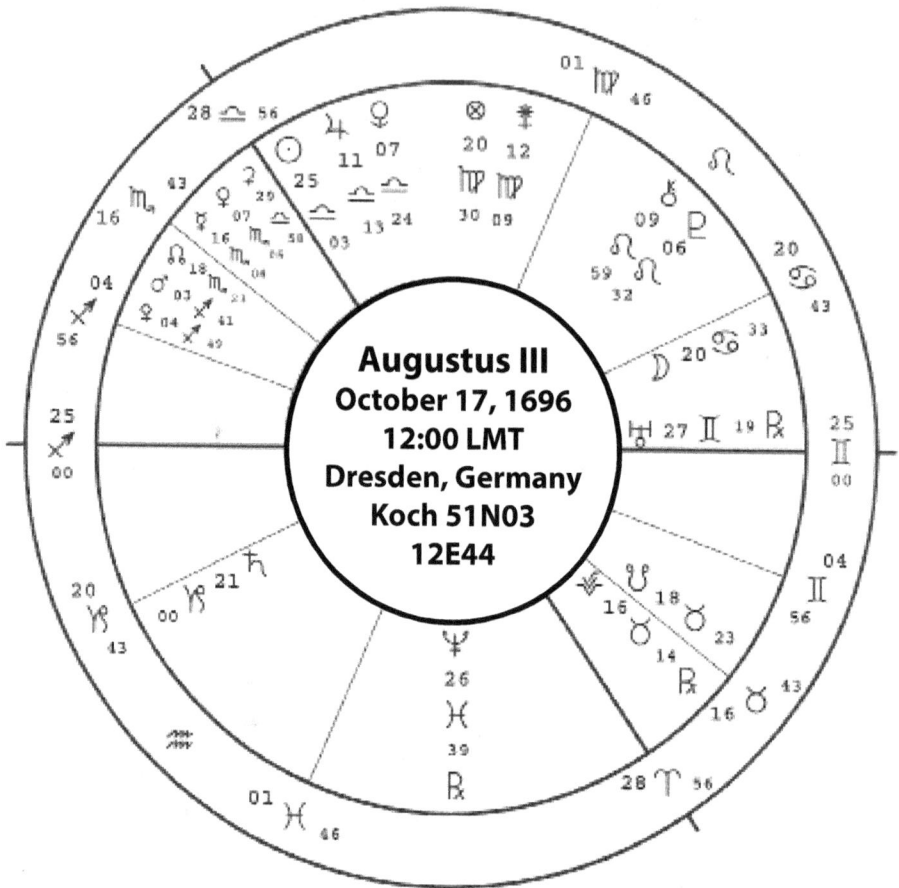

Zenger, and the lawyers who supported Zenger were disbarred.

However, Zenger's lawyers brought into the case an elderly lawyer named Andrew Hamilton, who was considered to be one of the best legal minds in the colonies. Hamilton gave a stirring defense, ridiculing the legal notion that "Truth makes a worse Libel than Falsehood."

Appealing directly to the jury, Hamilton spoke about the cause of Liberty and emphasized the significance of the case. Due to this speech, the jury found Zenger not guilty. He was able to

Augustus III

continue the attacks against corruption until Governor Cosby's death in 1736. The Zenger case served as a precedent for using Truth as a defense against libel charges, and it empowered juries to resist corrupt instructions by the courts, and deliver just verdicts. Ironically, when the next Eris-Pluto semi-sextile came about, it was the government of the United States which would prosecute libels, and the truth would be disregarded as a defense during those turbulent years.

Bibliography - Chapter 15
Internet Sources

War of Polish Succession
https://en.wikipedia.org/wiki/War_of_the_Polish_Succession
Stan
https://en.wikipedia.org/wiki/Stanis%C5%82aw_I
Gus
https://en.wikipedia.org/wiki/Augustus_III_of_Poland
History of Poland
https://en.wikipedia.org/wiki/History_of_Poland_in_the_Early_Modern_era_(1569%E2%80%931795)
Zenger case
https://en.wikipedia.org/wiki/John_Peter_Zenger

Book Sources

Barnett, Lincoln, *The Case of John Peter Zenger, New York, NY, American Heritage, Vol XXIII, No.1*, December, 1971, Pages 32-41, 103-105.

Ridpath, John Clark, LL.D., *Cyclopedia of Universal History: Being an Account of the Principal events in the career of the Human Race from the beginnings of Civilization to the Present Time. From Recent and Authentic Sources. Vol. II, Part II*, Cincinnati, OH, The Jones Brothers Publishing Co, 1885

Robinson, Nugent, *History of the World with all its Great Sensations together with Mighty and Decisive Battles and the Rise and Fall of its Nations from the Earliest Times to the Present Day, Vol. I*, New York, NY, P.F.Collier, Publisher, 1891.

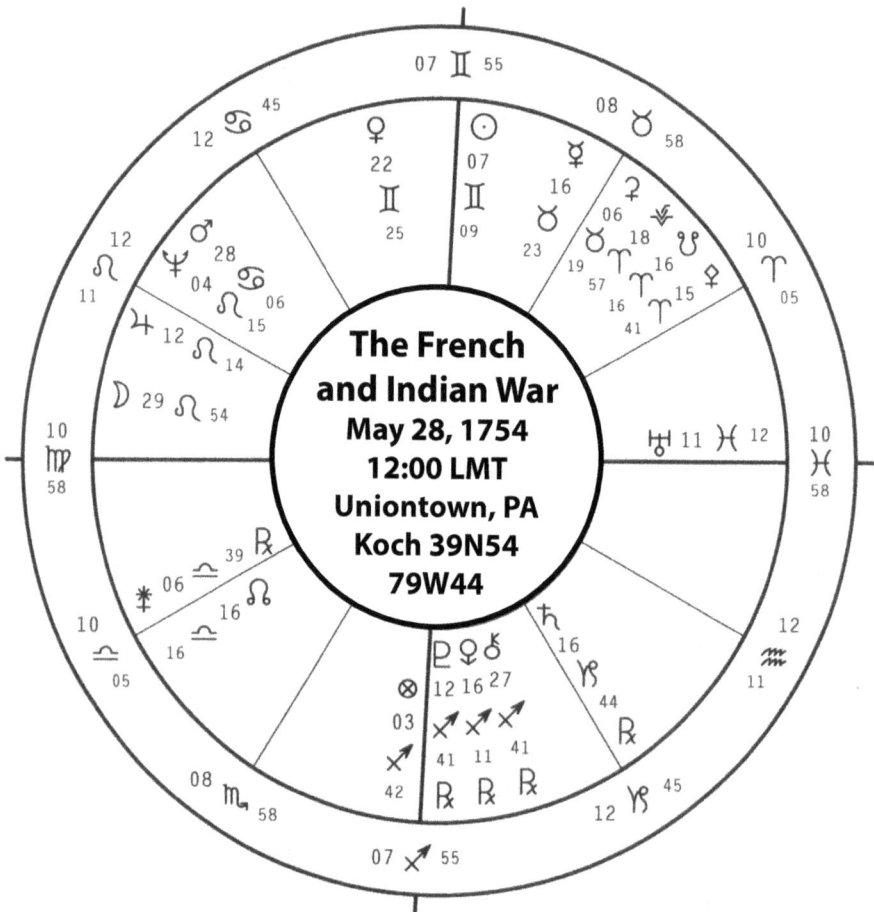

Chapter 16

Welcome to World War One
Eris conjunct Pluto

Winston Churchill once said that the Seven Years War (which history calls the French and Indian War) should have been considered the First World War. For the first time, a major European conflict spilled over to fighting in Asia, Africa, and the Americas. Of course, Australia was not involved with the war, and that might count against it being considered a "World War." Yet, as with the collapse of the Templars, with Eris conjunct Pluto, there was a conflict involving numerous nations, and a major reorganizing of power throughout Europe.

Like the 20th Century's, First World War, the Seven Years War was triggered by an "assassination" in an obscure, contested territory. In 1754, the governor of Virginia sent a young militia officer, George Washington, who then led the troops into Western Pennsylvania to fight against French encroachment in the territory.

Young George Washington

On May 28, 1754, Washington, his band of militia and their Indian allies, encountered a group of Indians who were traveling with a Frenchman. Assuming the Frenchman was a spy, Washington ordered his troops to attack. By the end of the battle the Frenchman had been killed by an Indian ally of Washington.

Upon examining the Frenchman's effects, it was discovered that he was not a spy, but instead was a diplomat who had been sent to negotiate with the governor of Virginia about the boundary dispute.

On July 4, 1754, Washington and his men had to surrender to the French at Fort Necessity. One of the men

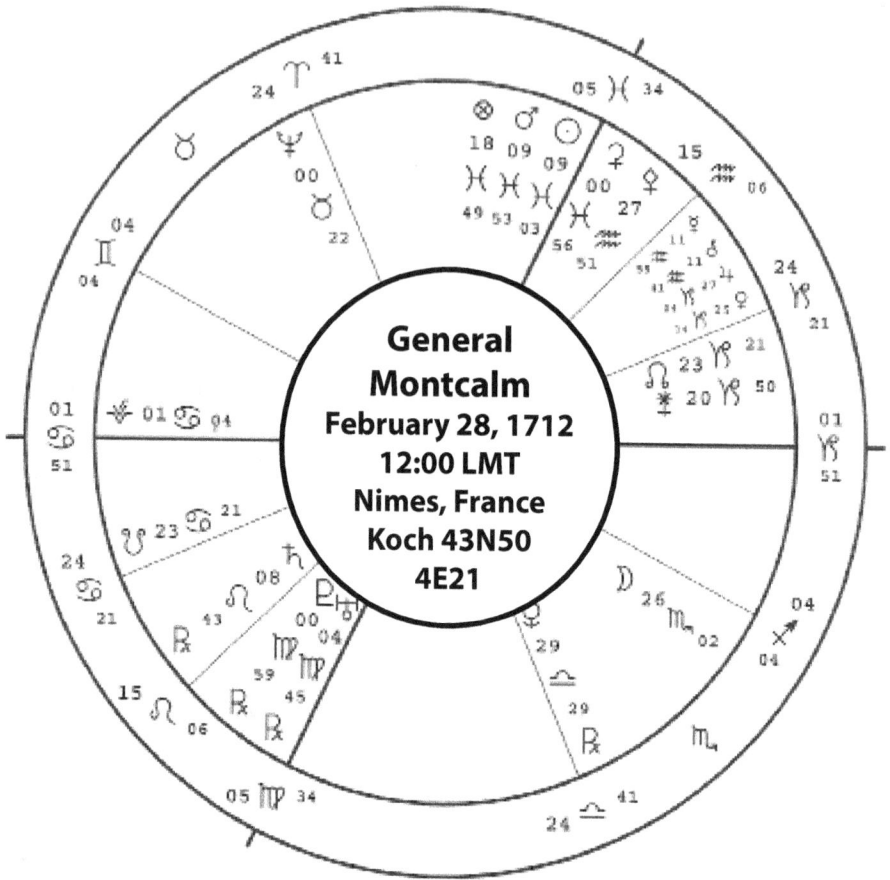

General
Montcalm
February 28, 1712
12:00 LMT
Nimes, France
Koch 43N50
4E21

whom Washington surrendered was the brother of the deceased French diplomat. He exacted a revenge against Washington by having him sign a document in French, which declared that the diplomat was "assassinated," thereby placing war guilt upon the British.

When word was received in France that their diplomats were being "assassinated," a war fever arose against the British. Fighting between the French and British continued for nearly two more years before the British got around to officially declare war on May 18, 1756.

General Montcalm

The Death of General Braddock, Battle of Fort Duquesne

This is the war that history calls The French and Indian War. The chart is for the date and the Pennsylvania town that is generally considered to be the onset of this war. In previous wars between France and Great Britain, the policy had been to concentrate the military campaigns in Europe, and let the American colonies fend for themselves. This time, both France and Britain began sending troops and supplies to their colonies.

The British army, led by General Edward Braddock, began its campaign by marching to attack Fort Duquesne (now the city of Pittsburgh,

Pennsylvania). Unfortunately, Braddock's army was ambushed by Indians and Frenchmen who were hiding in the forest. Braddock was among those who were killed. So, the only military glory that came out of that campaign was to the credit of George Washington (that guy again!) who organized survivors into orderly retreat.

The French military commander in America, Gen. Louis-Joseph de Montcalm, was an experienced and capable officer. With Sun conjunct Mars, Montcalm was born during the Eris-Pluto sextile, when Uranus was conjunct Pluto. (Some accounts of his birth say that he was born on Feb. 29, 1712, while others say it was February 28, but the differences of one day would not change the outer planet transits.) Eris square Jupiter marks a determined leadership talent, and Eris opposite Neptune suggests mental clarity in his preparations. Eris trine Pallas could indicate some unwise decisions, but Montcalm's success may be also accounted for by the lack of wisdom among his British opponents.

Montcalm joined the French army at age 15 in 1727, the year of birth of his nemesis, James Wolfe. In 1729, when transiting Eris was sextile his Juno and he was at the age of 17, Montcalm's father bought him a captaincy. His father died in 1735, when transiting Eris was sextile natal Venus, and Montcalm was given the title of Marquis. He was then able to contract a marriage to a wealthy heiress so as to ease the family debts. Although it was an arranged marriage, Montcalm and his bride, Angelique, got along well and had ten children, five of which survived to maturity.

Eris moved into Sagittarius by 1741, square Montcalm's Ceres and Pluto, and forming the point of a Yod from Neptune and Vesta. He showed his military talent by taking part in a campaign against Bohemia. Eris was square his Uranus in 1743 when he was promoted to Colonel. In 1746, Montcalm suffered from sabre wounds and was taken prisoner when Eris was trine his Saturn, but he was soon after that able to return to France on parole. The following year, when transiting Eris was square his natal Sun and Mars, he was given the rank of Brigadier General, but then suffered a wound from a musket ball.

Montcalm's next command did not come until 1756, when he was ordered to take charge of French troops in America. His first victory in America was the capture of Fort Oswego on Lake Ontario. Later he was embroiled in military disputes with the Governor General of Canada, which delayed his campaigns. Eris was approaching a semi-sextile to Montcalm's Juno, and he had many struggles over political issues, until word arrived from France that he was to take supreme command of the military.

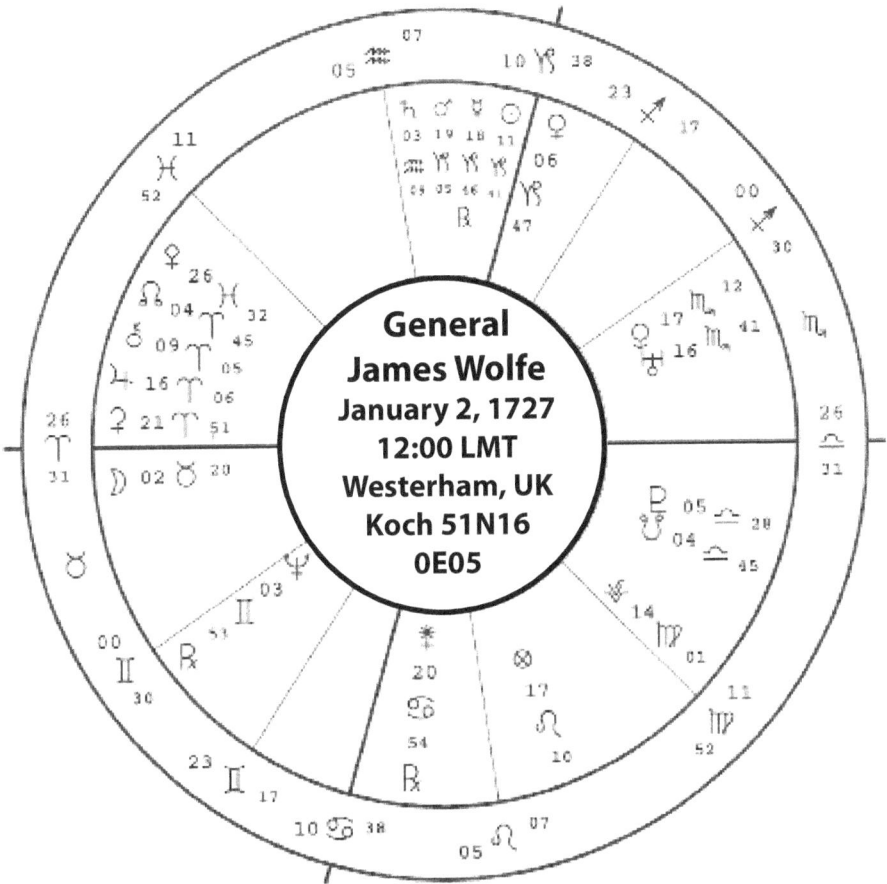

General James Wolfe
January 2, 1727
12:00 LMT
Westerham, UK
Koch 51N16
0E05

General James Wolfe

The British suffered a horrific defeat in 1757 with surrender of Fort William Henry at the southern tip of Lake George. General Montcalm had assured the garrison they could peacefully withdraw to another fort, but must leave their ammunition behind. When the British troops left the fort, they were ambushed by Montcalm's Indian allies. The bodies of the slaughtered troops were still on the ground when reinforcement troops arrived. The brutality of this inspired the British to take a more savage response against the French and Indians.

Yet, the military genius of Montcalm held off the British, especially at

The Death of General Wolfe

the battle of Ticonderoga in 1758. Under command of General Abercrombie, 15,000 men marched on the fort on the coast of Lake Champlain. General Montcalm had only 3,600 men to defend the fort. Rather than allow the British to march to the fort and lay siege to it, Montcalm fortified the isthmus leading to the fort, building a series of barricades along the way.

When the British managed to capture one barricade, they were faced with dealing with the French forces that had regrouped behind the next barricade. Such a fighting retreat might have seemed unwise in facing an enemy with heavy artillery, which could have blasted the barricades. However, General Abercrombie did not order the artillery brought up immediately, and he also missed an opportunity to outflank the enemy. Because the British did not wait until their artillery arrived, they suffered more than 2000 casualties, and had to retreat to Lake George. The French suffered about 1000 casualties, but ended up holding the fort until 1759, when they abandoned the fort to the British after blowing up all of the gunpowder.

After the Ticonderoga disaster, the dynamic British General James Wolfe was given command of British forces in America. With Eris conjunct Uranus, Wolfe was a popular leader, who had joined the military at the age of 13. He was noted for his fearless. sometimes reckless attacks, many of which were opposed by his more conservative superiors.

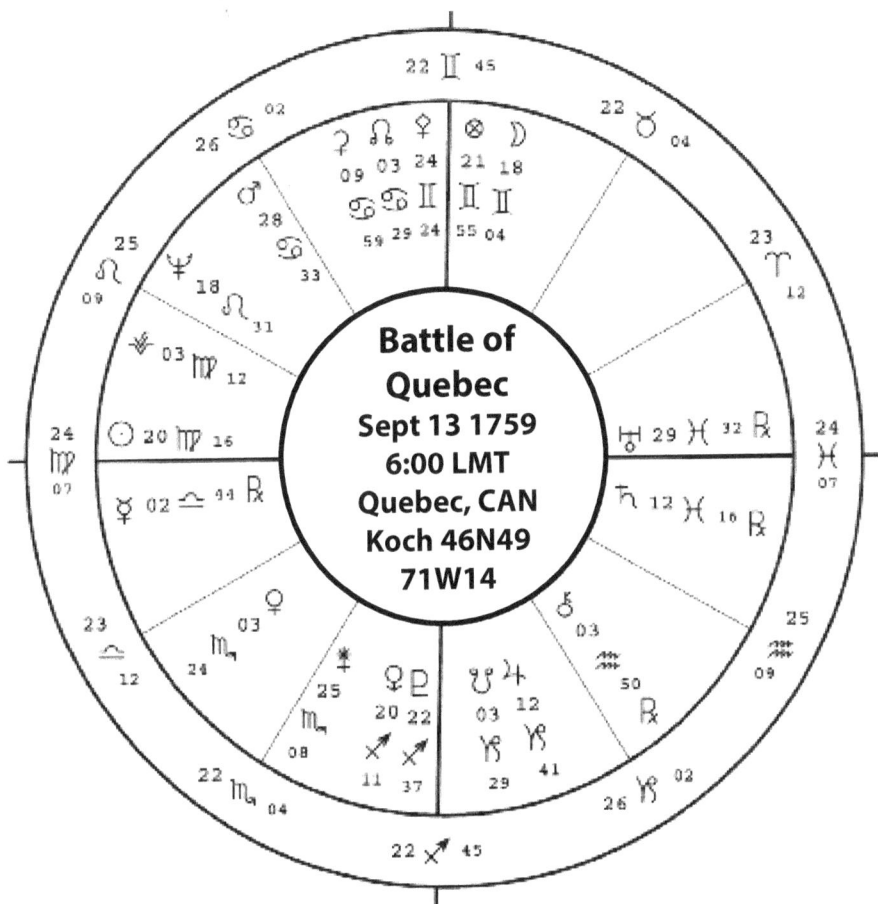

Battle of
Quebec
Sept 13 1759
6:00 LMT
Quebec, CAN
Koch 46N49
71W14

When one general said to King George II, "General Wolfe is mad," the king responded with, "I wish he would bite some of my other generals."

According to another story, after the battle of Culloden, Wolfe was ordered by his superior officer to shoot a wounded rebel highlander. Wolfe disobeyed the command, saying it was dishonorable (Jupiter quincunx Eris.) The officer ended up killing the highlander, anyway. The story boosted Wolfe's reputation as an honorable figure, and won him the loyalty of the Highlander troops when he was garrisoned in Scotland. Although he suffered from chronic ill-health (Pluto opposing Chiron), he was noted for his discipline, and would subject himself to the same demanding pace as his troops (Eris sextile Mars). Wolfe's private activities were more intellectual than romantic. He swore he would never marry (Eris trine Juno) and spent his time studying mathematics and foreign languages (Eris sextile Mercury).

The defining moment of the war was the attack on Quebec, September 13, 1759. Wolfe organized an amphibious force to take the British army down the St. Lawrence River to the base of the cliffs near Quebec City. Wolfe ordered his men to climb a 200 foot cliff, with Wolfe himself joining in the climb, and the army was then able to assemble in an area outside of Quebec known as "the Plains of Abraham." General Montcalm was astonished by this feat, because he never expected British troops would be able to climb the cliffs. Montcalm ordered an immediate attack in the hopes of scattering the British forces before they brought up more artillery. The battle was over in fifteen minutes with the British repelling the poorly organized French troops. Both Wolfe and Montcalm were wounded in the battle, and died shortly thereafter. According to accounts, the dying Wolfe was still giving orders to his men, but the dying Montcalm refused to give any orders and focused on receiving the last rites.

The battle of Quebec was followed up by the capture of Montreal in 1760. Without Montcalm's leadership, the war began turning badly against the French. In the end, France lost Canada to the British, and they were forced to pass on Louisiana to the Spanish in order to keep the British from getting control of it. With the Treaty of Paris in 1763, it was the beginning of the end for French global expansion. The French had lost their colony Senegal in West Africa to the British fleet. In India, the French were defeated by the legendary "Clive of India", thereby insuring British domination of the subcontinent for nearly 200 years.

There is a certain irony to the French defeat at this time of the Eris-Pluto conjunction. During the Eris-Pluto conjunction in the early 1300's, the French had destroyed the Templars, supposedly driving them into hiding in Scotland. In the early 1700's, a new organization called the Freemasons rose up, which claimed a spiritual descent from the Knights Templars. Many of the British officers who defeated the French in America were Freemasons, including the omnipresent George Washington. In that sense, the French defeats of the 18th Century Eris-Pluto conjunction were like a retribution for the actions taken during the 14th Century Eris-Pluto conjunction.

Like the 20th Century's "First World War," the Seven Years War spread through a series of entangling alliances. There had been much resentment towards the growth of Prussia under the dynamic leadership of Frederick the Great. In order to teach Frederick a lesson, in 1756 Austria, Russia, and France signed a triple alliance against Prussia. Just so he would not stand alone, Frederick signed an alliance with Great Britain. Once the alliance was concluded, Frederick began a war against Austria

Frederick the Great
January 24,
1712
11:30 LMT
Koch 52N30
13E22

and Pomerania. Frederick won initial victories by invading Bohemia and leading a bloody siege against Prague.

Like General Montcalm, Frederick was born during the Eris-Pluto sextile, with Eris in opposition to Neptune. With six bodies in Aquarius, he became noted as one of the most liberal-minded monarchs of the Age of Enlightenment. He invited the acerbic Voltaire to be a member of his court, though he did order Voltaire to be flogged when he got a little too disrespectful. Voltaire was given a receipt by the flogger to remind him of the punishment. After that, Voltaire parted company from Frederick, though they kept up their friendship by mail.

With Mars conjunct Pallas and Chiron, and sextile Venus, Frederick was one of the most dynamic military leaders of the century. He developed the German General Staff, the structure of which remained unchanged into the 20th Century. On the battlefield, he was fearless, always leading his men from the frontlines, and in constant danger of being shot. One of his tactics, which would be emulated by Napoleon, was to prevent enemy forces from uniting so that the different sections of the armies could be defeated separately. Yet, with Mars opposed by Saturn and the Moon, even Frederick had his setbacks on the battlefield, and these were manifested early in the war when transiting Eris was conjunct his Venus and sextile his Pallas.

At the battle of Kolin, the Austrians were able to score a major military victory against Frederick, mainly because fog kept Frederick from seeing which direction the Austrians were maneuvering. To add to Frederick's problems in 1757, the Russians invaded Memel with 75,000 men, and then Sweden declared war against Prussia, sending 17,000 troops to occupy Pomerania. However, Frederick was not known as "the Great" for nothing, and he quickly took the offensive. After defeating a French army at the battle of Rossbach, he defeated an Austrian army at the battle of Leuthen. The Russians decided to withdraw their forces from Eastern Prussia until the following year. Frederick then turned his forces to Pomerania and kicked out the Swedes.

Frederick did suffer one major embarrassment in October, 1757, when transiting Eris was sextile his Ceres. A Hungarian General named Count Andras Hadik commanded a force of 5000 hussars (light cavalry) in a maneuver around Frederick's army, and managed to capture Frederick's capital, Berlin. The city of Berlin was spared by payment of a ransom of 300,000 thalers, which Count Hadik divided among his troops. When Frederick heard about the capture of Berlin, he sent a huge army to liberate the city, but by the time they got there Count Hadik and his men had retreated to the Austrian lines. Because of his dauntless deed of derring-do, Count Hadik was made a Marshal in the Austrian army.

From 1758 to 1762, Frederick fought a back-and-forth war, sometimes gaining victories and territories, and then losing the land back to the Austrians, Russians, and Swedish. Great Britain provided minor aid to Frederick with a subsidy of 670,000 pounds and 9000 troops. However, the British threatened to cut off the aid unless Frederick started negotiating for peace. By 1762, the Prussian army was reduced to 60,000. Relief finally came with the death of the Russian Czarina Elizabeth, and the new Czar, Peter III, was an admirer of Frederick. Czar Peter III withdrew the Russian army, and negotiated a truce between Prussia and Sweden. Morale in France and Austria was declining, and in 1763 Frederick was able to negotiate a victorious peace.

Spain was a latecomer to the war, declaring war against Great Britain in 1761. Portugal joined the war on the side of the British, and received British aid when Spain invaded Portugal. Some Portuguese col-

Frederick the Great

onies in South America were attacked by the Spanish. In the 1763 peace settlement, Spain made out the best by having Louisiana territory ceded to them. They did have to give up Eastern Florida to the British, but were able to get it back again 20 years later.

France suffered the most loss of territory when they had to give up Canada to the British. However, France managed to hold on to colonies in the Caribbean. In spite of the gain of Canada, the British were left with a crippling war debt. They attempted to ease the debt by raising taxes on the American colonies. This caused a resentment which brought about a boycott of British goods, organized by George Washington (him again!), and finally an outright rebellion against Great Britain, which was led by (who else?) George Washington. The Eris-Pluto conjunction seemed to have propelled George Washington onto the fast track of glory, but as we will see in the following chapter, even he would feel the affliction of Eris-Pluto.

The Eris-Pluto conjunction from 1754 to1759 also brought forth a generation that would take part in major political changes. Two American Founding Fathers with this aspect were Alexander Hamilton and Aaron Burr. Although they served together during the American Revolution, after the war they became political rivals, and each one had ambitions that were blocked by the other. This rivalry culminated in 1804, when Burr killed Hamilton in a duel. Burr became a political outcast when his schemes for conquering Mexico collapsed, after he was betrayed by General James Wilkinson, who also had the Eris-Pluto conjunction. Years later it would be discovered that Wilkinson was actually a Spanish secret agent, leaking American secrets to Spain.

In France, leaders of the French Revolution had this aspect, and we will read about their accomplishments and actions in the next chapter.

Bibliography - Chapter 16

Internet Sources

The Seven Years War
  https://en.wikipedia.org/wiki/Seven_Years%27_War
The French and Indian War
  https://en.wikipedia.org/wiki/French_and_Indian_War
George Washington
  https://en.wikipedia.org/wiki/George_Washington
General Edward Braddock
  https://en.wikipedia.org/wiki/Edward_Braddock
General Louis-Joseph de Montcalm
  https://en.wikipedia.org/wiki/Louis-Joseph_de_Montcalm
General James Wolfe
  https://en.wikipedia.org/wiki/James_Wolfe
The Battle for Quebec City
  https://en.wikipedia.org/wiki/Battle_of_the_Plains_of_Abraham

Frederick the Great
  https://en.wikipedia.org/wiki/Frederick_the_Great
Count Andras Hadik
  https://en.wikipedia.org/wiki/Andr%C3%A1s_Hadik

Book Sources

Fleming, Thomas J., G. *Washington Meets a Test*, New York, NY, American Heritage, Vol. XIV, No. 2, February, 1963, Pages 56-59, 79-81.

Flexner, James Thomas, Washington: *The Indispensable Man*, New York, NY, Little, Brown, and Company, 1974, Pages 19-38.

Flexner, James Thomas, *The Miraculous Care of Providence*, New York, NY, American Heritage, Vol. 33, No. 2, Feb/March 1982, Pages 82-85.

Parkman, Francis, *Montcalm and Wolfe: The Decline and Fall of the French Empire in America*, New York, NY, The Crowell-Collier Publishing Company, 1969.

Ridpath, John Clark, LL.D., *Cyclopedia of Universal History: Being an Account of the Principal events in the career of the Human Race from the beginnings of Civilization to the Present Time. From Recent and Authentic Sources. Vol. II, Part II*, Cincinnati, OH, The Jones Brothers Publishing Co, 1885

Robinson, Nugent, *History of the World with all its Great Sensations together with Mighty and Decisive Battles and the Rise and Fall of its Nations from the Earliest Times to the Present Day, Vol. I*, P.F.Collier, Publisher, New York, NY, 1891.

Snow, Richard F., *The Debacle at Fort Carillon*, American Heritage, Vol. XXIII, No. 4, New York, NY, 1972, Pages 80-87.

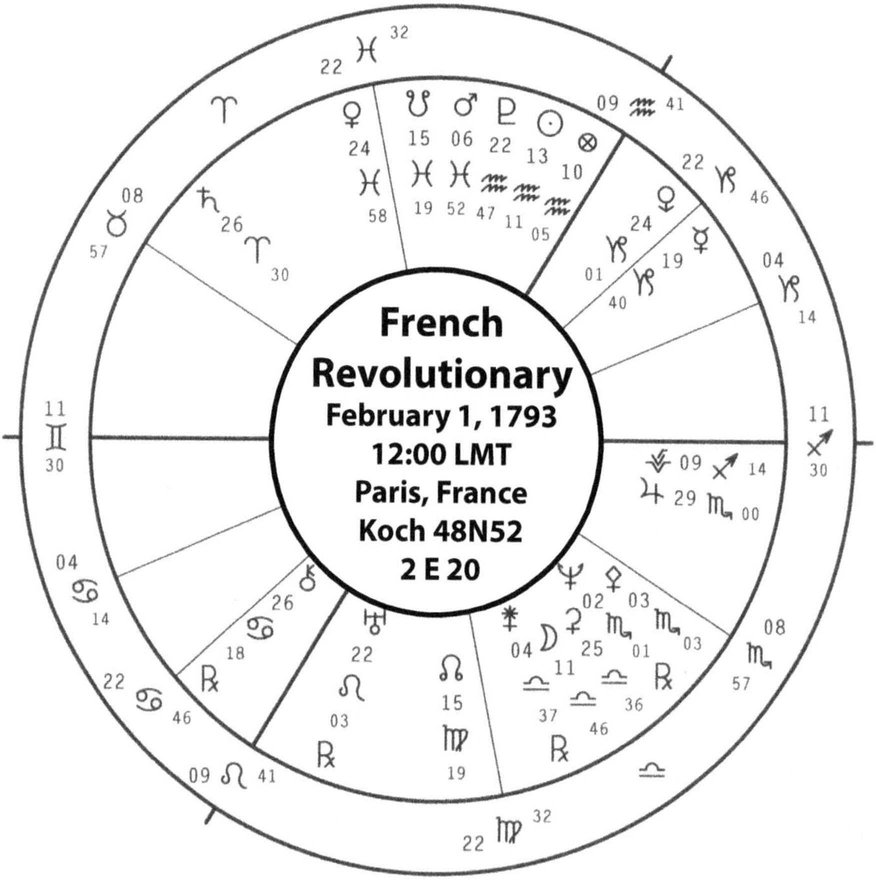

French
Revolutionary
February 1, 1793
12:00 LMT
Paris, France
Koch 48N52
2 E 20

Chapter 17

Revolutionary Wars
Eris semi-sextile Pluto

Although the French Revolution began in 1789, the most violent years were from 1792 to 1799, corresponding with Eris semi-sextile Pluto. It was the time of the "Reign of Terror" as well as the rise of Napoleon Bonaparte to the European theater of war. The violence of the French Revolution even had its repercussions in America, with the rise of political factions (Pro-French versus Anti-French), and the passing of the Alien and Sedition Acts, which limited freedom in an attempt to prevent war. Great Britain experienced its own form of hysteria, committing to a war that would last about twenty years.

After the fall of the Bastille, the new government of France looked to the example of the American army. During the American Revolution, British regulars were defeated by an army of citizen recruits. Rather than rely on professional soldiers, who were of the noble class, the French government began conscripting single men between the ages of 18 and 25. Married men and older men were still required to provide some non-combat services for the army.

Training for the revolutionary army was difficult, because many of the officers and non-commissioned officers had fled France rather than be imprisoned for their noble positions. The result was that the conscripted soldiers received inadequate military training, especially in the area of obedience. When France invaded the Netherlands in 1792, the revolutionary army actually took a vote to decide whether or not to attack a certain target. The soldiers had been taught that their allegiance was to the revolutionary government, and not to a general who happened to be leading the army. In one instance, when an attack was ordered upon a target the soldiers did not approve of, they murdered the commanding general.

Generals also had problems in dealing with their own government. Because some of the remaining generals had been of the noble class, whenever they lost a battle, it was suspected that the loss was deliberate to aid the enemies of the republic. As a result, when generals lost battles, they were sent to the guillotine. One commander who came under suspicion was the legendary Marquis de Lafayette, who surrendered to the Austrians before he could be arrested. Lafayette remained a prisoner of war for years, and his wife was imprisoned in Paris under suspicion of aiding the enemies of France. Fortunately, the intervention of Elizabeth Monroe, wife of the American ambassador James Monroe, prevented Madame Lafayette from being sent to the guillotine.

Although France had been fighting the Austrian and Prussian armies in 1792, from 1793 onward the wars became more intense as the nation took on the First Coalition. On Feb. 1, 1793, France went to war with Great Britain, Spain, Portugal, and Sardinia. In the chart for the French Revolutionary War (also called First Coalition), Eris was sextile Venus and both were quincunx Uranus. It would become a revolution more bloody than the world had ever seen. Pluto was in opposition to Uranus, marking the revolution with the spirit of death, as the guillotine became the symbol for French power, even after more moderate regimes came to power. Eris formed a Grand Cross by opposing Chiron, and squaring both Saturn and Ceres.

Ironically, the guillotine was supposed to be a merciful invention, providing a quick death without the lingering pain of hanging or shooting. Dr. Joseph Guillotin did not invent the device, but his name became associated with it because he promoted it as the humane method of capital punishment. It was by this device the "ancient regime" was done away with, and it brought public entertainment to the "tricoteuses", the knitting ladies, who got their Erisian jollies by watching the heads fall from the guillotine, including that of King Louis XVI and his family. The fear of losing more royal heads prompted the members of the First Coalition to attack France.

The coalition forces attacked and occupied the port city of Toulon, bottling up the French fleet in the harbor. It was during the siege of Toulon that a young Napoleon Bonaparte stepped upon the military scene, beginning his notorious career as a conqueror. By capturing the British position known as "Little Gibraltar," Napoleon was able to command the heights at the entrance to the harbor, making the British fleet vulnerable to artillery attack. The coalition forces were forced to flee the city, but not before burning the French fleet.

While the French army was battling the First Coalition (as well as a civil war in the Vendee), the French Revolution had reached a point where it started consuming its own children. The Committee of Public Safety was run by Maximilien Robespierre and Georges Couthon, both of whom had Eris conjunct Pluto in their charts. They used their power to arrest and execute revolutionary leaders like Georges Danton, Camille Desmoulin, and Jacques Hebert, who also had Eris conjunct Pluto. At the time, it was said of Robespierre, "He will execute everyone, even the executioner." In July, 1794, Robespierre and his friends were overthrown by Paul Barras, Joseph Fouche, and Jacque Billaud-Varenne, who also had Eris conjunct Pluto in their charts.

Barras ruled France for five years as leader of the Directory, an infamously corrupt government. His regime saw the end of the First Coalition against France by signing separate peace treaties with Spain and Prussia. Barras installed Charles Maurice de Talleyrand as foreign minister, which had a detrimental effect on relations with the United States. Barras was instrumental in the rise of Napoleon Bonaparte, calling upon him to quell the Vendemiaire rebellion in October, 1795, and then supporting his appointment to command the Army of Italy in 1796. Barras introduced Napoleon to Josephine de Beauharnais, his former mistress, thereby creating a famous historical love match.

Napoleon began his invasion of Italy two days after his marriage to Josephine. His army was outnumbered by the Austrian army. Still Napoleon had devised the tactic of attacking the enemy in the weakest spots. He moved his army at rapid speed to attack Austrian positions with few defenders. Before the main body of the Austrian army could counterattack, Napoleon would be off to another target. He was able to increase the mobility of the French army by limiting the supplies they carried,and allowing his soldiers to "live off the land" by seizing food and supplies from farms and villages. He also started the practice of stealing art treasures, which were sent back to Paris, thus pleasing the corrupt Directory.

The Directory governed by bribery, graft and rigged elections. The lascivious private life of Barras also added to its unpopularity. For a while, the government could distract the public with news of the military success of Napoleon Bonaparte in Italy, and then later in Egypt. However, when Napoleon returned to France in 1799, he found out that the Directory was extremely unpopular. People looked to Napoleon as "the man on horseback" who could bring about a change. In November of 1799, Napoleon seized power in the coup of 18 Brumaire, and Barras was forced into exile. Talleyand remained in power, as did Joseph Fouche, who headed the

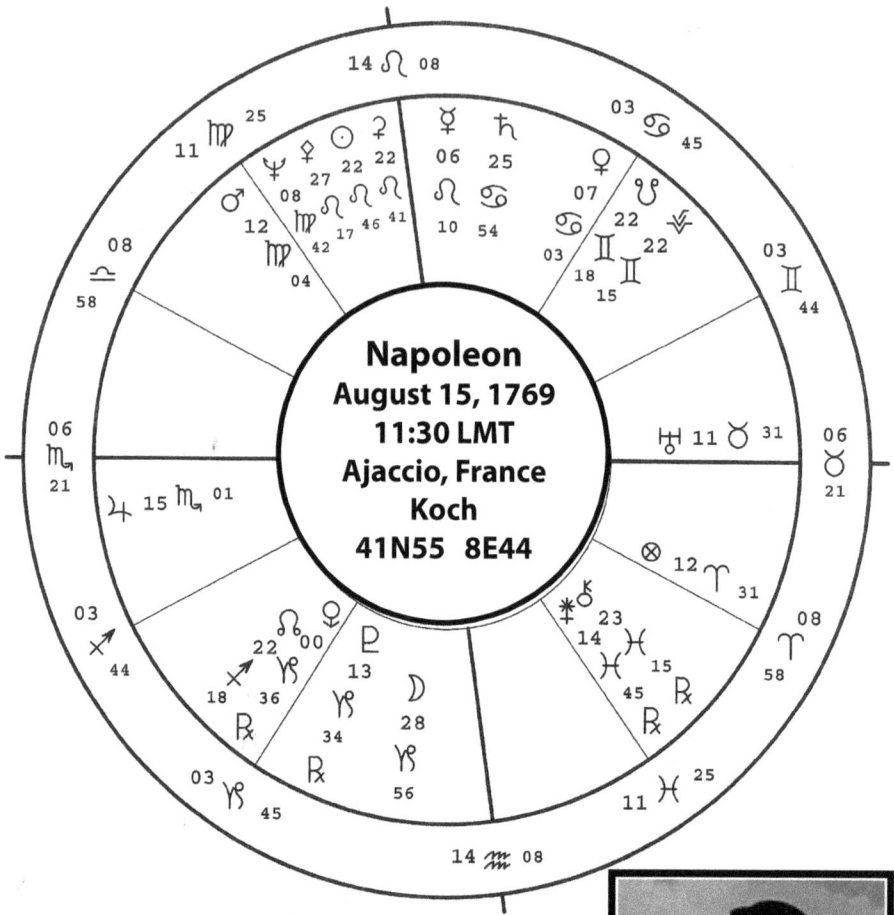

Napoleon
August 15, 1769
11:30 LMT
Ajaccio, France
Koch
41N55 8E44

secret police. Both men had Eris conjunct Pluto in their charts.

Napoleon became First Consul of France, and began dealing with the problems facing the nation. After defeating the Austrians in 1800, he was able to break up the Second Coalition attacking France. In 1802, as the Eris-Pluto semi-sextile was starting to separate, he concluded the Peace of Amiens, which ended the war with Great Britain. For a year, British tourists came to visit Napoleon and express admiration for him. The Peace of Amiens proved to be a short truce, however, because hostilities with Great Britain resumed in 1803, and continued until Napoleon was defeated at Waterloo twelve years later.

Napoleon

In the natal chart of Napoleon, there are no natal Eris aspects, but transiting Eris aspects marked developments in his career. During his childhood, he had Eris quincunx Mercury, Eris opposing Venus, and Eris trine Neptune. Having been born in Corsica to a large family, Napoleon might have seemed destined to live a provincial lifestyle. However, in the year transiting Eris was trine his Neptune, his father, Carlo Bonaparte, became the Corsican representative to the court of King Louis XVI. The result was that more opportunities began opening up for young Napoleon. He was taken to the mainland and instructed on how to speak French, though he retained a Corsican accent the rest of his life.

From 1779 to 1784, Napoleon had many Eris transits—trine Uranus and his Mars, square his Part-of-Fortune and conjunct his Pluto. During this time he attended Brienne-le-Chateau, a prestigious military academy. Here he developed his warrior spirit, not only through his studies, but through conflict with other students, who teased him for his Corsican accent. Still, he made one life-long friend at the academy, Louis de Bourrienne, who later became Napoleon's secretary and biographer. At Brienne, Napoleon did so well in his studies of geography, history and mathematics that one of his teachers made the comment that he would be an excellent sailor!

After his graduation in 1784, Napoleon went to the Ecole Militaire, which was the military academy for the elite. Unfortunately, Eris was sextile his Juno and his Jupiter, and at that time his father died, leaving the family in financial difficulty. Napoleon had to complete a two-year course in just one year, and became the first Corsican to graduate from the Ecole Militaire. He became a second lieutenant artillery officer, who was stationed at obscure garrisons, until the French Revolution broke out. He then took a leave of absence from the French army and returned to Corsica to make his career there.

By 1792, transiting Eris was at the focal point of a Yod formed by Napoleon's South Node and Vesta sextile his Sun and Ceres. It was at this time that the whole Bonaparte family was exiled from Corsica, due to a political quarrel among factions that wanted Corsica to become an independent nation. The Bonapartes settled in France, and then Napoleon resumed his military career to help support his family. In 1793, when Eris was sextile his Chiron, he had his breakthrough success at Toulon. It also marked the first time in his career that he was wounded in battle, having been stabbed in the chest by a British bayonet.

In 1796, when Eris was opposing his Saturn, Napoleon was able to overcome the nay-sayers, take control of the Army of Italy, and begin the Italian campaign that would make him world famous. In 1798, with Eris quincunx his Pallas, he started his invasion of Egypt, which did not end too well, so he had to abandon his army. By 1799, Eris was conjunct his Moon. Napoleon had become the toast of France, having developed a cult of personality that enabled him to overthrow the Directory. With the entry of Eris into Aquarius a consulate government in France negotiated the Peace of Amiens with Great Britain, and brought about the Louisiana Purchase with the United States.

By 1810, when Eris was opposing Napoleon's Mercury, he was the master of Europe, having dominated Austria, Prussia, and Russia. Only Great Britain and Spanish guerillas stood against him. His judgment started to wane at this time, when he decided to divorce Josephine and marry the Austrian princess, Marie-Louise. By 1811, when Eris was quincunx his Venus, he had fathered a son to further the Bonaparte dynasty, and made an alliance with Austria that he hoped would keep the peace in Europe.

Unfortunately, in 1812, when Eris was quincunx his Neptune, political disputes prompted his invasion of Russia. At first, all seemed to go well, and Napoleon was able to capture Moscow. However, he did not reckon with the severity of the Russian winter and the determination of the Russian people. The Russians had maintained a "scorched earth" policy of destroying anything that might aid the French. This included the city of Moscow, which was set on fire to chase out the French. Napoleon began a long retreat from Russia, which was followed by numerous military defeats. This resulted in his abdication, the brief exile to Elba, the triumphant return for the 100 days, and the final defeat at Waterloo.

By the time Eris was square his Uranus, Napoleon was held as a prisoner by the British, but it was the beginning of a new struggle, namely the forging of the Napoleonic legend. During his stay on Saint-Helena, Eris was sextile his Part-of-Fortune and quincunx his Mars. Napoleon and his followers helped create the image of himself as a modern Prometheus, chained to a lonely rock for the crime of challenging the powers that be. It was a masterful propaganda campaign to win the hearts and minds of posterity. Napoleon's death in 1821 took place as Eris was at the bottom of his chart, opposing his Midheaven, and applying to a square with Jupiter. In his death, his reputation won the final victory as a figure of glory who managed to stand up to the crowned heads of Europe, but was beaten and yet not broken.

In Great Britain, the period of the Eris-Pluto semi-sextile, helped bring a unifying element to the nation. The 1780's had been a time of uncertainty, beginning with the loss of the American colonies, and ending with the bout of madness suffered by King George III. In the 1790's, the monarch had regained most of his sanity, and with help of William Pitt the Younger, he was able to promote the war against revolutionary France. After the excesses of the Reign of Terror, most citizens of Britain were ready to rally behind "King and Country." There were economic hardships, such as higher taxes because of the war. Pitt did make the tempts to negotiate a peace with France, but the talks always fell through because of the details.

William Pitt the Younger was born at the end of the Eris-Pluto conjunction in the 1750's. He was the son of the Earl of Chatham (William Pitt the Elder), who was a popular figure in America for speaking in favor of American interests in Parliament. William the Elder became the Earl of Chatham about the time transiting Eris was square Uranus in the young William's chart. This opened a world of prestige and opportunity for young William. When Eris was opposing his Moon, he became a paragon of home schooling, developing an expertise in Latin and Greek. In the 1770's, when Eris was quincunx his Sun, trine his Pallas, and conjunct his South Node, Pitt was studying at Pembroke College in Cambridge, where he advanced his studies with chemistry, trigonometry, and political philosophy. While there, he made friends and contacts which bolstered his career. As a member of the elite, he was allowed to graduate from Cambridge without taking final exams.

When Eris was in opposition to his Venus, his father died, and Pitt began studying the law. He was called to the bar in 1780, and in 1781 was able to enter Parliament by means of a "pocket borough,"a corrupt political practice that Pitt later denounced. At first, Pitt made common cause with Charles Fox and other Whigs, who were fighting Lord North over the war in America. When Lord North's ministry fell, both Fox and Pitt served in the Rockingham ministry. When Rockingham was replaced by Lord Shelburne, Fox dropped out and made common cause with Lord North. Pitt was made Chancellor of the Exchequer at age 23, and his work at such a young age attracted the attention of King George III, who asked Pitt to form a government when the Shelburne ministry collapsed.

So it was that at age 24, William Pitt became the head of a new government. Transiting Eris was opposing his Vesta, quincunx his Part-of-Fortune and Neptune, sextile his Saturn, and trine his Mars. Pitt's youth

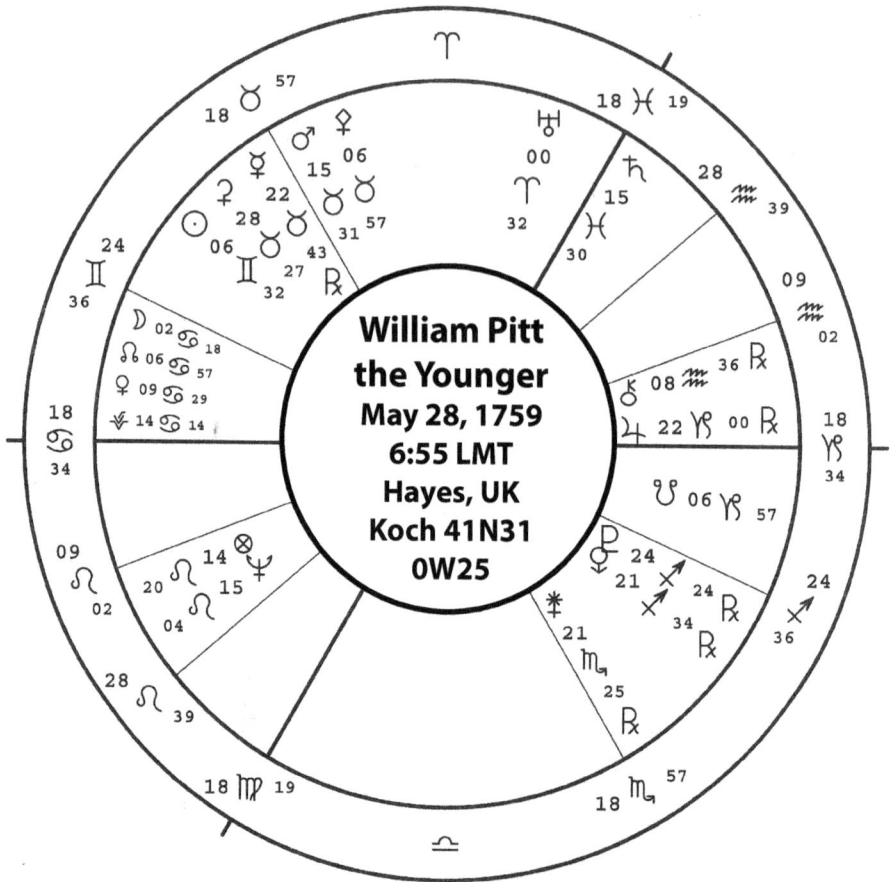

William Pitt the Younger
May 28, 1759
6:55 LMT
Hayes, UK
Koch 41N31
0W25

attracted the abuse of the older politicians, who mocked him as "the infant Atlas." A friendlier cartoon depicted Pitt as infant Hercules, strangling the vipers Fox and North. For months, Pitt was subjected to verbal abuse in the House of Commons. One politician declared that Pitt's ministry would be gone by Christmas. (He was off by 17 years!)

Pitt's roughest time came in 1788, when Eris was sextile his Midheaven. King George III experienced a period of madness, and there was a danger he would be removed from power, with the Prince of Wales serving as regent. Charles Fox was a close friend of the Prince of Wales, and it was likely that Pitt would have been replaced as head of the government. Fortunately for Pitt, King George III recovered from madness before the Regency bill got through Parliament.

William Pitt the Younger

In the 1790's, Eris was trine Pitt's Mercury and conjunct Jupiter. It was a time of new honors and successes. The King gave him the sinecure post of Lord Warden of the Cinque Ports, making Pitt responsible for the security of coastal defenses. The King offered the knighthood of the Garter, but Pitt turned it down in favor of his elder brother, the Earl of Chatham. Once Great Britain entered war with France, the Pitt government became oppressive, banned "seditious" writings, and suspended *habeas corpus.*

In 1798, there was panic due to rumors that Napoleon Bonaparte was preparing an invasion of England. Napoleon had considered the idea, but decided that Egypt would be a better target, since it would disrupt Britain's trade route to India. The British did have cause to fear from a rebellion in Ireland, which was supported by the landing of 1,100 French troops. Originally, 14,000 troops were to have been landed, but storms scattered the French fleet. The insurrection was ended by 1799 due to the attacks by the British army, which had a skilled advantage over the ill-trained and poorly organized rebels.

The most significant result of the rebellion was the creation of the United Kingdom. In 1707, the Kingdom of Great Britain had come into existence with the union of England, Wales and Scotland. Ireland remained a separate country, ruled by an Irish parliament under the control of the British parliament. Pitt realized that this was the time to bring Ireland into the kingdom, and on Jan. 1, 1801 (the day Ceres was discovered) the Act of Union took place, making Ireland officially part of the Kingdom of Great Britain, and the establishing the name of the United Kingdom.

Unfortunately for Pitt, he could not convince King George III of the need for Catholic emancipation. Since the deposing of King James II, there had been more laws passed against the rights of Catholics, preventing them from taking part in public service and keeping them from joining the military. The result of the reluctance by King George III was that only Irish Protestants could serve in Parliament, and Irish Catholics were reduced to the level of second-class citizens. With transiting Eris trine his Ceres, Pitt resigned his office over this issue, and was replaced by Henry Addington, who concluded the Peace of Amiens with France.

Rather than serve in Addington's ministry, Pitt joined the opposition, making common cause with his old nemesis, Charles Fox, which took place when Eris was sextile Pitt's Uranus. He was able to form a second ministry when Eris was quincunx his Moon, but its position was weaker than his previous administration. Pitt lasted less than two years in office, until his poor health finally finished him off on January 23, 1806. Catholic emancipation would not come until 1827, after King George III had been replaced by his son, King George IV.

In the United States, the Eris-Pluto semi-sextile took place during years of consolidation for the new Federal government, but also marked a period of hysteria and dissension. George Washington was the first president under the new constitution, and his greatest task was in setting up the executive branch of government, keeping in mind that actions on his part would be setting a precedent for future presidents. He was assisted by Secretary of the Treasury, Alexander Hamilton, who established the financial security of the government by assuming all of the debts incurred by the states during the American Revolution. To help pay these debts, a new tax on whiskey was passed, which proved to be very unpopular.

Farmers in western Pennsylvania were the hardest hit by the Whiskey Tax. Because transportation costs were too great to send most of their crops to market, the farmers would distill their corn into whiskey, and even use it as a form of currency. The Whiskey Tax, and the interference by revenue agents took away the advantages of this system. By 1794, the anger of the farmers was so great they attacked tax collectors, causing a fear that a new revolution was about to break out. When the farmers formed a militia with several hundred members, President Washington sent requests to Maryland, New Jersey, Pennsylvania, and Virginia to raise troops to put down the rebellion.

An army of 13,000 men marched on western Pennsylvania, and President Washington went into the field to inspect the troops. The farmers realized that they were outnumbered, and they sent peace commissioners to negotiate a settlement. Most of the towns in western Pennsylvania accepted the Federal terms, though some rural areas maintained resistance. Some of the leaders of the rebellion ended up fleeing the area. In the end, 20 men were arrested for attacking tax collectors. Ten men were charged with treason, but only two were found guilty and sentenced to hang. Both were pardoned by President Washington.

Breaking the Whiskey Rebellion demonstrated that the Federal government was here to stay, though some still resented the power of the central government, and formed a faction of "Anti-Federalists" to oppose it. Former Secretary of State Thomas Jefferson (who had resigned after clashing with Hamilton) began supporting states rights over those of the Federal government. Rather than speak out himself, since he was a bad public speaker, Jefferson employed newspapers to attack the Federal government, with editorials warning about the potential threat of "a monarchy."

160. Brother Pluto, Sister Eris

The most obnoxious editorial writer was Benjamin Franklin Bache, the grandson of Benjamin Franklin. He was born with Eris quincunx Mercury, and he had a quick, brilliant mind, worthy of his grandfather. With Venus opposing Eris, he was beloved as a child, especially by his grandmother, Deborah Read Franklin. Unfortunately, she died when he was age 5 in 1774. The following year he met his illustrious grandfather, and was taken into his sphere of influence. When transiting Eris was trine Benjamin's natal Neptune, he joined his grandfather on a trip to France, which was made perilous by storms and threat of capture by British warships.

Young Benjamin went to boarding school with other American children, including young John Quincy Adams. When transiting Eris was trine his natal Uranus and Mars, he assumed a heavy workload, but managed to work his way through it. By age 13, with transiting Eris conjunct his Pluto, he was immersed in dead languages, translating Latin into French. He would later receive an award from the Geneva school for excellent work.

In 1783, with transiting Eris sextile young Benjamin's Jupiter, the elder Franklin achieved his greatest accomplishment as a diplomat by signing the peace treaty between the United States and Great Britain, assuring America's role as an independent nation. In 1785, transiting Eris was sextile young Bejamin Juno. When the Franklins had returned to Philadelphia, young Benjamin found it to be foreign and provincial after his Paris education. He graduated from the University of Pennsylvania in 1787, and then went about the mundane task of working in his grandfather's print shop.

In 1790, when transiting Eris was quincunx young Benjamin's natal Sun and natal Vesta, this Yod aspect marked a major change in his family life. The elder Benjamin Franklin died that year, and in his will he left his books and printing press to his grandson. That year, Benjamin Franklin Bache started the *General Advertiser, and Political, Commercial, and Agricultural Literary Journal*. The following year, when Eris was quincunx his Ceres, he dropped the word "Agricultural" from the banner. In 1793, when Eris was sextile his Chiron, he maintained a pro-French editorial policy, in spite of stories about the "Reign of Terror." It was the beginning of an upheaval in the body politic of the young nation.

As transiting Eris approached an opposition to his Saturn and quincunx his Pallas, Benjamin Franklin Bache changed the name of his newspaper to *Aurora*, and printed numerous articles attacking George Washington. The President was accused of wanting to be a king, of being

Benjamin
Franklin Bache
August 12 1769
12:00 LMT
Koch 39N57'08
75W09'51

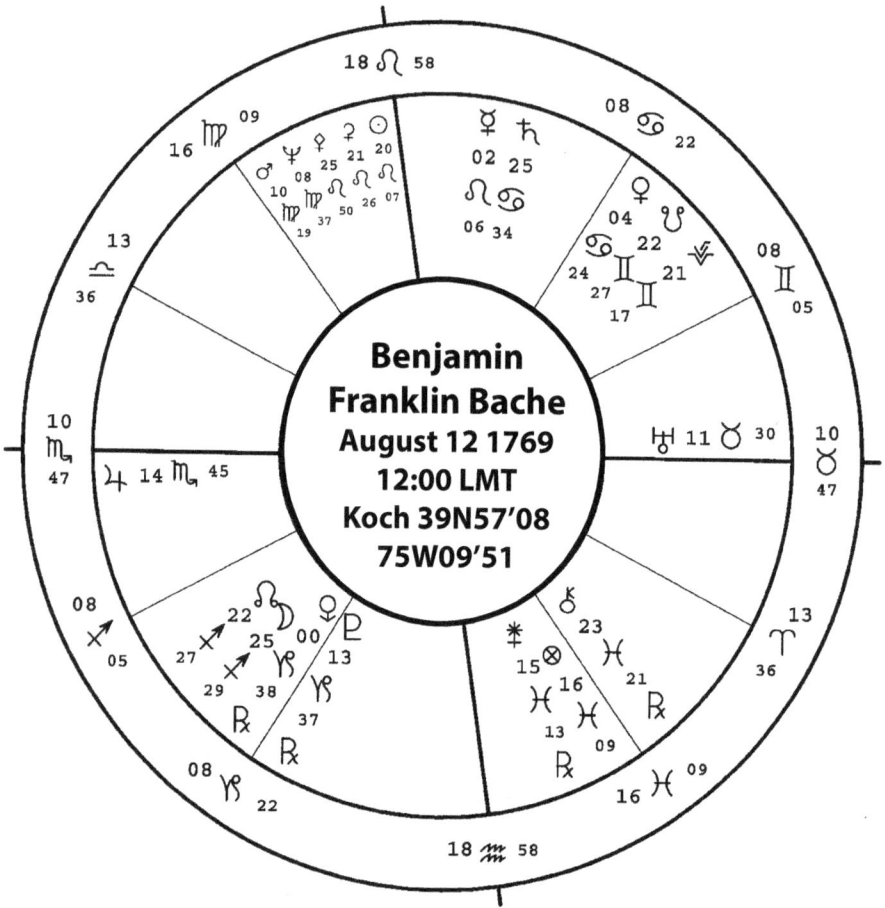

a friend to England, and of wanting to suppress French sympathizers. Bache's articles became so offensive that Washington decided not to run for a third term, thus establishing a precedent that lasted until Franklin Roosevelt came along. Bache eased up on the editorials once Washington announced his decision to retire. Bache was saving his worst pieces for when John Adams became president.

As a young man, Bache had witnessed the contention between his grandfather and John Adams as they served as diplomats in Europe, and he got a good look at the moods and tantrums of Adams when Ben Franklin would not agree with him. As

political factions became more vocal, Bache began denouncing him as "bald, fat, blind, and mad Adams." John Adams' response was, "I am not mad." Bache received attacks in return from Federalist newspapers. He was even physically attacked by Federalists, as the rancor grew worse between the Federalist and the Anti-Federalist parties.

Part of the contention was over the French Revolution. The Federalists saw the French as bringing about anarchy. Washington's administration tended to favor the British, while maintaining outward neutrality. Jefferson and his party maintained a pro-French attitude, comparing the French Revolution to the American Revolution. Unfortunately, events were soon to change that would cripple the power of the anti-Federalists.

In 1797, three American diplomats were sent to France to negotiate with Talleyrand over the containment of American ships that had been seized by the French fleet. The diplomats were visited by three associates of Talleyrand, (referred to in dispatches as X, Y, and Z) who let it be known that the foreign minister would fairly consider their case in return for a gratuity. When word of this was released, the American public was outraged by the demand for a bribe, and responded with the slogan, *Millions for defense, but not one cent for tribute*. A wave of anti-French feeling swept across the nation, and new ships were built to fight the "quasi war" with France.

The Adams administration took advantage of this mood change by passing the Alien and Sedition Acts. French immigrants, who were thought to be potential revolutionary agents, could easily be deported. Newspaper editors who dared to criticize the government could be arrested. Matthew Lyons, a Congressman from Vermont, was thrown into jail on the sedition charge, but he managed to get re-elected, even from a jail cell. Benjamin Franklin Bache was put into prison, then made bail, and finally died during the Yellow Fever outbreak of 1798, shortly before his Saturn return.

Thomas Jefferson once referred to this period as *The Reign of the Witches*, as it seemed that reason and common sense were being sacrificed to a political agenda. Fortunately, President Adams did not intend to fight a war with France, even though there were events of American ships and French ships engaging in combat. In 1800, Adams sent new diplomats to France, and the new government of Napoleon was willing to negotiate any differences without bribery. In 1801, Thomas Jefferson became President, and he repealed the Alien and Sedition Acts, as well as the tax on whiskey.

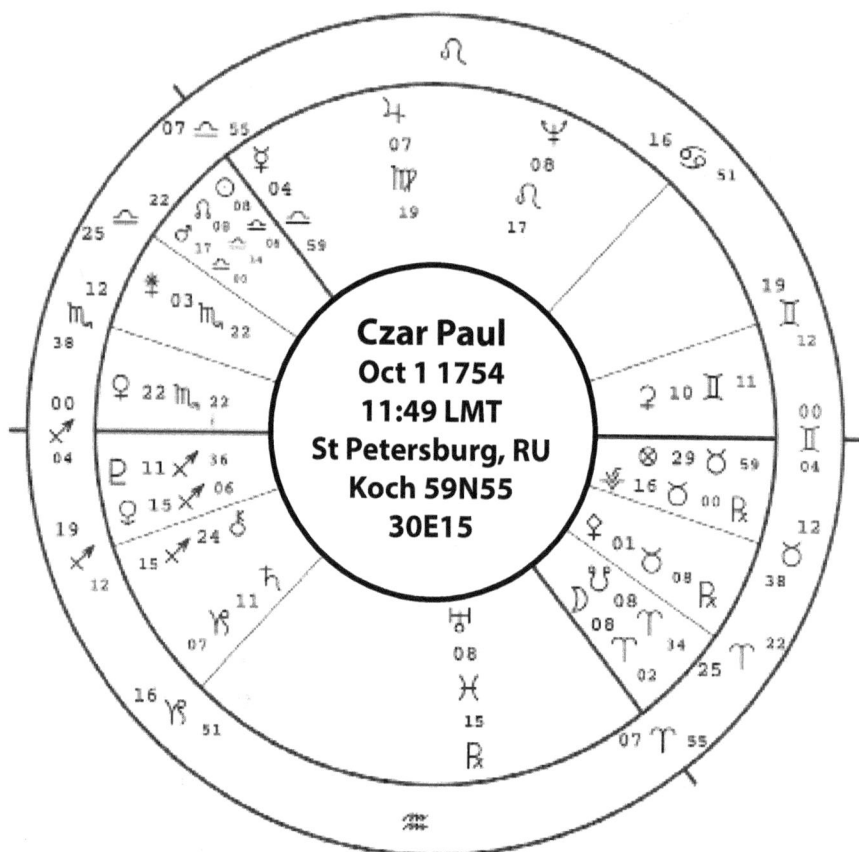

Czar Paul
Oct 1 1754
11:49 LMT
St Petersburg, RU
Koch 59N55
30E15

In Russia, the Eris-Pluto semi-sextile marked the reign of Czar Paul I, the son of Catherine the Great, who had Eris conjunct Pluto in his chart. By some accounts, Paul may have been mentally ill, since it was said that he often spoke and acted without reflection. Czarina Elizabeth had removed him from his mother's care soon after he was born. Some accounts say that she spoiled him, but that treatment ended as transiting Eris went over his Chiron. Czarina Elizabeth died, and when Catherine the Great came to power, she kept Paul isolated in the care of servants, who only brought him to court for special events.

Czar Paul

Catherine arranged two marriages for Paul. The first took place when Eris was sextile his Juno. The marriage ended when his wife died in child birth in 1776, when Eris was trine his Jupiter. A second marriage took place the same year, when Eris was square his Sun, sextile his Uranus and quincunx his Neptune. This marriage produced ten children, and his elder sons were raised by Empress Catherine. As Paul became older he would criticize his mother's policies, and rather than take part in court life, he spent his time at his estates, forcing his guards to go through Prussian military drills. This isolation took place as Eris was conjunct his Saturn and semi-sextile his natal Pluto.

By 1787, when Eris was square Paul's Mars and trine his Vesta, it was Catherine's intention to groom the eldest son, Alexander, to become her successor, keeping Paul away from the throne. In 1796, Catherine died (not because of a horse, but because she suffered a stroke) and Paul worked to seize the throne. He refused to have his mother's testament released, out of fear that it would proclaim Alexander to be the czar. He worked to change the laws of inheritance so that the throne of Russia would go through primogeniture rather than have it bequeathed by the previous ruler.

An invasion of Persia that was planned by Catherine was called off by Czar Paul, who then released some of Catherine's political prisoners, and his commands became a bit strange. He demanded that his guards parade each morning, no matter what the weather. The army was obliged to wear Prussian style uniforms, even though both the weather and the uniforms were quite uncomfortable and also more difficult to maintain than the Russian style uniforms. Finally, he insisted that Russian nobles should maintain a code of chivalry, hearkening back to the medieval knights.

This love of chivalry was to cause for Czar Paul one of his oddest foreign policy moves. He was approached by the Order of Knights Hospitaller in regard to priories in Poland that had not been producing revenue. After the partition of Poland in 1772, all of the knights had been stationed in Russia. Czar Paul was impressed with the knights, and to help their order he relocated the Polish priories to St. Petersburg. The Knights Hospitaller were so grateful to the Czar that they gave him the title of "Protector of the Order." He was both surprised and touched by this title, so he took additional interest in the affairs of the order.

One issue involving the Order was the sovereignty of Malta, which had been under their control since 1530. When Napoleon was on his way to Egypt, he stopped in Malta, and the French occupied the island. The Grand Master of the Knights Hospitaller gave the sovereignty of Malta to the French, and Napoleon spent six days making reforms on the island before sailing off to Egypt. (If he had stayed one more day on the island, he would have been trapped by Lord Horatio Nelson's fleet.)

Czar Paul felt that the French had no right to Malta. This was echoed by the Priory of St. Petersburg, and shortly after they declared that Czar Paul was now the Grand Master of the Order. The other priories had a hard time accepting this, because he was a member of the Russian Orthodox Church, and the Knights Hospitaller was a Roman Catholic order. It was a divisive act for the order, but it gave Czar Paul an additional excuse for going to war against France. He formed an alliance with Austria to fight in the Second Coalition against the French. Russian troops were sent to fight alongside the Austrian troops in Italy.

Russian troops stopped fighting in Italy after political disagreements with the Austrians. The Russians wanted to install Italian nobles as the rulers for the lands abandoned by the French. The Austrians just wanted to keep the lands for their empire. The Russians did try to remove French troops from Switzerland, but the campaign proved to be a stalemate. The Second Coalition started to break up in 1800, and Czar Paul was able to come to terms with Napoleon. In fact, he liked Napoleon so much he began fighting against the British, and offered to send a Cossack army to attack India. The British countered this threat by signing treaties with Persia to block any attack against India.

With Eris trine his Part-of-Fortune, Czar Paul began organizing the Baltic kingdoms into a coalition against England. He started seizing British ships, and ordered their crews to be put into prison camps. He helped the Danes assemble a fleet that would be larger than the British fleet, but in March, 1801 Lord Nelson attacked Copenhagen and destroyed the Danish fleet. Lord Nelson was then preparing to sail to St. Petersburg to attack the Russians, but circumstances changed that plan.

By the time Eris was sextile Czar Paul's Ascendant, he had earned the enmity of the noble class with his decrees and fancies towards chivalry. When he started to expose corruption in the royal treasury, a group of conspirators began plotting against his life. On the evening of March 23, 1801, a band of dismissed officers burst into Czar Paul's bedroom to assassinate him. They found him hiding behind curtains. He offered them restitution and rewards, and some of the officers were willing to believe him. However, one officer pointed out that if Czar Paul was allowed to live, he could have revenge against them all. Czar Paul was stabbed with a sword, strangled, and then trampled by the conspirators. His son, Alexander, was proclaimed to be the new czar. Negotiations were begun with Lord Nelson to prevent a British attack on St. Petersburg.

By the end of the Eris-Pluto semi-sextile, political transformation had taken place in France, England, the USA, and Russia. Barras, Pitt, Adams, and Czar Paul were cast out to make way for more decisive leaders. Pitt regained power temporarily, but would pass away as Britain engaged in new battles with Napoleon. Jefferson came to terms with Napoleon in the Louisiana Purchase, which doubled the size of the United States. Czar Alexander would fight Napoleon, then come to terms with him, and then fight him again in what became the decisive defeat for the French Army. For 40 years after the fall of Napoleon, the nations of Europe managed to live in peace, with a diplomatic balance of power preventing major conflicts, until the next Eris-Pluto aspect.

Europe and America were not the only areas to experience revolutions during the Eris-Pluto semi-sextile. In China, a major rebellion broke out by the White Lotus Society in 1794. This secret society had been around for about 500 years, mixing Buddhist principles with Persian Manichaeism. It also became involved in political matters. The society allowed men and women to interact freely, and they would meet at night for incense burning ceremonies. Over the centuries, they had caused some rebellions, but nothing as vast as what took place during the Eris-Pluto semi-sextile.

The White Lotus rebellion began as a tax protest, fighting against the extortion of local officials. This stand against corrupt authority brought in thousands of peasants to the cause. The Qing dynasty sent troops to suppress the rebellion, but the guerilla tactics of the White Lotus Society hampered their progress. The rebellion was broken by a means of "resettlement," which meant placing peasants who had surrendered into stockade villages to keep them from joining the White Lotus Society. The Qing Dynasty also punished the local officials who had been extorting money, thereby satisfying the grievances of the peasants. It was not until 1804 that the White Lotus Society was defeated, with 100,000 casualties. The result of the rebellion was to weaken the power of the Qing dynasty, which would lead to further rebellion with the next Eris-Pluto aspect.

Bibliography - Chapter 17
Internet Sources

French Revolution
https://en.wikipedia.org/wiki/French_Revolution

The Reign of Terror
https://en.wikipedia.org/wiki/Reign_of_Terror

Guillotine
https://en.wikipedia.org/wiki/Guillotine

Tricoteuse
https://en.wikipedia.org/wiki/Tricoteuse

Robespierre
https://en.wikipedia.org/wiki/Maximilien_Robespierre

Barras
https://en.wikipedia.org/wiki/Paul_Barras

Napoleon Bonaparte
https://en.wikipedia.org/wiki/Napoleon

Talleyrand
https://en.wikipedia.org/wiki/Charles_Maurice_de_Talleyrand -P%C3%A9rigord

Joseph Fouche
https://en.wikipedia.org/wiki/Joseph_Fouch%C3%A9

The Directory
https://en.wikipedia.org/wiki/French_Directory

William Pitt the Younger
https://en.wikipedia.org/wiki/William_Pitt_the_Younger

Catholic Emancipation
https://en.wikipedia.org/wiki/Catholic_emancipation

United Kingdom
https://en.wikipedia.org/wiki/United_Kingdom_of_Great_Britain and_Ireland

Charles Fox
https://en.wikipedia.org/wiki/Charles_James_Fox

The Whiskey Rebellion
https://en.wikipedia.org/wiki/Whiskey_Rebellion

The XYZ Affair
https://en.wikipedia.org/wiki/XYZ_Affair

Benjamin Franklin Bache
https://en.wikipedia.org/wiki/Benjamin_FranklinBache_(journalist)

Czar Paul
https://en.wikipedia.org/wiki/Paul_I_of_Russia

Russian Tradition of the Knights Hospitaller
https://en.wikipedia.org/wik_Russian_tradition_of_the_Knights_Hospitaller

Catherine the Great
https://en.wikipedia.org/wiki/Catherine_the_Great

Alexander I of Russia
https://en.wikipedia.org/wiki/Alexander_I_of_Russia

The White Lotus Rebellion
https://en.wikipedia.org/wiki/White_Lotus_Rebellion

Book Sources

Dos Passos, John, *Lafayette's Two Revolutions*, New York, NY, *American Heritage, Vol. VIII, No. 1, December 1956*, Pages 4-9, 104-116.

Flexner, James Thomas, *Washington: The Indispensable Man*, New York, NY, Little, Brown, and Company, 1974, Pages 312-320.

McCullough, David, John Adams, New York, NY, Simon & Schuster, 2001.

Paschall, Rod, MHQ: The Quarterly Journal of Military History, August, 1999, Leesburg, VA, *Napoleon's First Triumph*, Pages 6-17.

Ridpath, John Clark, LL.D., *Cyclopedia of Universal History: Being an Account of the Principal events in the career of the Human Race from the beginnings of Civilization to the Present Time. From Recent and Authentic Sources. Vol. II, Part II,* Cincinnati, OH, The Jones Brothers Publishing Co, 1885

Robinson, Nugent, *History of the World with all its Great Sensations together with Mighty and Decisive Battles and the Rise and Fall of its Nations from the Earliest Times to the Present Day, Vol. I,* New York, NY, P.F.Collier, Publisher, 1891.

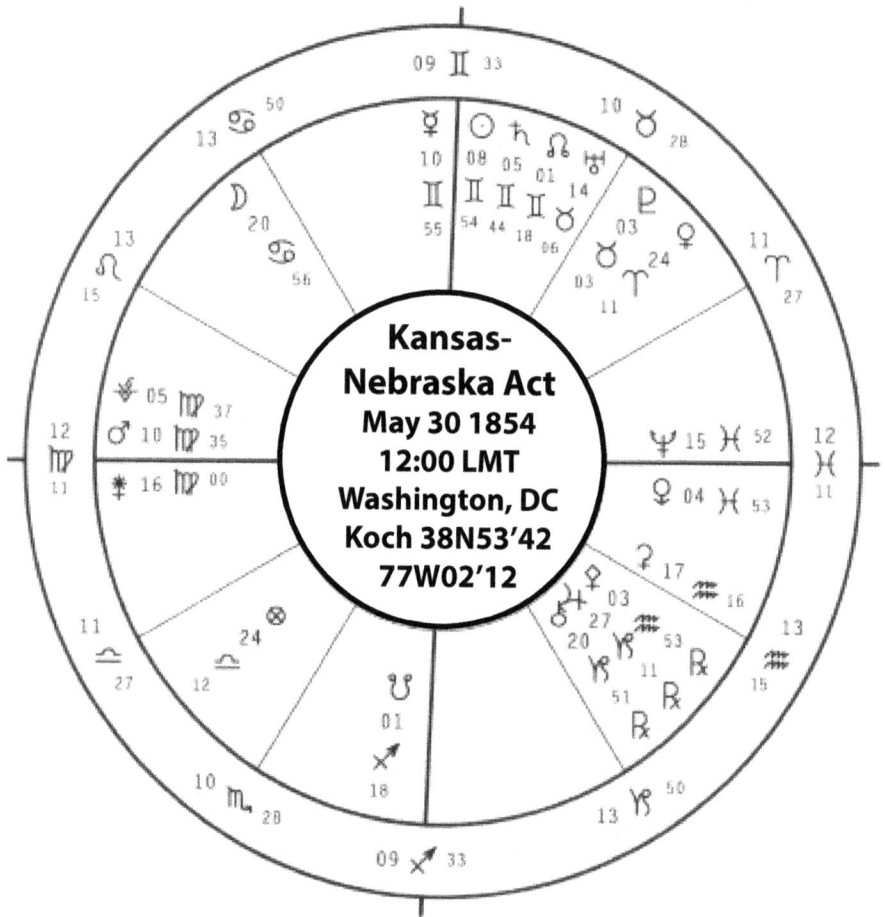

Inner chart text:

Kansas-
Nebraska Act
May 30 1854
12:00 LMT
Washington, DC
Koch 38N53'42
77W02'12

09 ♊ 33

13 ♋ 50

♀ 10
08 05
♂ 01
♅ 14
♉ 28

10 ♊ 55   ♊ 54   ♊ 44   ♊ 18   06   10 ♉

☽ 20

♋ 56

♇ 03   ♉ 24

♉ 03   ♈ 11

13 ♌ 15

11 ♈ 27

♄ 05   ♍ 37
♂ 10   ♍ 35
⚷ 16   ♍ 00

12 ♍ 11

♆ 15 ♓ 52

♀ 04 ♓ 53

12 ♓ 11

♃ 17 ♒ 16

☿ 03   ♒ 27
⚷ 20   ♑ 53 ℞
♑ 11 ℞

13 ♒ 15

11 ♎ 27

⊗ 24

12 ♎

☊ 01
♐ 18

13 ♑ 50 ℞

10 ♏ 28

09 ♐ 33

Chapter 18

"Theirs not to reason why"
Eris sextile Pluto

For nearly 40 years after the fall of Napoleon, the European powers managed to live in peace, though there were some internal rumblings of revolution in 1848 when Eris was conjunct Neptune. The revolutions were suppressed, but there were new struggles brewing, which finally burst out in the 1850's and lasted until 1865, during which time Eris in Pisces was sextile Pluto in Taurus. It was a time of three bloody wars around the world. First was the Taiping Rebellion in China, which may have cost 20 million lives, with disease and famine being factors as well as warfare. Also at this time was the Crimean War, which showed the professional incompetence of rigid military planning. Finally, there was the American Civil War, which had fewer deaths than the Taiping Rebellion, but which received better coverage due to telegraphed newspaper reports and photographs of the battle scenes.

The origins of the Taiping Rebellion dated back to the mid-1830's, when a civil servant applicant named Hong Xiuquan failed to pass the imperial examinations. The examinations were so hard, only five percent of the applicants ever passed them. Hong Xiuquan failed four times, and in 1837 he suffered a nervous breakdown. Upon his recovery, he became a teacher, and in 1843 he began studying Protestant Christianity tracts that he had received during his illness. His study of Christianity filled him with messianic zeal, and in a short time he began telling people that he was the brother of Jesus Christ, and he had come to remove the "devils" of Confucianism and Buddhism.

It is interesting that Hong Xiuquan's religious zeal developed at the same time as other religious/millennial movements around the world. In America, William Miller and Joseph Smith were convincing thousands of people that the 1840's were the Latter Days. In Persia, a holy man named the Bab was predicting the coming of a new prophet. From these

Charles George Gordon
January 28, 1833
9:53 LMT
Woohwich, UK
Koch 52N29
0E05

preachers would come the religions of Seventh Day Adventists, the Mormons, and the Baha'i. Hong Xiuquan's preaching became more violent and more appealing to an unsettled population. China had lost the First Opium War, thereby allowing European merchants to encourage opium addiction among the people. The ruling Qing dynasty was bending more to foreign pressure, and it seemed there was a power vacuum being created. The preaching of Hong Xiuquan appeared to fill that vacuum.

At first the Taiping movement was like a militant reform movement, and

Chinese Gordon

its first victims were bandits and river pirates. Part of the appeal of the new movement was its break from China's feudal order. Women were considered to be socially equal to men, though the movement did keep them segregated, and polygamy was outlawed. There were beliefs that all property should be held in common, that opium should be outlawed, and that Christian teachings should replace the older Chinese beliefs. By the 1850's, Hong Xiuquan had more than 10,000 followers, and they were able to overwhelm the local imperial army. The new movement marched on Nanjing, which was proclaimed to be the new capital.

The Qing dynasty started sending armies against the rebels, but many of the generals were trained in antiquated tactics, and they could not fight against the guerilla tactics of the rebels. In order to maintain the war, the Qing dynasty needed foreign assistance. Militia groups were organized by the European powers that had been trading with Shanghai. The military command of the rebels was taken over by another erstwhile prophet, Yang Xiuquing, who claimed to be getting information from God, but who had a very efficient spy network. Hong Xiuquan resented the preaching by his subordinate, and in 1856 he ordered Yang Xiuquing to be put to death, along with the members of his family.

The tide began to turn against Hong Xiuquan in 1861. The British sent Captain Charles George Gordon to train the Chinese troops, for which he received the nickname,"Chinese Gordon." Gordon had trained at the Royal Military Academy in Woolwich when transiting Eris was semi-sextile his Jupiter and Pallas, and square his Mars. He entered the British Army as a second lieutenant in 1852, when Eris was sextile his Moon. He became a full lieutenant in 1854, and his talents for constructing fortifications were put to good use during the Crimean War. After the war, he was part of a surveying team establishing the boundary between Russia and Turkey. He later became an instructor, and was promoted to captain in 1859. When Eris was trine his Part-of-Fortune and sextile his Ceres, he left England for service in China against the Taiping Rebellion.

Gordon brought the latest rifle and artillery pieces to China, making sure his troops were well equipped. The army of the Qing Dynasty began pushing into the rebel territory. By 1864, Eris was semi-sextile Gordon's Sun and Pluto, and Gordon had his greatest success in capturing the Taiping military base at Changzhou. Hong Xiuquan was trapped inside of Nanjing, with the Chinese army making a siege to the city. Hong Xiuquan predicted a miracle would save the city, but he ended up dying from eating spoiled food. Some accounts claimed he committed suicide by poison. His fifteen-year-old son was left as his successor, but the city was soon captured and the rebellion was broken. As for Gordon, he was promoted to lieutenant colonel and given honors by the Chinese government, including an imperial yellow jacket, for bringing about the fall of Hong Xiuquan.

Ironically, twenty years later, when Eris was sextile his Chiron and his Mercury, as well as semi-sextile his Uranus, Major General Charles George "Chinese" Gordon would meet his death at the hands of another religious fanatic. Gordon was commanding troops in the Sudan, and the city of Khartoum was under attack by a Muslim leader, Muhammed Ahmad, calling himself the "Mahdi." who was supposed to be the prophesized redeemer of Islam. A relief expedition from Egypt was too late to save Gordon, who was beheaded when the Mahdi's troops captured the city. His head was presented to the Mahdi, and then placed on display in a tree for public ridicule. Gordon was avenged when the Mahdi was killed six months later.

Returning to the 1850's, it was also a religious issue that sparked the second conflict of the Eris-Pluto sextile, the Crimean war. Since the Eris-Pluto sextile at the time of the siege of Malta in 1565, the Ottoman Empire had been in a state of steady decline. By the 19th century, it had lost much of its European territories in the Balkans, and Greece fought a successful war of independence, thereby freeing Athens, which had been taken during the Eris-Pluto trine in 1458. The Ottoman Empire still controlled the Straits of Bosphorus leading to the Black Sea, and most of the lands in the Middle East, including the holy cities of Jerusalem and Mecca.

The conflict began with Russian demands that the Orthodox Church should have control over Christian holy sites in the Middle East. Napoleon III, who had just come to power in France, insisted that the Roman Catholic Church should have control over the holy sites. When Turkey signed a treaty with France, the Russians placed troops on the borders of Turkish territories. From there the conflict escalated to questions over the ownership of certain areas. France and Great Britain urged the Turks to stand up against the Russians. When the Russians occupied Turkish lands along the Danube, France and Great Britain declared war on Russia. It was the first time in more than 600 years that the two countries had formed an alliance against a common enemy.

The Russian advance along the Danube was forced back when the Austrians entered the war. Previously, the Russians had helped the

Florence Nightingale

Austrians during a revolution in 1848. However, the Austrians did not trust the Russians to have them alongside their territories, and Austria came to regard the Ottoman Empire as a bulwark against Russian expansion. After an Austrian advance, the Russians were forced to retreat from the Danube region.

The whole war might have ended there, but in France and Great Britain there had been war fever growing for most of the year, and it was felt that a punitive expedition against Russia would prevent future attacks on the Ottoman Empire.

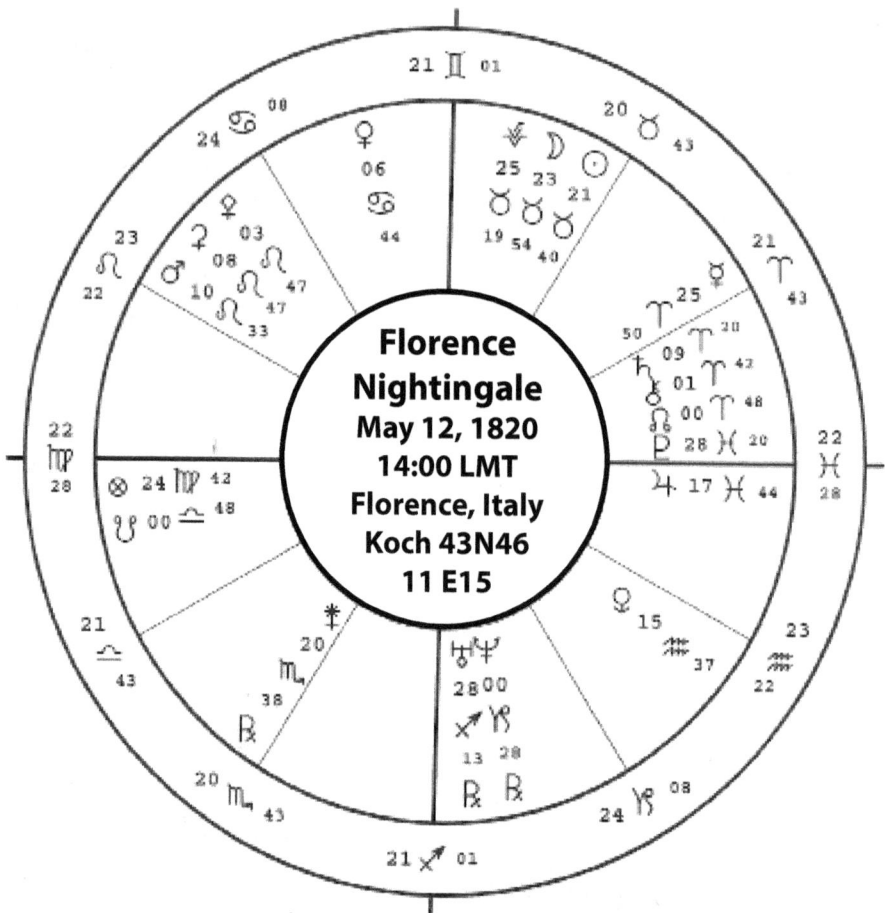

Florence Nightingale
May 12, 1820
14:00 LMT
Florence, Italy
Koch 43N46
11 E15

The Russians had disabled the Turkish fleet in the Black Sea, and the British and French sent naval forces into the area to support the Turks. In September 1854, an invasion force landed on the Crimean peninsula, consisting of British, French, and Sardinian soldiers. (The Sardinians joined in because they were trying to curry favor with the French over the issue of Italian unification.) Their mission was to capture the Russian naval fortress at Sevastopol, which would destroy the major Russian base on the Black Sea. Unfortunately, the plans for attack were soon revealed to be inadequate.

The Crimean War was the first to receive major newspaper coverage. Forty years earlier, it had taken a week for news of the battle of Waterloo to reach London. Thanks to a telegraph line laid by the French, it only took a few hours for the war news to get to London. The result of this constant attention was that the British public was given a first-hand look at the incompetence of military planning for the campaign.

Supplies and distribution were disorganized, but worst of all was the poor planning for sanitation and medical relief. Wounded soldiers were given rudimentary first aid, and then left to lie on the floor in their bloodstained uniforms where they would be vulnerable to infection. To be wounded was tantamount to a death sentence.

If there was one truly heroic figure of the Crimean War, it was the nurse Florence Nightingale, forever remembered as "the lady with the lamp." She organized the first nursing medical corps to serve in a military conflict. Before her efforts, nursing was considered to be a disreputable profession. In his novel, Martin Chuzzlewit, Charles Dickens caricatured the pre-Nightingale image of a nurse with his comical Mrs. Gamp. She was an alcoholic old woman, whose function was to sit up with the sick, and to perform menial tasks like bringing food and water.

Before Florence Nightingale, there was no medical training for nurses, and socially they were considered to be little better than thieves or prostitutes. The Crimean War changed those notions, with descriptions of Florence Nightingale's sanitary and organized hospitals for the wounded soldiers. The result was that women from respectable families began to consider nursing as a career.

It was mysticism and messages from God that set Florence Nightingale on her path. Having been raised in an upper class family, she had no need for considering a career other than making a good marriage. Yet, with natal Eris semi-sextile her Jupiter, she began to question the worth of wealth and gentility. During the 1830's, when transiting Eris was square her Sun and Moon, she received an education at home. In 1837, when Eris was quincunx her Part-of-Fortune, she began having mystical experiences which set her on the path to helping others. In 1838, when Eris was sextile her Mercury and square her Vesta, she made the acquaintance of an eccentric lady in Paris, Mary Clarke, who taught her to set aside convention, and that women could be the equals of men.

In 1844, when Eris was sextile her Uranus, she created an uproar by announcing that she wanted to train as a nurse. Her mother and sister were mortified by her career choice. (Also, Martin Chuzzlewit, with its account of the nursing talents of Mrs. Gamp was published at that time.) Florence Nightingale was insistent upon nursing, and as Eris went into Pisces, sextile her natal Neptune, as well as conjunct transiting Neptune, she took up the career of nursing, though she had to travel outside of England to get the training she needed. During her travels, she made a friendship with Mr. & Mrs. Sidney Herbert, which proved to be very beneficial. During the Crimean War, Sidney Herbert was the War Minister, and a leading supporter for Florence Nightingale's innovations.

When Eris was semi-sextile her North Node and Chiron, Florence Nightingale received her best training in Germany, at a Lutheran religious community, Kaiserswerth-am-Rhein. She worked alongside the "deaconesses" who administered to the sick and elderly. She received four months of medical training while in Germany. Upon her return to England, she was given a position of superintendent at the Institute for the Care of Sick Gentlewomen, which she held until the coming of the Crimean War.

Florence Nightingale was prompted to volunteer for the Crimean War when horrific stories came to England about the poor treatment of wounded soldiers. Leading a contingent of 38 volunteers (including her own aunt), she arrived in the Crimea in November 1854, as Eris was quincunx her Pallas. Immediately, she started sending back reports on the poor sanitation, ventilation, and nutrition of the wounded. Although the British Navy had eradicated scurvy with rations of fruit juices, the British Army had not learned that lesson, and many of the troops came down with scurvy. After her letters were printed in the London Times, the government responded by sending a prefabricated hospital and paying more attention to the health needs of the army.

Florence Nightingale gained an international reputation for her care of the wounded, but her most important work was the gathering of information and statistics on hygiene and hospital conditions. It became the basis of her work on hospital sanitary care, and set standards for cleanliness that the medical world had not seen before. After she had been in the Crimea for a year, her friends set up the Nightingale Fund, which was to pay for the training of nurses. In 1860, as Eris was trine her Venus, she published a book on nursing and established a school for nursing. Unfortunately, her experience in the Crimea left her with depression and a case of hypochondria, which caused her to withdraw from public life. For the next 50 years, she would act in an advisory capacity for hospitals and nursing schools, as well as having an extensive correspondence, but she would not take a personal role in nursing as she did in the Crimea.

In the early 20th century, as Eris passed into her Seventh House, and was sextile her Sun and Moon, she did have to deal with major publicity. In 1904, she was made a Lady of the Order of St. John, a chivalric order that was a Protestant offshoot of the Knights Hospitaller. In 1907, she became the first woman to receive the Order of Merit, a new order created by King Edward VII for distinguished service to the armed forces, and for advancements in art, science, and literature. Florence Nightingale passed away on August 13, 1910, when transiting Eris was sextile her Vesta and semi-sextile her Mercury. The British government offered to bury her in Westminster Abbey, but her family turned down the offer for a simpler burial in a churchyard.

Another bit of heroism from the Crimean War has brought about constant debate regarding the nature of warfare. On October 25, 1854, British troops were fighting Russian troops at the Battle of Balaclava. The commander, Lord Raglan, had issued orders for the cavalry to advance and to prevent Russian troops from removing cannons from the battlefield. The wording of the order was imprecise, and when the command reached Lord Cardigan of the Light Brigade, it was interpreted as being a full charge at the enemy cannons. The result of the charge was a slaughter, with almost half of the Light Brigade becoming casualties to the Russian cannon fire. Alfred Lord Tennyson would immortalize the scene in his poem, "The Charge of the Light Brigade."

Theirs not to reason why,
Theirs but to do and die:
Into the valley of Death
Rode the six hundred.

The shock of the destruction of the Light Brigade brought repercussions to the British government, and a bill to investigate the military was passed. On January 30, 1855, the Prime Minister, Lord Aberdeen, resigned, and was replaced by the Foreign Secretary, Lord Palmerston. A little ditty of the time said, "If the Devil ever had a son, he surely would be Lord Palmerston." His method of power politics was to take a more militant stance on the war, and to extend it to a war that would annihilate Russian power forever. He began seeking more allies for the war, and stirred up interest in Prussia and Sweden to join the war.

The Russians were demoralized by the idea that all of the European powers were uniting against them. In the Ukraine, a Cossack revolt against the war drained more resources from the battlefield. Czar Nicholas I died in 1855, and was replaced by his son, Alexander II. (Like Hong Xiuquan, there were rumors that Nicholas poisoned himself.) Finally, in September 1855, Sevastopol fell to the allied forces. The French, who had supplied the most troops, began urging an end to the war. In 1856, the Russians signed a peace treaty, which prevented them from having a Black Sea naval fleet.

George McClellan
Dec 3 1826
12:15am
Philadelphia, PA

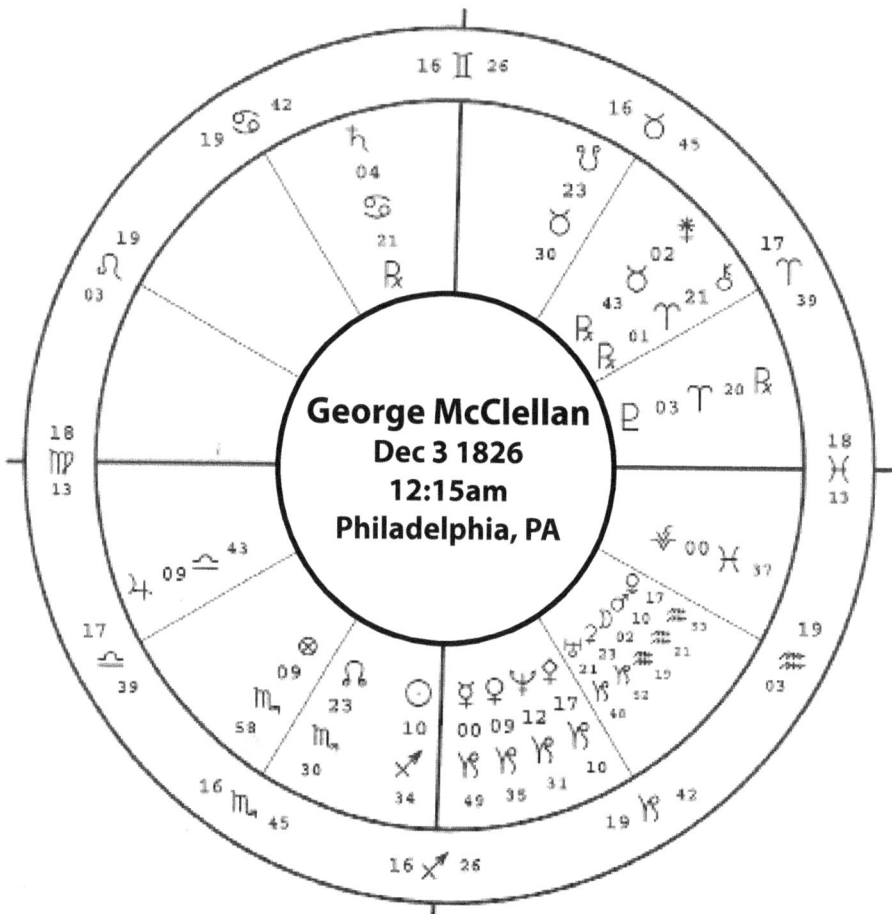

During the Crimean War, an American army officer named George McClellan observed many of the major battles. Upon returning to the United States, he wrote a military report critical of the war, as well as a cavalry manual based on Russian regulations. The U.S. Army would use the cavalry manual as long as it had horses on the battlefield. In a few years, McClellan was able to use his skills for proper planning in setting up the Army of the Potomac. Unfortunately, his career would be haunted by a lack of daring actions like the charge of the Light Brigade.

George McClellan was born with Eris trine his Midheaven, quincunx his Ascendant, and semi-sextile his Pallas. He had a brilliant mind, and entered the University of Pennsylvania, later switching to the West Point Academy at age 15, the only student admitted below the minimum age of 16. While at West Point, he became friends with southern cadets, who later became opposing Confederate generals. (One future general, A.P. Hill was actually McClellan's rival for the hand of Mary Ellen Marcy.) McClellan claimed that he could understand the "Southern mind", but that did not help him with defeating the Confederate army.

During the Mexican War, when Eris was conjunct his Vesta and sextile his Mercury, McClellan served in Zachary Taylor's army in northern Mexico. McClellan did not see any action, but he came down with dysentery and malaria, which afflicted him later on in his life. The 1850's was a busy decade for McClellan with Eris sextile his Juno and trine his Saturn. He performed surveying missions for railroad building, translated a French manual on bayonet tactics, and made his trip to the Crimea. For a short time, he left the army and became chief engineer and vice-president of the Illinois Central Railroad, which put him in contact with a corporate lawyer named Abraham Lincoln. Relations between Lincoln and McClellan were strained to the point that Lincoln had to sue the railroad in order to get his fees.

McClellan rejoined the army in time for the Civil War, and because of his experience and background he was given the rank of Major General to replace the ailing Winfield Scott. McClellan's first goal was to train the Union army so that they would be the top fighting force. The battle of Bull Run had been an embarrassment for the North, with Union soldiers running away from the battle, in what became known at "The Great Skedaddle." McClellan was expert at training his troops, but to the fury of now President Abraham Lincoln and his cabinet, he was hesitant about taking them into battle. Part of the reason may have been that his intelligence agents kept inflating the numbers of Confederate troops so that McClellan believed he was facing an army of 100,000 men, though the actual size of the rebel army was closer to 75,000.

McClellan's campaigns in 1862 were marked by hesitation, delays, and a painful slowness, which allowed Robert E. Lee to outfox the Union Army. McClellan lost a golden opportunity at the battle of Antietam, when presented with Lee's battle plans, showing how the Confederate Army was divided. If McClellan had acted to block Lee's retreat, the Confederate Army would have been defeated, but he hesitated too long. This was too much for Lincoln, who had McClellan removed from command.

In 1864, McClellan ran as the Democratic candidate for President. At first, it seemed likely he would defeat Lincoln, and even Lincoln prepared for that possibility by gaining pledges from cabinet members that they would help President-elect McClellan to end the war. However, the Democratic Party was divided between Union Democrats and "Copperheads" who supported the South. Many soldiers resented McClellan's association with "Copperheads" and ended up voting Republican. Victories by the Union Army raised morale in the North and helped insure Lincoln's re-election.

After the war, McClellan had Eris sextile his Venus, trine his Part-of-Fortune, and quincunx his Jupiter. He and his wife traveled in Europe for four years, and started raising a family. Upon his return to the USA, with Eris squaring his Sun and semi-sextile his Mars, McClellan was made Chief Engineer of the New York City Department of Docks. In the 1870's, when Eris was sextile his Neptune, he became President of the Atlantic and Great Western Railroad, which was followed by a three-year trip to Europe. The most distinctive honor he had in the post-war years was to serve one-term as the governor of New Jersey. After that, he traveled and then wrote his memoirs, which were published after his death in 1885. His lethargic career as a general may serve as a warning of what may happen if there are no Eris transits inspiring a desire for battle.

The American Civil War has been so well documented, it has been estimated that one book per day has been written about the war since its ending in 1865. The battles of Shiloh, Antietam, Fredericksburg, and Gettysburg were the bloodiest in USA history. Gettysburg had the odd distinction of being the largest land battle ever fought in the Western Hemisphere. There have been debates over the war leadership, and who was the most incompetent general. One debate has been over exactly when the war started. Although most historians mark the shelling of Fort Sumter as the official start of the war, there are some who consider the Kansas-Nebraska Act of 1854 to be the start.

For 75 years, the free states of the North had coexisted with the slave states of the South in an uneasy state of compromise. Henry Clay had set the pattern in 1820, with an arrangement which allowed a slave state to join the Union at the same time when a free state joined. This balance of power came to an end in 1850, when California entered the Union as a free state, but there was no corresponding slave state. To mollify the South, a Fugitive Slave Act was passed, which would allow trackers to bring back slaves who had escaped to the North. The result of this act was to galvanize the abolitionist movement, bringing about more militant action to free the slaves. One of the most powerful advocates was a religious fanatic named John Brown, who believed that the curse of slavery could only be removed by the shedding of blood.

In 1854, Senator Stephen Douglas introduced the Kansas-Nebraska act, which was to bring the Kansas and Nebraska territories into the Union and help open up the route for a transcontinental railroad. In regard to slavery, Douglas introduced the concept of "Popular Sovereignty" (later ridiculed as "Squatter Sovereignty"), which said that the people of the territories could vote to determine whether they were to become a free state or a slave state.

In the chart for the Kansas-Nebraska Act, Saturn was square Eris. The purpose of the act was to appease the conservative ideal that the practice of owning slaves was a personal choice, and by such appeasement a war could be avoided. Pluto was square Pallas, suggesting poor planning and a lack of wisdom. Mars was square Mercury, and the news of the act helped to stir up militant propaganda on both sides. Mars opposing Neptune brought out fanciful fears to inspire both sides. The South feared slave rebellions and a massacre of slave owners. The North

John Brown
May 9, 1800
3:00 LMT
Torrington, CT
Koch 41N48'02
73W07'18

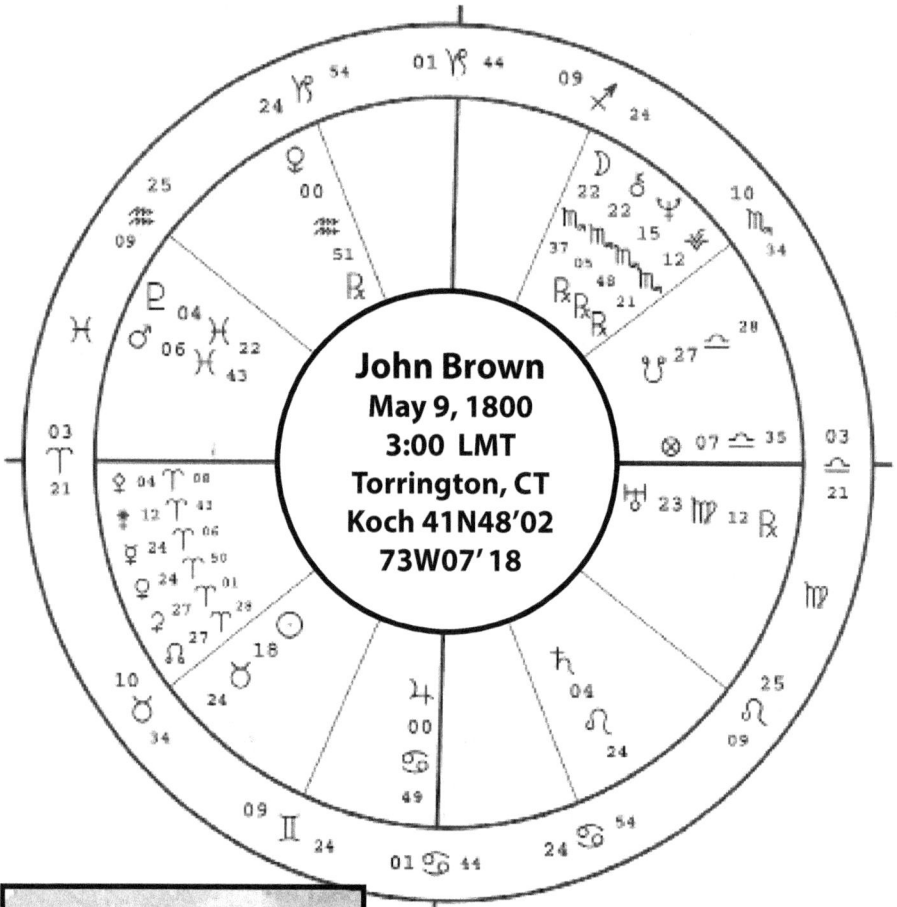

feared an increase of the slave power, with changes in laws that could possibly even enslave white people.

It was a policy meant to please everybody, but in the end it pleased nobody. Pro-slavery settlers came to Kansas from the South, while abolitionist settlers came from the North, including John Brown and his followers. Pro-Southern and pro-Northern communities began attacking each other, resulting in a period of warfare known as "Bleeding Kansas." John Brown wreaked an Old Testament vengeance upon pro-slavery settlers in Pottawatomie by slashing them to death with a sword.

John Brown

John Brown was born with Eris quincunx Jupiter. All through his life he lost at most business ventures. He tried to become a farmer, then a tanner, a wool manufacturer, and even a Congregational minister, but each venture failed. His leanest years were the result of the Panic of 1837, when Eris was sextile his Mercury and Venus. It was at this time that he developed his fervent anti-slavery attitudes, and was shocked by the murder of abolitionist Elijah Lovejoy. Brown was good at bringing children into the world, having fathered 20 children with two wives.

When Eris went into Pisces and was trine Brown's Jupiter, he set up his wool company in Springfield, MA. It was there that he made contacts with anti-slavery figures, and became a noted speaker against slavery. He became involved in the Underground Railroad, and purchased land in New York State where freed slaves could settle. By the time Eris was semi-sextile his Ascendant, he was ready to move to Kansas to stop the raids by pro-slavery Border Ruffians from Missouri.

His warfare in Kansas was just a preparation for his ill-fated attack on the arsenal at Harper's Ferry in an attempt to start a slave rebellion. Transiting Eris was conjunct his Pluto, semi-sextile his Pallas, and quincunx his Saturn. Part of his plan was to create a new state ruled by liberated slaves. He and his followers wrote a new Constitution, and planned to set up their own provisional government within the conquered territory. Through the summer of 1859, Brown toured and lectured in the North to drum up support for his cause. When he attacked Harper's Ferry on October 16, 1859, Brown had only 21 men with him. The U.S. Army under Colonel Robert E. Lee defeated John Brown, and he was hanged for his efforts. Abolitionists kept his spirit alive with the song, "John Brown's Body," which later morphed into "The Battle Hymn of the Republic."

Eris sextile Pluto also marked other conflicts around the world, such as the Sepoy Rebellion in India (which had more than 100,000 casualties), the fight for Italian Unification (more than 10,000 casualties), and the Second Opium War (which ran concurrent with the Taiping Rebellion, so casualties are hard to determine.) Another element rising at the time was the "Blood and Iron" mentality, promoted by the Prussian statesman, Otto Von Bismarck. During the final years of the Eris-Pluto sextile, Prussia began a few conquests, which were just a prelude of what would come once German states united to form an empire under the Prussian crown. One conquest made was the removal of the Schleswig-Holstein province from Denmark. This was the area that included Dithmarschen, and had been dominated by the Danish crown for 300 years.

Eris-Pluto remained in sextile until 1865, when the fighting of the American Civil War ended and the period of Reconstruction began. Instead of the slave power, the people now had to deal with the rise of corporations, and a pattern of bribery and pay-offs to public officials to maintain those corporations. Actual slavery became replaced by wage slavery. The plantation gave way to the corporate boardroom as a center of power. It was the beginning of a time of robber-baron capitalism, best summed up by the epithet of banker J.P. Morgan, "The public be damned."

Another side event for the Eris-Pluto sextile was the signing of the Treaty of Kanagawa, which opened up diplomatic relations between Japan and the United States. Japan had been isolated since the Eris-Pluto semi-sextile marking the Thirty Years War. The United States saw the opening of Japan as a measure to help the increase of trade with Asian nations. The Japanese accepted it reluctantly, but with the pragmatic reasoning that their nation needed to learn about the new military technology of the other nations. So skillful was the Japanese study of technology that by the time of the next Eris-Pluto aspect, Japan would become one of the world's leading military powers.

Diplomacy and education were also policies at this time in Thailand, under the reign of King Mongkut, who was far wiser than depicted by Anna Leonowens, or the Broadway musical based on her work. King Mongkut signed treaties with European powers and the United States, bringing missionaries and educators for the betterment of his kingdom. Contrary to legend, he did not offer to send war elephants to Abraham Lincoln to fight in the Civil War. Apart from being a Buddhist scholar, King Mongkut was also a master of astronomy and mathematics, accurately predicting the location of a solar eclipse in 1868. His expansion in education reform impressed people around the world with the erudition of the people of Thailand. As a result, Thailand was never subjected to the "white man's burden" of colonization. (Of course, it is possible all of the upheaval during the Eris-Pluto sextile may have distracted the other powers from colonization.) King Mongkut's policies were continued by his son, King Chulalongkorn, who ended slavery in Thailand, and weakened the power of nobles who threatened the kingdom. His reign lasted until the next Eris-Pluto aspect in the early 20th century.

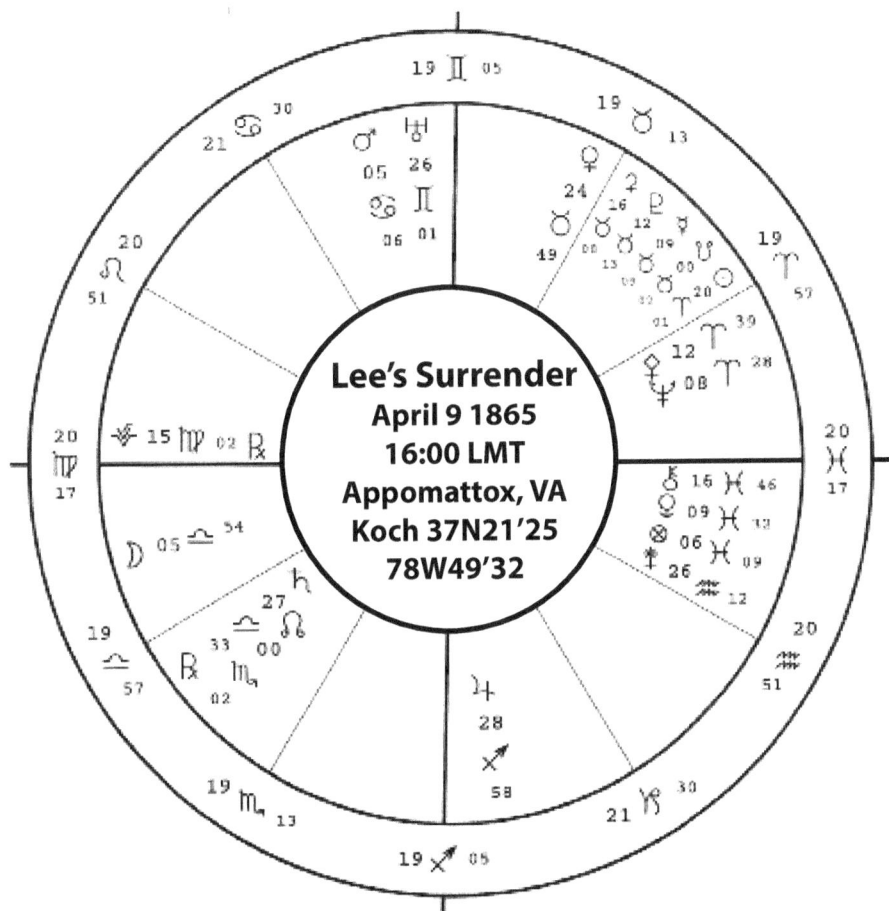

Lee's Surrender
April 9 1865
16:00 LMT
Appomattox, VA
Koch 37N21'25
78W49'32

Bibliography - Chapter 18
Internet Sources

Taiping Rebellion
  https://en.wikipedia.org/wiki/Taiping_Rebellion

Hong Xiuquan
  https://en.wikipedia.org/wiki/Hong_Xiuquan

Yang Xiuqing
  https://en.wikipedia.org/wiki/Yang_Xiuqing

Chinese Gordon
  https://en.wikipedia.org/wiki/Charles_George_Gordon

The Crimean War
  https://en.wikipedia.org/wiki/Crimean_War

Charge of the Light Brigade
  https://en.wikipedia.org/wiki/

Florence Nightingale
  https://en.wikipedia.org/wiki/Florence Nightingale

George McClellan
  https://en.wikipedia.org/wiki/George_B._McClellan

American Civil War
  https://en.wikipedia.org/wiki/American_Civil_War

Kansas Nebraska Act
  https://en.wikipedia.org/wiki/Kansas%E2%80%93Nebraska_Act

John Brown
  https://en.wikipedia.org/wiki/John_Brown_(abolitionist)

Raid on Harper's Ferry
https://en.wikipedia.org/wiki/JohnBrown%27s_raid_on_Harpers_Ferry

Blood and Iron
  https://en.wikipedia.org/wiki/Blood_and_Iron_(speech)

Robber Barons
  https://en.wikipedia.org/wiki/Robber_baron_(industrialist)

Kanagawa Treaty
  https://en.wikipedia.org/wiki/Convention_of Kanagawa

King Mongkut
  https://en.wikipedia.org/wiki/Mongkut

Book Sources

Carmer, Carl, *The Death of the Prophet*, New York, NY, American Heritage, Vol. XIV, No. 1, December, 1962 Pages 42-48, 85-89.

Catton, Bruce, *Crisis at the Antietam*, New York, NY, American Heritage, Vol. IX, No. 5, August, 1958, Pages 55-57, 93-96.

Fleming, Thomas J., *The Trial of John Brown*, New York, NY, American Heritage Vol. XVIII, No. 5, August, 1967, Pages 28-33, 92-100.

Larrabee, Harold A., *The Trumpeter of Doomsday,* New York, NY, American Heritage Vol. XV, No. 3, April, 1964, Pages, 34-37, 95-100.

Nevins, Allan, *The Needless Conflict,* New York, NY, American Heritage, Vol. VII, No. 5, August, 1956, Pages 4-9, 88-90.

Regan, Geoffrey, *Snafu: Great American Military Disasters*, New York, Avon Books, NY, 1993, Pages 105-121, The Battle of Gettysburg

Ridpath, John Clark, LL.D., *Cyclopedia of Universal History: Being an Account of the Principal events in the career of the Human Race from the beginnings of Civilization to the Present Time. From Recent and Authentic Sources. Vol. II, Part II*, Cincinnati, OH, The Jones Brothers Publishing Co, 1885

Robinson, Nugent, *History of the World with all its Great Sensations together with Mighty and Decisive Battles and the Rise and Fall of its Nations from the Earliest Times to the Present Day, Vol. II*, New York, NY, P.F.Collier, 1891.

Sears, Stephen W., *The Terrible Price of Freedom, Battles and Leaders*, New York, NY, American Heritage supplement, 1994, Pages 18-30.

Stone, Irving, *They Also Ran*, New York, NY, Pyramid Publications Inc., 1964, Pages 180-197, George B. McClellan.

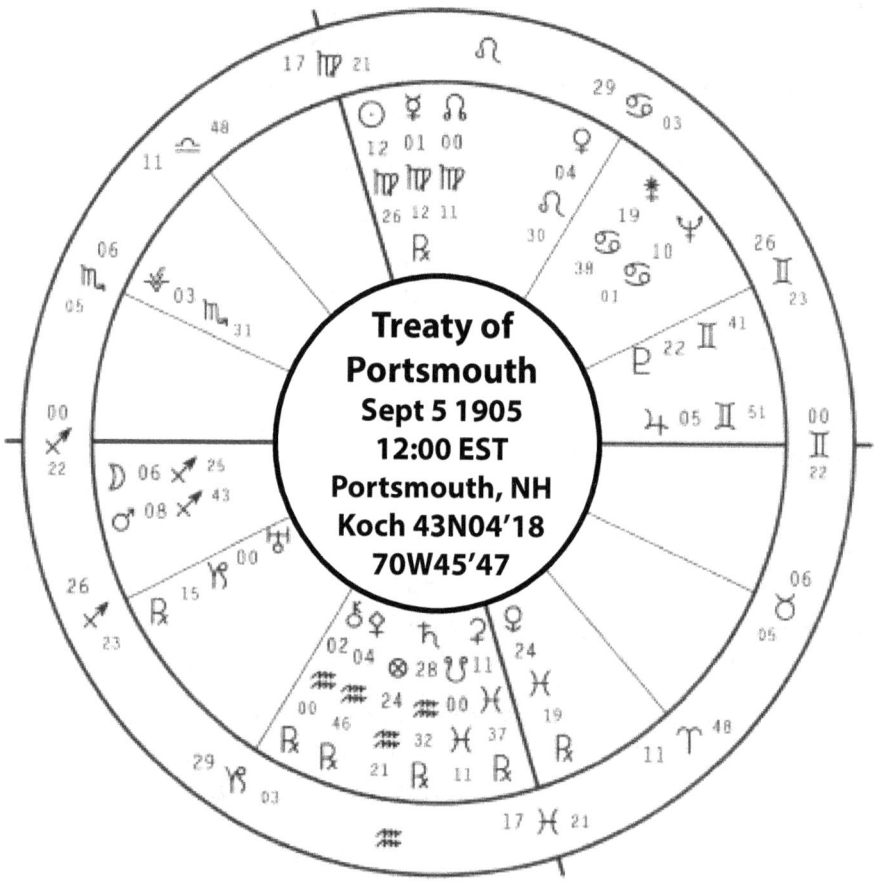

Treaty of
Portsmouth
Sept 5 1905
12:00 EST
Portsmouth, NH
Koch 43N04'18
70W45'47

Chapter 19

World War 1/4?
Eris square Pluto

Could the First World War have taken place a decade earlier? In 1904, Eris and Pluto were square each other, and the square lasted for ten years, with the two dwarf planets separating in August, 1914, just as World War One was breaking out in Europe.

Yet, for the preceding decade, there were incidents which could have started the war, but they fizzled out before an explosion took place. With the challenging aspect between Eris and Pluto, it might be said that Pluto represented transformation without the warmongering.

The first major blow-up could have happened in 1904, when Russia and Japan were involved in a localized war in the Pacific. The Russo-Japanese war began when the two empires ran into conflicts over control of Manchuria. Russia needed Port Arthur as an ice-free port to bring more foreign goods into the empire. Japan saw Manchuria as an area to be exploited and developed. After a surprise attack on the Russian fleet, the Japanese dominated the fighting in Manchuria. Russia suffered a major disaster by sending the Baltic Fleet to the Pacific, only to have it destroyed by the Japanese fleet. Afterwards, Russia and Japan listened to Theodore Roosevelt's offer of mediation, and the war ended with the Treaty of Portsmouth in 1905.

Yet, there were circumstances which could have expanded the war, leading to a world wide fight. Great Britain had signed a naval treaty with Japan, promising to aid the Japanese if they were attacked by more than one European power. During the Russo-Japanese war, the British provided naval intelligence to the Japanese. The Japanese were receiving loans from Britain, and the United States as well. A loan of 200 million dollars was made by the New York banker Jacob Schiff, partly as revenge against Russia for the way they persecuted the Jews.

On the other side, Russia was receiving loans from France, and some material support from Germany. The British saw German-Russian cooperation as an attempt to upset the balance of power in Europe, and German naval power was considered to be such a threat that the British began to modernize and expand their fleet. In reality, Kaiser Wilhelm II tried to convince his cousin, Czar Nicholas II, to start negotiations. The Czar was not willing to do so until after the Baltic fleet was destroyed at the battle of Tsushima. If the Russian military had been more competent and less over-confident, the war might have lasted longer, with the possibility of another European power joining in and dragging others into the conflict as well.

The Treaty of Portsmouth remains as one of Theodore Roosevelt's greatest accomplishments, which made him the first U.S. President to win the Nobel Peace Prize. For Japan it was an unsatisfying end to the war, since Japan did not gain territory or reparations from Russia. For the Russians, the end of the war shook national confidence, leading to a revolution marked by strikes, mutinies, and anarchist attacks, with the public making demands for reforms. An attempt was made to set up a Duma (parliament), but the same old corrupt courtiers remained in power, leading Czarist Russia to collapse a decade later.

Part of Russia's problem may have been the vacillating nature of its leader, Czar Nicholas II. He was born with Eris trine his Venus and Uranus. He was the sort who wanted to please everyone, but ended up pleasing no one. Many political decisions ended up being made by his wife, under the influence of Grigori Rasputin. In the end, Nicholas came under the sway of reactionary forces, which brought him and the nation into the violent path of the First World War.

In 1881, when transiting Eris was sextile his Pluto and semi-sextile his Moon, Nicholas lost his grandfather, Czar Alexander II, when anarchists threw bombs at the royal coach. Nicholas witnessed the death of his grandfather when the wounded Czar was brought to the palace. The new czar, Alexander III, kept his entire family in seclusion to prevent further assassination attempts. The royal family moved to Gatchina Palace outside of St. Petersburg, and only entered the city when they needed to be present at ceremonial events.

Nicholas had Eris semi-sextile his Neptune in 1884, when he went through a coming of age ceremony, which affirmed his role as heir to the throne. The same year he met Alexandra (Alix) of Hesse-Darmstadt, and he fell in love with her at once. For years, he wrote to her, expressing his love. She responded with statements of love, but declined marriage because she was a Lutheran and she would not convert to the Russian Orthodox Church. The romance might have ended had it not been for the

Czar Nicholas II
May 19, 1868
0:15 LMT
St. Petersburg,
Russia
Koch 59N55
30E15

Czar Nicholas II

intervention of Kaiser Wilhelm II, who told Alix that it was her duty to convert and be a good wife to Nicholas. Their engagement took place when the transiting Eris was trine Vesta in the chart of Nicholas. At that point, events were getting out of hand to prevent Nicholas from having a happy home life.

In 1894, Czar Alexander III died from an illness, and 26-year-old Nicholas became the new czar. He did manage to have his wedding during the period of mourning, by planning it for the same day as the birthday celebration of his mother.

Sadly, the new czar's coronation was tragic, when about 100,000 people

193.

attended the event, and more than 1,300 were trampled to death while getting the free food and drink on Khodynka Field. Nicholas wanted time to mourn the deaths, but protocol required him to attend a party given by the French ambassador. Such an action made him appear cold and callous to his subjects.

As the 20th century began, Czar Nicholas II had Eris trine his Juno. He followed an imperialistic political path. To unite the people behind him, a series of anti-Jewish pogroms (riots) took place. For diplomatic reasons, Nicholas and the Orthodox Church denounced the violence. Still, the Russian government continued with anti-Jewish propaganda, including the infamous "Protocols of the Elders of Zion," which became the anti-Semitic source book for the 20th century.

The imperialist policies brought Russia on a collision course with Japan, resulting in the Russo-Japanese war. The failure of the war caused riots, which ended with bloodshed. The popularity of Nicholas declined as the nation became stuck in the First World War, and conditions brought about his abdication and the rise of revolutionary governments in Russia. The royal family was imprisoned, and in 1918, with Eris semi-sextile his Mars and Ceres, sextile his Sun, and approaching a conjunction to his Chiron, Nicholas and his family were gunned down and buried in the forest of Yekaterinburg. It was not until 1979, when transiting Eris was square his Venus, that the bodies of Nicholas and other royal family members were located and exhumed. During the 1980's, when Eris was conjunct the Moon and Neptune of Nicholas, there was a debate over whether the royal family should be considered saints. This was officially declared by the Russian Orthodox Church in the year 2000.

In the early 20th Century, part of the danger of Russian policies was the number of treaties made for military intervention with other countries. Russia was diplomatically tied to Serbia and France, with extensions bringing Great Britain and Italy into any crisis. On the other side, Germany was tied to Austria and Turkey, with a tentative tie to Italy. No one stopped to question whether this arrangement of treaties could lead to a general war. The instability of the diplomatic situation was not helped by the quirky, autocratic behavior of Kaiser Wilhelm II of Germany.

In the natal chart for the Kaiser, Eris and Pluto are sextile, with Sun also in a semi-sextile with Eris, Ceres and Vesta. Eris was quincunx Saturn, and Pluto was square Saturn. The nativity of Wilhelm was an unfortunate event, with his left arm being dislocated during the birth. Improper care caused the arm to wither, so Wilhelm had to wear bulky uniforms to hide his deformity. He also developed an over-bearing ego, and a sa-

Kaiser
Wilhelm II
Jan 27 1859
3:00 LMT
Potsdam, GER
Koch 52N24
13E04

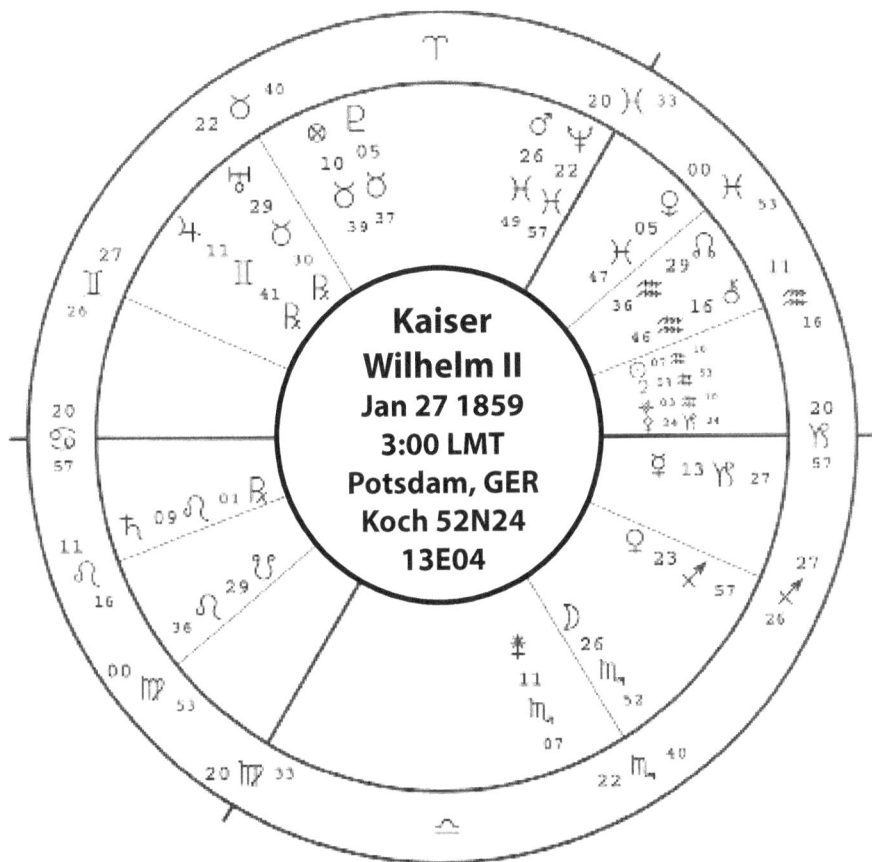

distic sense of humor, even making his generals perform comical dance routines. One general died during a dance performance while wearing a ballerina's tutu!

When Wilhelm came to power at the time of his first Saturn return, one of his first goals was to remove Otto von Bismarck as Chancellor. Known as the "Iron Chancellor," Bismarck had dominated the government during the reign of Kaiser Wilhelm I, bringing about a war with France and the unification of Germany under the Prussian crown. The new Kaiser did not like Bismarck's attacks on the Catholic

Church and on the Socialists. Bismarck was forced to resign in 1890. A year before Bismarck's death, when Eris was entering Wilhelm's Tenth House, the Kaiser had a final meeting with Bismarck. At the time, Bismarck made a curious prophecy pointing out that it was 20 years after the death of Frederick the Great that Napoleon wrecked the power of Prussia at the battle of Jena. Bismarck expected that Wilhelm's empire would last only 20 years after Bismarck's death. The prediction came true, just as Wilhelm was experiencing his second Saturn return in 1918.

During the early years of the 20th century, when Eris was conjunct his Neptune, Kaiser Wilhelm began an expansion program for building up the German fleet. The plan was to have a navy that would rival the British navy, which would allow Germany to put pressure on Great Britain during diplomatic squabbles. Later, when Eris was square his Venus, the Kaiser tried to be diplomatic, but his blunt manner of speaking caused more problems. When sending troops to China to fight against the Boxer Rebellion, Kaiser Wilhelm urged them to fight like Attila and his Huns, offering no mercy to the enemy. The enemies of Germany would later seize upon that phrase and refer to the Germans as "the Huns."

The Kaiser also stirred up a crisis in 1905, when he learned that France and Spain had made a secret treaty to take control of Morocco. When he was traveling towards Morocco in his Imperial yacht, the Kaiser made a ham-handed attempt at intervention, promising German support for Morocco. He was forced to back down when it was revealed that Great Britain was supporting France and Spain. Austria was not willing to support the Kaiser in this effort, and the Germans backed away from involvement with Morocco, at least for a few years.

When Eris was sextile his Pallas, the Kaiser made an upsetting remark during an interview for a British newspaper by saying he had supported Great Britain during the Boer War, whereas his subjects had supported the Boers in South Africa. This statement aroused public sentiment against Wilhelm in Germany, with some calling for his abdication. Wilhelm also declared that his naval build-up was not meant to be a threat to Great Britain, but for war with Japan.

Wilhelm's military build-up increased as Eris passed over his Mars. By 1914, when Eris was trine his Moon, Germany was fully armed and ready for war, which came because of a lack of diplomacy. The result was a disaster for Germany and Kaiser Wilhelm. After four years of horrific fighting, when Eris was sextile his Uranus, Wilhelm was forced to abdicate and go into exile in the Netherlands. He lived long enough to see Germany invade the Netherlands in 1940, and he died in 1941, when Eris was sextile his Vesta and Ceres. (To Hitler's fury, the S.S. guards who watched over Wilhelm served as an honor guard and used to call him "Your Majesty.") Would Wilhelm's fate (and that of Nicholas) have been dramatically different if major European war had broken out before 1914?

Another near miss of the First World War took place from 1906 to 1909, over a local conflict called "The Pig War." In the Balkan kingdom of Serbia, the economy had been dominated by the neighboring Austrian empire. In particular, the Austrians had the corner on the Serbian pork market, with shipments of pork going directly to Austria, and the Serbs receiving little in return. To break this control, the Serbians built two new meat-packing plants, and began negotiations to export pork to France and Bulgaria. Austria responded by starting an economic blockade against Serbia, not allowing any goods to cross the border. However, the Serbs had been buying French munitions, and were in a position where they could militarily stand up to Austria. To further complicate matters, Russia backed Serbia's stand against Austria, and it seemed that Austria would have to go to war over pigs.

The Austrian Emperor Franz Joseph contacted the German Kaiser and asked for his support in the matter. Kaiser Wilhelm II was not eager to go to war over pigs, but he did send a diplomatic letter to Russia, demanding that they back away from supporting Serbia. Also, the Serbs were buying munitions from Germany, and the Germans did not want to lose a good market. Austria finally had to back down, and the Serbian pig market became more profitable.

Another threat of war came in 1908 with what was called "the Bosnian Crisis." Since 1878, Austrians had occupied the provinces of Bosnia and Herzogovina, that had been taken from the Ottoman Empire. For years, the Austrians had to deal with Turkish, Bosnian, and Serbian nationalists. It was finally decided that the best way to handle the problem was to officially make Bosnia-Herzogovina part of the Austrian Empire. The announcement coincided with the declaration of independence of Bulgaria from Turkish control. Both news items were seen as major blows against Turkey, which was undergoing a revolution and not able to respond with their military.

Yet, the Austrians nearly came to blows with Russia. The Russian foreign minister was willing to accept the Austrian annexation in exchange for Austrian support against Turkey for Russia to gain control of the Straits of Bosphorus. However, the Austrian foreign minister announced the annexation before negotiations could be made, and the Russian foreign minister took that as an affront. There was saber-rattling between the two empires, until Germany entered the discussion and demanded the Russians accept the annexation. The Russians agreed to back down, and the Austrians appeared to have their way in the matter. However, what they did not realize was that they had aroused Serbian nationalists, who would make a violent statement on June 28, 1914.

Germany stirred up more trouble in 1911 with what became the Second Morocco Crisis, and was a little more serious than the one the Kaiser had caused earlier. The French had received a request from the Sultan of Morocco to send troops to Fez to rescue the Sultan from a tribal rebellion. Germany took this time to send the cruiser "Panther" to Morocco, ostensibly to guard German interests. Spain and France accused each other of working with the Germans to seize all of Morocco. However, the discord died down when the Kaiser realized he could not get allies to help seize Morocco, and there were demonstrations by socialist organizations opposed to the war. The cruiser "Panther" was ordered back to Germany. France and Spain were able to carry on negotiations for dividing Morocco.

In 1911, another flashpoint took place with a war between Italy and Turkey. The Italians were seeking to control Libya, which was part of the Ottoman Empire. The Italians wanted a cheap and easy victory, but the war proved a little more costly than expected. Italy did save money on prisoner of war camps by massacring any Turks who tried to surrender. This war also marked the first time that aerial bombs were dropped from airships and an airplane, which proved effective, although the Turks used rifles to shoot down the Italian airplane. The war also featured trench warfare, which foreshadowed what was to come with World War One.

The Italians ended up taking Libya and there was further desire for African colonies. The Italians had signed treaties with major powers of Europe. When the First World War began, Italy found itself committed to both sides. The balance for Allied powers was turned when they promised African colonies to Italy after the war. But, as it turned out they did not follow through on the promise. As for Turkey, the beating they received from Italy inspired others to take on the remains of the Ottoman Empire.

In 1912, another threat took place with the First Balkan War, when Serbia, Bulgaria, Montenegro, and Greece formed the Balkan League, and, with the blessing of Russia, began an attack against Turkey. The Ottoman Empire was known as "the sick man of Europe," and the goal of the Balkan League was to remove more European territory from Turkish control.

The major powers tried to stay clear of involvement in the struggle. Great Britain had strong diplomatic ties to Turkey, but also had royal ties to the King of Greece. Britain remained neutral, but secretly encouraged the Balkan League. France was ill-prepared and not eager to be involved in the war, so they sent a diplomatic note to Russia saying that they would not back up any Russian involvement in the Balkans.

Once again, Austria proved to be a trouble-maker, wanting to go to war to support Turkey and to humble Serbia. However, the Austrians would not act without a commitment from Germany. The Kaiser was willing to support Austria, but the German General Staff warned the Kaiser that it would be about two years before the military was ready for a major war. The Kaiser backed away from Austria, and the Austrians dropped their plans for entering the war. In 1913, a peace treaty was signed in London, and with the territory gained from Turkey, the new kingdom of Albania was created.

No sooner was the Treaty of London signed than a new flashpoint erupted. Bulgaria accused Serbia of violating terms of a secret treaty made before the war. The Bulgarians were not happy with the division of territory taken from the Ottoman Empire. The result was that in June, 1913, the Bulgarians turned on their former allies and declared war on Serbia, Montenegro and Greece. If the Bulgarians were hoping for a quick and easy victory, they were disappointed when their forces were stopped by the Greeks and Serbs at the end of July.

In July, 1913, Romania and Turkey entered the war to gain territory from Bulgaria. The Bulgarians realized they were trapped in a multi-sided war, and they began peace negotiations. At first, they wanted Russia to mediate, but the Russians did not want to get involved in the Balkan dust-up. The Bulgarian government collapsed and was replaced by one with anti-Russian sympathies.

The Romanian army had gotten all the way to Sofia, the Bulgarian capital, and then was willing to make an armistice so negotiations could go forward. The negotiations were moved to the Romanian capital of Bucharest, and the Romanians would not allow the Turks to attend. Bulgaria had to negotiate with Turkey on a separate basis.

During negotiations, Austria and Russia supported Bulgaria, while Germany and France supported Serbia and Greece. The Bulgarians were forced to make significant territorial concessions. Greece received a 68%

increase in territory, and Montenegro received a 62% increase. Serbia nearly doubled its territory, while Romania only received a 5% increase. Serbia came out of the war as the strongest military power in the Balkans.

Turkey regained a small amount of territory from Bulgaria. The Bulgarians were so sick of their former Balkan allies, they entered into a secret treaty with Turkey. The result was that when the First World War broke out, Bulgaria joined Turkey in fighting for Germany and Austria, even though Russia had been one of the few supporters of Bulgaria. It was a set-up of strange bedfellows, made possible by Bulgarian greed and the dreams of glory in starting another regional war.

During this decade from the Russo-Japanese war until World War One, the powers of Europe were involved with major military build-ups. It was expected that all of these machine guns and battleships would be put to use, but the question was when and how. From the Pig War to the Second Balkan War, power politics could have set the major nations at each other. It was not until an Austrian archduke was shot at Sarajevo that the major conflict began.

There were attempts at diplomacy during July, 1914, but by August, when Pluto moved from Gemini into Cancer, war fever swept all across Europe, and there was no way that the conflict could be stopped. All of the militarism, the bombast, and speeches of glory from the past decade now erupted into a bloody reality, which would turn out to be just the overture to an even more destructive war that came with the next Eris-Pluto aspect.

Perhaps the war could have been avoided if people had recalled one of Bismarck's predictions—"One day the great European War will come out of some damned foolish thing in the Balkans."

Chapter 19 - Bibliography
Internet Sources

Russo-Japanese War
https://en.wikipedia.org/wiki/Russo-Japanese_War

Treaty of Portsmouth
https://en.wikipedia.org/wiki/Treaty_of_Portsmouth

Czar Nicholas II
https://en.wikipedia.org/wiki/Nicholas_II_of_Russia

Kaiser Wilhelm II
https://en.wikipedia.org/wiki/Wilhelm_II,_German_Emperor

Otto von Bismarck
https://en.wikipedia.org/wiki/Otto_von_Bismarck

The Pig War
https://en.wikipedia.org/wiki/Pig_War_(1906%E2%80%9308)

Italo-Turkish War
https://en.wikipedia.org/wiki/Italo-Turkish_War

First Balkan War
https://en.wikipedia.org/wiki/First_Balkan_War

Second Balkan War
https://en.wikipedia.org/wiki/Second_Balkan_War

Origins of World War 1
https://en.wikipedia.org/wiki/Causes_of_World_War_I

Print sources

Joll, James, *The Origins of the First World War*,
     The Silver Library-Longmans, Edinburgh, UK, 1992.

World War II
September 1, 1939
5:00 CET
Berlin, Germany
Koch 42N30
13E22

Chapter 20

The Big One: WW2
Eris trine Pluto

Although there were a variety of events leading up to World War II, and military actions by various nations, most of the war guilt has been focused on Adolf Hitler. Militarism and anti-Semitism were not invented by Hitler, but he used those systems and carried them to a genocidal extreme. The result was that Hitler has gone down in history as an insane and violent figure. For issues such as tyranny, racism, and mass murder, the name of Hitler will always be raised.

In the birth chart of Hitler, Eris is sextile his Mars, Venus, and Vesta. The conjunction of Mars and Venus indicates a passionate figure, and he did have a way of charming ladies. One of the reasons he did not marry Eva Braun until the end of his life was because he feared taking a wife would end his control over the female population. Yet, he carried this passion too far, creating a hypnotic effect with his speeches which roused the masses.

Eris sextile Vesta could indicate difficulties in living conditions. In his early adult years, Hitler was homeless, living in flophouses in Vienna. During the World War One years, he lived in trenches with the troops, and during the early party years he lived at the homes of party members. It was not until the Nazi party became successful that Hitler built his estate at Berchtesgaden, but constant work kept him traveling.

Eris quincunx his Uranus was an influential aspect, because Hitler was able to make use of the electronic media. After the conjunction of Uranus and Eris in 1927, major advancements were made with radio networks, talking movies, and experiments with television. Hitler was able to use these to his advantage, especially the talking newsreels, which presented his speeches around the world. Eris was also trine his North Node, raising issues about his values and what ideals he was fighting for.

Hitler became acquainted with strange racial theories that depicted the Germans as part of a pure Aryan race, and declared that Slavic or Semitic people were "untermenschen" or lesser beings from an impure race.

Hitler explored these theories in the early years of the 20th Century when transiting Eris was opposing his Juno and semi-sextile his Mercury. He was struggling in Vienna in order to get admitted to an art school, but his works were not appreciated. He blamed his failure on the "Jews" who ran the academy. He seemed to have little focus in life until the outbreak of World War One. Having moved to Munich, he joined the German Army, and proved to be an exemplary soldier, even winning the coveted Iron Cross. At this time, transiting Pluto had moved into Cancer, and was conjunct Hitler's Pallas and Part of Fortune. Hitler admitted later that the war years were the best years of his life.

Hitler's wartime pleasure came to an end in the autumn of 1918, when he was blinded in a gas attack. At that time, Eris was trine natal Ceres, and Hitler seemed to have lost everything once the war came to an end. He faced an uncertain future, not sure if he would be able to continue in the army. Yet, when transiting Pluto was conjunct his Chiron, he went through a major life change. He was hired to be an informant for the army, and assigned to investigate small political groups that were springing up. One of his assignments was to check out a new organization called the German Workers Party.

When Hitler attended a public meeting of the party, he found the proceedings to be dull. Most of the speeches were about proposals for improving life in Munich and Bavaria. Just as Hitler was getting ready to leave, one loudmouth character got up and suggested that Bavaria should secede from Germany and join Austria. Having developed a nationalistic pride in Germany (despite being born in Austria), Hitler got up and shouted down the loudmouth, citing historic and cultural ties that Bavaria had with Germany. Everyone at the meeting was impressed with Hitler's speaking talents. They gave him a pamphlet on their political goals, and asked him to join the party.

Hitler was not impressed with the pamphlet, but he did think the political group could be of service to the army, so he joined the party, and started to influence its positions. Before long, he was chosen as leader of the party, and set a new course when he insisted upon nationalism and anti-Semitism. His speeches attracted new members, even wealthy members of society. Following the example of Mussolini, Hitler tried to overthrow the local government in November, 1923. The "putsch" failed, and Hitler was thrown in prison. Because the judges sympathized with

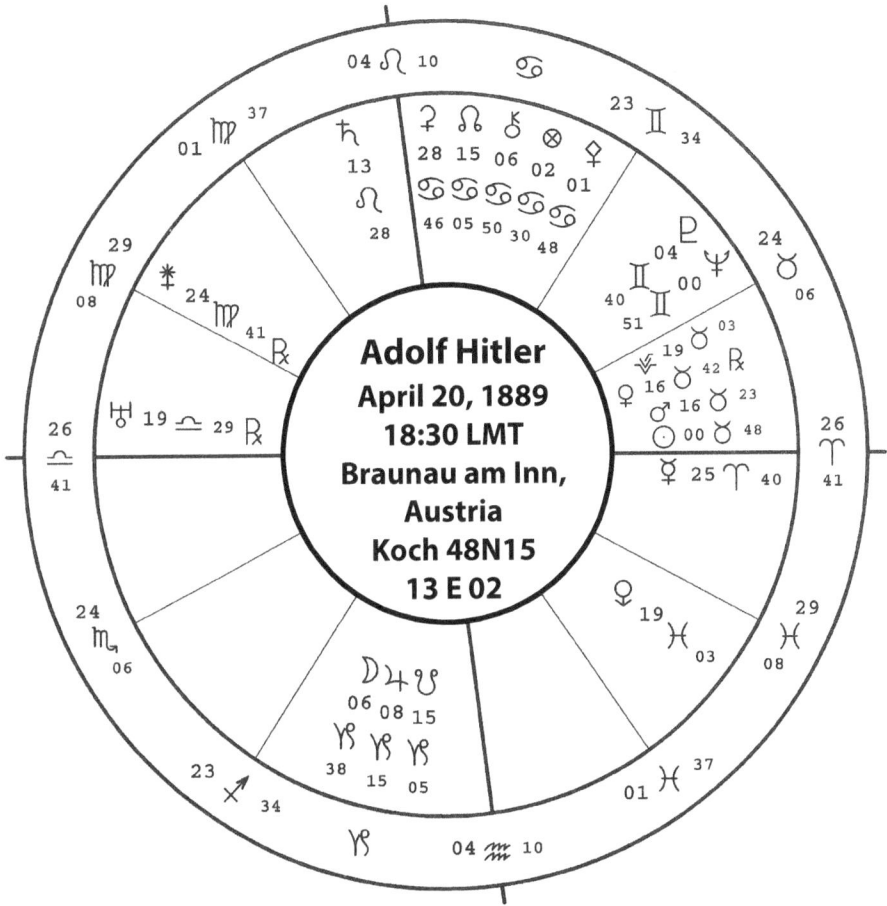

Adolf Hitler
April 20, 1889
18:30 LMT
Braunau am Inn,
Austria
Koch 48N15
13 E 02

his views, he was only imprisoned for a few months, during which time he wrote his autobiography, *Mein Kampf*.

It was after the Eris-Uranus conjunction in 1927 that Hitler's career really took off. Eris-Uranus were semi-sextile his Sun, sextile his Neptune, and square his Pallas. By the late 1920's, more and more people started to know who Hitler was, though many regarded him as a comical, posturing figure. His plans became more visionary, and in 1928 he wrote a sequel to *Mein Kampf* (not published in his lifetime) in which he described plans for an eventual war against the United States.

Although Hitler and the Nazis were a minority party in the 1920's, Hitler rose to greater fame by making a political alliance with a conservative group run by millionaire Alfred Hugenberg, who helped finance Nazi programs. By 1933, when Eris was square Hitler's Part-of-Fortune, he was made Chancellor of Germany, and he was on his way to setting himself up as complete leader or "fuhrer."

In the autumn of 1937, Pluto made a brief entry into Leo, forming a trine with Eris in Aries. On November 5, 1937, Hitler conducted a meeting with his military and diplomatic advisers. The minutes of the meeting were preserved in the "Hossback Memorandum," which Hitler considered to be his political testament. At the meeting, Hitler declared that he was willing to go to war to provide "Lebensraum" (living space) for Germany. The intention was expressed to add Austria and Czechoslovakia to the Third Reich. The expansion was to begin in 1938, but Hitler was willing to wait as late as 1943 to go to war.

The members of the General Staff stated that they could not build up the armed forces in such a short period of time. In 1938, they were removed from power and replaced by officers who were more agreeable to Hitler's will. Circumstances were taking place that hastened Hitler's plans. Austrian Nazis had started a terror campaign to destabilize the Austrian government. In March, 1938, Hitler sent troops into Austria, with the pretext of stabilizing the nation so that there would not be a major civil war like the one in Spain.

During this time, Pluto had gone retrograde into Cancer again. There was very little opposition to the "Anschluss" or "annexation" of Austria, and it was seen as a local matter between two German states. In August, 1938, Pluto entered Leo again, and once again Hitler began to act on his plans for conquest. Charges were made that the Czechoslovakian government was persecuting Germans living in the Sudetenland. Hitler threatened a war against Czechoslovakia, but that nation had made treaties with France and Great Britain. Through the peace negotiations of British Prime Minister Neville Chamberlain, the Germans agreed not to attack Czechoslovakia, and the Czech government was forced to turn the Sudetenland over to Germany.

In early 1939, Pluto had gone retrograde into Cancer again, and there was a sense that "Peace with Honor" had prevented another World War. There was some dismay when Hitler sent in troops to occupy the remainder of Czechoslovakia in March, 1939. Although it violated the Munich agreement, Britain and France did not declare war on Germany, although Chamberlain publicly questioned whether Hitler was really a "Gentleman."

Pluto returned to Leo in June, 1939, as Hitler set his sights on a new target. The city of Danzig (now Gdansk) in Poland was supposed to be a free city, but Hitler made claims that the Germans in Danzig were being persecuted by the Poles. Atrocity stories were spread of Germans living in Poland who were being forced out to the border. Finally, a

Adolf Hitler

German radio station near the border was attacked by Polish troops, who were then gunned down by German troops. Later, it was revealed that the "Polish troops" were really German concentration camp prisoners who had been dressed up in Polish uniforms. This false flag operation gave Hitler the excuse he needed to invade Poland on September 1, 1939. At that time, transiting Eris was sextile Hitler's natal Pluto, and also trine his Midheaven. He had started down a path that would become fatal, both to himself and to Germany.

Great Britain and France acted by declaring war on Germany, but they did not respond to help Poland. That country was conquered in less than a month. Russians occupied the Eastern part of Poland, according to the agreement of the Non-Aggression Pact that Russia and Germany had signed in August. Britain's first "attack" against Germany was to drop leaflets urging the Germans to overthrow Hitler. France placed its army behind the Maginot Line, a series of fortresses, and waited for a German attack.

In November, 1939, Pluto went retrograde again, but this time remained in Leo. All remained quiet on the Western front, during a period known as "The Phony War." When Pluto went direct in April, 1940, the Phony War came to an end with the Germans invading Denmark and Norway. In May, attacks began against the Netherlands, Belgium, and France. The Germans were able to flank the Maginot Line by sending an army of lumberjacks into the Ardennes forest, chopping down trees to create roads so that the tank divisions could get through.

By the autumn of 1940, only Great Britain remained as the sole opponent of Germany. The world waited to see if Germany would invade England. Luftwaffe attacks against London and other cities were on the increase, leading to stiff determination during "the Battle of Britain." By November, 1940, Pluto went retrograde again, and there was no invasion force. It was not expected that a naval attack would occur during the winter months, but the air attacks continued. By April, 1941, when Pluto went direct again, the RAF had scored significant victories over the Luftwaffe, and the number of air raids decreased. The resistance to the German air force convinced other nations that Great Britain was not to be defeated.

In June, 1941, Hitler made his greatest gamble by turning his forces to the East and invading Russia. The Soviet government was caught by complete surprise, and millions of soldiers were killed or captured in a matter of weeks. It was thought that the "blitzkrieg" or "lightning war" would cause Russia to collapse, as had happened with Poland, Norway, France, and other countries. However, Pluto went retrograde again in November, 1941, and one thing the Germans had not counted on was the brutality of the Russian winter. During the Pluto retrograde from November, 1941 to April, 1942, German advances towards Leningrad, Moscow, and Stalingrad were delayed by the cold weather, which even froze the oil in the tank engines.

It was during the Pluto retrograde that Germany's ally, Japan, made a surprise attack against the U.S. naval fleet at Pearl Harbor. Following their old tactic, the Japanese were to cut off diplomatic relations just a few hours before the attack, but a failure in communication prevented the diplomatic message from getting through until after Pearl Harbor had been bombed. Germany had signed a treaty, offering to intervene if Japan had been attacked. The Germans were under no obligation to declare war on the United States since Japan had done the attacking. Hitler went ahead and declared war, anyway, thereby sealing his doom with the industrial might of the USA directed against him.

Once Pluto went direct in April, 1942, Germany began making further advances into Russia. More resources were poured into gaining control of the Caucasus region and the oil fields. It was because of this zeal that Hitler made a strategic blunder. An armored panzer division had been sent to support the Sixth Army under General Friedrich Paulus for the attack on Stalingrad. Hitler ordered the panzer division to the Caucasus front. If the panzer division had accompanied the Sixth Army, Stalingrad would have been taken in a short time. As it was, the Soviet army was able to surround Stalingrad and trap the Sixth Army. The panzer division sent to the Caucasus turned out to be a nuisance, blocking the crowded roads.

By November, 1942, when Pluto went retrograde again, the Soviet army launched Operation Uranus, which cut off the German Sixth Army and slowly began to destroy it inside of Stalingrad. Germans were being massacred in the rubble of the city. Hitler ordered General Paulus not to surrender, and even promoted him to the rank of Field Marshal on the grounds that no Field Marshal in history had ever surrendered. Paulus was not concerned with historical niceties, and at the end of January, 1943, he surrendered the Sixth Army to the Russians. (It was also at this time that the U.S. military took Guadalcanal, thereby changing the course of the war in the Pacific.)

For Germany, the loss of Stalingrad was the beginning of the end. By the time Pluto went direct in April, 1943, the German forces were in retreat. In July, 1943, they regrouped for a major offensive near Kursk, which the Russians were able to stop, and then turn around for their own offensive. At the same time, the British and American troops had performed an invasion of Sicily, and then Italy, which brought about the collapse of Mussolini's regime. By that time, Pluto was no longer applying to a trine with Eris, and was starting to separate from Eris.

Pluto, retrograde from November, 1943, to April, 1944, marked more losses for Germany and Japan. In June, 1944, the Eris-Pluto trine was within one degree as the D-Day invasion began. Eris and Pluto started separating as British and American troops marched through France, and Russian troops went through Poland. There was one major attempt to stop the invasion at the Battle of the Bulge, but by that time Pluto was retrograde again, and the German attack failed. Through the winter, the Germans fought for a stalemate, but by the time Pluto went direct in April, 1945 (on Hitler's birthday), the end had come.

Adolf Hitler committed suicide in his Berlin bunker on April 30. His suicide took place as Eris was trine his Chiron and square his Moon, with an extreme situation probably comforted by his marriage to Eva Braun and the knowledge that one person would die with him.

The victors of World War II went on to be designated as "the greatest generation." However, not all of the winners were angelic, nor regarded with unquestioning hero worship. One controversial figure who would emerge from the war was British Field Marshal Bernard Montgomery. He was affectionately known as "Monty" by his troops and the general public, but his fellow officers and British politicians could not stand him. In his later years, a series of unpopular political positions left him shunned as an embarrassing character.

Part of Monty's unpopularity may have been due to Saturn on his Ascendant. He did have a reputation for strict discipline, even in his personal life. He was notorious for not smoking nor drinking, which may have cut down on his social life. There was speculation that his abstinence was caused by injuries from the First World War. He did give out cigarettes to his soldiers as gifts, but he also embarrassed society hostesses by insisting upon a glass of water rather than table wine. Natal Eris was semi-sextile his natal Juno, and trine his natal Jupiter. Monty often alienated social contacts and world leaders with his crass remarks and inconsiderate attitudes. He was too willing to speak his mind when a diplomatic silence would have served him better.

Monty was born with Eris opposing his Mars, and he was skilled in the art of warfare and battlefield planning. One of his nicknames was "The Spartan Warrior." He also had a good understanding of the psychology of war, and how to motivate his men to fight. Monty was the sort of general who would visit his men on the eve of battle, giving them the impression that he was on the front lines of the fight just as they were. His most famous command was at the second battle of El Alamein, where

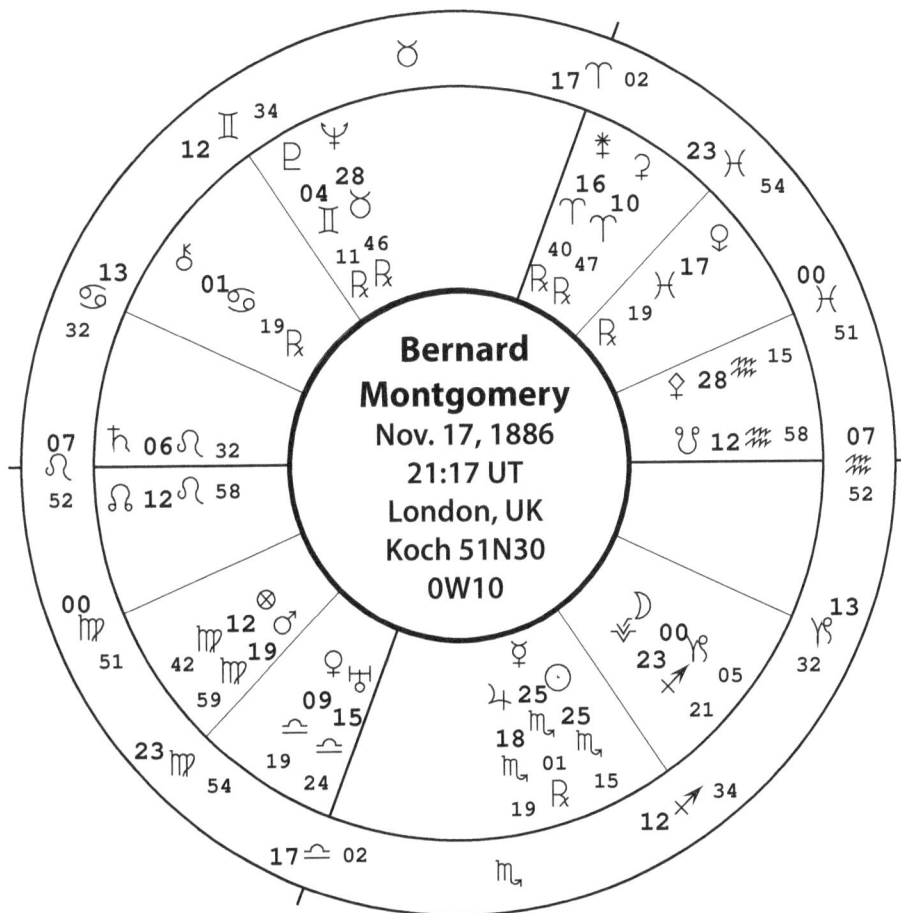

Bernard Montgomery
Nov. 17, 1886
21:17 UT
London, UK
Koch 51N30
0W10

Bernard Montgomery

he scrapped plans for a possible retreat, declaring that the British Army would die on the spot rather than run away.

Monty's martial spirit may have been sparked by an abusive upbringing. In the 1890's, when the transits of Eris made more exact aspects to his natal Mars and Jupiter, his family was living in Tasmania. His father was the local bishop, whose duties kept him traveling for months. Monty grew up in the care of his emotionally distant mother. The only contact she had with him was to punish him brutally for his wild behavior. As a result of this treatment, Monty became a bully to the other children. In his later years, he expressed regret for his behavior. He never forgave his mother for her treatment, and he would not allow his son to visit her. When his mother died in 1949, he did not attend the funeral.

The Montgomery family returned to England in the late 1890's, and in the early 1900's (when Eris and Pluto were square) it was decided that Bernard Montgomery would seek out a military career. He entered the Royal Military College, Sandhurst, but was nearly expelled because of his fighting with other students. In 1908, when transiting Eris was trine his Mercury and Sun, he graduated and was sent to India to start his military career. With the coming of World War I, his career started on the fast track. First he had to survive the war to get his career going. In 1914, he was shot through a lung, and later shot in the knee. While he was recovering, he became a brigade major, and was made a general staff officer.

When Eris was sextile his Neptune and semi-sextile his Pallas, he was a lieutenant colonel, and busy working for the general staff. In the 1920's, he served in Ireland during the years of rebellion, and eventually agreed with the government that freedom for Ireland was the best solution.

Although personally distant, Monty had some emotional healing in 1927, when he married a widow, Elizabeth Carver. Eris was then square his Moon. A year later, when Eris was square his Chiron, he celebrated the birth of his son, David.

Monty became a full colonel in 1934, and was given assignments in Palestine and India. He returned to England in 1937, when transiting Eris was sextile his natal Pluto. Unfortunately, his wife died that year from an infected insect bite. Monty requested more military assignments to escape from grieving. In 1939, when transiting Pluto was sextile his natal Neptune, he helped subdue an Arab revolt in Palestine. Monty was forced to return to England because of illness, but he regretted leaving Palestine because he enjoyed the war.

With the start of World War II, Monty was one of the commanders of the British Expeditionary Force in France. During the 1940 blitzkrieg, his division protected the left flank of the British army, enabling them to reach Dunkirk for the famous evacuation. Monty's division only had minimal casualties, and was the strongest division in Britain after Dunkirk. He was rewarded with the Order of the Bath, and given assignments for developing war plans for possible invasions of the Azores, the Cape Verde Islands, and even neutral Ireland. None of these plans were used, but Monty was given command of troops in southeastern England in preparation for fighting off a possible invasion. He demanded that his troops be physically fit, and he was noted for dismissing numerous officers who did not match up to his standards.

In 1942, when transiting Eris was approaching a trine to his Saturn, and transiting Pluto was conjunct his Saturn and Ascendant, Monty's name was put forward during a change of command in North Africa, and he was given command of the Eighth Army at El Alamein. He became a dynamic figure at the front, visiting his men in every area and personally examining the military situation. It was at this time that Monty stopped wearing his British officer's cap, and started wearing a black beret that became his trademark. His presence encouraged the men, and raised morale for the prospects of victory. Monty spent months in preparation for an offensive, even though the British government wanted swift action. Monty's meticulous methods were shown to be effective in October, 1942, when the British swept away the Germans and Italians at the second battle of El Alamein

Monty was promoted to full General in 1943. His forces soon joined up with the American forces in kicking out Rommel's army from Africa. In planning the invasion of Sicily, Monty offended the American commanders by his fussy planning, and his relegating Americans to a supporting role. General George Patton got even with Monty by pushing an attack to capture Palermo, thereby gaining all the glory. In the autumn of 1943, Monty began leading British troops onto the Italian mainland, but he was not happy with the lack of coordination. He gladly left Italy for a greater assignment in England.

In 1944, Monty worked with General Dwight Eisenhower in preparation for Operation Overlord, the D-Day invasion. There was friction between Eisenhower and Monty since Eisenhower was Supreme Commander, and Monty resented his command. After D-Day, there was a "sack Monty campaign", which was even supported by leading British officers. Monty had a private meeting with Churchill and Eisenhower in which he convinced them that he should not be sacked.

Part of Monty's resentment was that he was not allowed to give commands to American troops. Churchill promoted him to Field Marshal to assuage his feelings. Ironically, during the Battle of the Bulge, two American armies were placed under Monty's command until the situation on the front was stabilized, and the bulge in the Allied lines was reduced. Monty's contribution to the battle was to assess the German attacks, and to prepare a concentrated plan of counter-attack, removing the chaos caused by localized counter-attacks. In 1945, Monty's army entered Germany and began attacks that seized Hamburg, Rostock, and the entrance to the Danish peninsula. The German commanders for northeastern Germany surrendered to Monty on May 4, 1945.

After the war, when transiting Pluto was sextile his Uranus, Monty was made a Viscount, and was a member of the Allied Control Council. However, by the 1950's, with transiting Pluto square his Jupiter, and Eris trine his Saturn and Ascendant, Monty's egotistical lack of tact made him very unpopular in leading circles. He sent a secret report to the Atlee government, which showed how Britain could exploit the natural resources of Africa to make up for the loss of colonies in Asia. Monty had a racist contempt for Africans, dismissing them as "complete savages."

In 1958, when transiting Pluto was square his natal Pluto, Monty published his memoirs, which further showed his talent for tactless thought. Monty criticized Eisenhower (who was by then President of the United States), saying that the decisions by Eisenhower had prolonged the war for a year. (Monty had been made an honorary citizen of Montgomery, Alabama, but after the attack on Eisenhower the honor was rescinded.) He also criticized Field Marshal Auchinleck, saying that Auchinleck was ready to retreat from El Alamein. Auchinleck threatened a lawsuit against Monty, until Monty gave a radio interview praising Auchinleck and dismissing the view that Auchinleck would have retreated.

In the 1960's, when transiting Eris was opposing his Venus and conjunct his Ceres, Monty continued to upset the public with his tactless views. After a visit to South Africa, he publicly supported apartheid, when most politicians were beginning to deplore it. He praised the leadership of Chairman Mao, just before the Chinese Cultural Revolution began. In a meeting with Israeli General Moshe Dayan, there was a discussion about the Vietnam War, and Monty was appalled by the fact that all of the military activity was localized and there was no clear-cut objective. Monty told Dayan to tell the Americans they were "insane." His last major controversy, when transiting Pluto was conjunct his Mars, was when the British government decided to legalize homosexuality in 1967. Monty opposed legalization and declared that sort of behavior was for the French, not for the British. After that, he lived an isolated existence until his death in 1976, when transiting Pluto was opposing his Ceres.

As for Japan, from 1943 on their empire was rolled back, one island at a time. American troops regained the Philippines, and launched an attack on Iwo Jima. The bloodiest battle was the taking of Okinawa, which was to be a major base for the invasion of the Japanese mainland. The defenders of Okinawa fought with such fury, it was expected the invasion of Japan would be even more deadly. The U.S. Military considered different options, including the use of poison gas against Japan. Suddenly, all planning was forgotten with the dropping of the atomic bomb.

It was a weapon that no nation could defend against. The Japanese were facing the possibility of complete annihilation. By the middle of August, 1945, when Eris and Pluto were separating from their trine, the Japanese command realized the war could not continue. Emperor Hirohito made a radio broadcast to the nation, announcing the end of hostilities. The final documents were signed on September 2, 1945, six years after the war had begun in Europe.

By default, the United States had emerged as the leading power in the world, mainly because it was the only major nation that did not have its infrastructure destroyed during the war. With the Marshall Plan, the United States was able to help European nations rebuild after the war. Even Japan underwent a reconstruction. The Soviet Union remained suspicious of American intentions, and a Cold War developed for more than 40 years. This Cold War mindset would have a negative effect on the post-World War II generation, with an embarrassing conflict starting with the next Eris-Pluto aspect.

JAPANESE SURRENDER; WORLD WAR II ENDS

Pearl Harbor Is Avenged!

AMERICAN POWER OVERWHELMS FOE

Brother Pluto, Sister Eris

Bibliography - Chapter 20
Internet Sources

World War II
https://en.wikipedia.org/wiki/World_War_II

Causes of World War II
https://en.wikipedia.org/wiki/Causes_of_World_War_II

Adolf Hitler
https://en.wikipedia.org/wiki/Adolf_Hitler

Mein Kampf sequel
http://www.historynet.com/mein-kampf-the-sequel.htm

World War II database
http://ww2db.com/event/timeline/

Timeline of World War II
http://ww2db.com/event/timeline/

Field Marshal Bernard Montgomery
https://en.wikipedia.org/wiki/Bernard_Montgomery

Book Sources

Allen, Thomas & Polmar, Norman, MHQ: *The Quarterly Journal of Military History, Autumn, 1997*, New York, NY, Pages 38-43, Gassing Japan.

Gorman, Edward, *The End on Okinawa*, New York, NY, *American Heritage, Vol. 46, No. 3*, May/June, 1995, Pages 34-38.

Large, David Clay, MHQ: *The Quarterly Journal of Military History, Autumn, 1997*, New York, NY, Pages 56-67, Present at the Creation.

Lukacs, John, *The Transatlantic Duel, Battles and Leaders*, New York, NY, *American Heritage Supplement, 1994*, Pages 38-42.

Maddox, Robert James, *The Biggest Decision: Why we had to drop the Atomic Bomb*, New York, NY, *American Heritage, Vol. 46, No. 3*, May/June, 1995, Pages 69-77.

Schramm, Percy Ernest, *Hitler: The Man and the Military Leader*, Chicago, IL, Quadrangle Books, 1971.

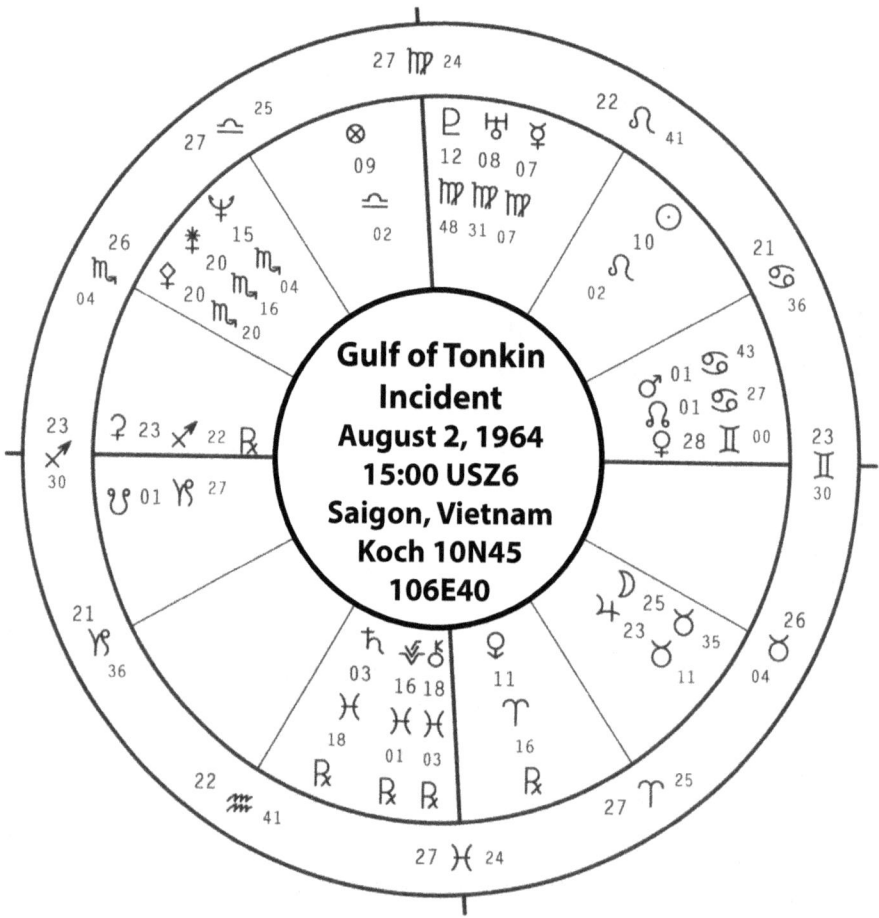

Gulf of Tonkin
Incident
August 2, 1964
15:00 USZ6
Saigon, Vietnam
Koch 10N45
106E40

Chapter 21

Honkin' on the Tonkin
Eris quincunx Pluto
(and Neptune and Uranus)

From October, 1943 to October, 1947, Eris was in opposition to Neptune. World War II entered its bloodiest struggles as the Third Reich and Japanese Empire were in their death throes. The public faced a stark realism about ending the war, and were admonished not to have "fancies in the firelight." Yet, the Neptune role was to be a visionary one, with ideas being brought forward to make the post-war world a better place. Perhaps the most idealistic bit of legislation passed at this time was the G.I. Bill, which provided help for returning veterans.

On the dark side were thoughts regarding "our valiant Russian ally." Joseph Stalin's post-war plans were not too clear, and there was a resurgence of the anti-Communist attitude that the Russians were out to "rule the world." George Orwell tried to warn the world about Stalin in his political fable "*Animal Farm*," but the story did not interest the public until after the war. Arguments about Russian intentions were postponed until after Germany and Japan were defeated.

Adding to the role of Eris in the post-war years was a trine from Saturn in Leo. The trine began in the summer of 1946, as political parties were running conservative candidates for Congress. In Massachusetts, Joseph Kennedy pushed his son, John F. Kennedy, to run for congress. In California, Richard Nixon answered a want-ad looking for political candidates. Because he was a veteran, his local party bosses chose him to be the Congressional candidate. Nixon defeated New Deal Democrat, Jerry Voorhees, with the help of late night phone calls from mysterious callers who declared that Jerry Voorhees was a "Communist."

The stage was being set for a different kind of war, the Cold War, which was fueled by conservative fears and public delusions. When the Russians occupied most of Eastern Europe, and did not seem to be in a hurry to leave the territory, Winston Churchill declared that an "Iron Curtain" had fallen over most of Europe. The House Un-American Activities Committee began an investigation into "Communist infiltration" of Hollywood. They were welcomed by studio heads and created a stir by indicting the "Hollywood Ten", who were noted directors and screen writers accused of "Communist sympathies." The result of the investigations was the creation of a blacklist which would remove from Hollywood anyone who had the slightest connections to "Communists." Even the classic film *"It's a Wonderful Life"* became labeled as "Communist propaganda" by the FBI because mean Mr. Potter was considered a Communist caricature of an evil capitalist.

The Cold War continued through the 1950's, with fears and delusions on both sides of the Iron Curtain. Was Alger Hiss really a spy? Did doctors conspire to kill Stalin? Were the Rosenbergs really secret agents? Did the CIA infiltrate European Communist parties? Delusions soared in 1957, when the Russians launched Sputnik, and there was a fear that America would have to sleep under a "Communist Moon." By the autumn of 1960, when Eris was quincunx Pluto, Presidential candidate John F. Kennedy, was able to exploit the fear by declaring there was a "missile gap", suggesting that the Eisenhower administration had not kept up with nuclear arms against the Soviets. This issue helped Kennedy to get elected, after which it was revealed there was no missile gap.

Eris quincunx Pluto remained in aspect throughout Kennedy's administration. One of his accomplishments was to overcome the anti-communist ideology with a "real politic" attitude based on common understanding. Kennedy was suckered by the anti-communist ideology at the beginning of his term, when the CIA prepared an invasion of Cuba by anti-Castro exiles. The Bay of Pigs invasion turned out to be a fiasco, which some tried to blame on Kennedy because he would not allow U.S military aircraft to be used to cover the invasion. Kennedy took the responsibility for the failure, even though the planning had been done under the previous administration.

Oddly enough, in the autumn of 1961, Neptune was also quincunx Eris. On September 29, 1961, Neptune and Pluto formed their closest sextile, while both were quincunx Eris, forming a Yod aspect. On that day, President Kennedy was given a secret 26-page letter from Nikita

Khrushchev. In June, Kennedy and Khrushchev had met at a summit in Vienna to discuss major issues such as the Berlin crisis, a nuclear test ban treaty, Laos, and Cuba. Kennedy had gotten into an ideological argument with Khrushchev, who publicly humiliated the young president. In his secret letter, Khrushchev apologized to Kennedy for his behavior and expressed a willingness to keep negotiating on the Berlin Crisis. Kennedy responded by a secret letter on October 16, when Neptune and Pluto were still forming a Yod to Eris.

The Eris Yod continued into 1962, when sensible solutions were made to difficult problems. The Russians were trying to prevent East Germans from fleeing into the free city of West Berlin, creating a "brain drain" in the East German economy. The only solution they could come up with was the notorious Berlin Wall, which would have a 28 year history as a symbol of repression. Yet, for the Russians, it was a solution to a serious problem. Regarding Laos, it was agreed to allow a neutral government to take over the country. The nuclear test ban treaty was the most successful outcome, with the United States and Russia reaching an accord to prevent more nuclear explosions in the atmosphere.

Cuba remained a continuing problem, with a constant worry that the United States would attempt another invasion. After the failure of the Bay of Pigs, the Joint Chiefs of Staff submitted a plan for a war with Cuba, which included a number of false flag scenarios. Cuban refugees were to dress up in Cuban uniforms and stage an "attack" on Guantanamo Bay. Mortars were to be fired, and an ammunition dump and some planes were to be destroyed. Another scenario involved disguising an American fighter plane as a Cuban MIG, and using it to shoot down an American airliner. The Kennedy administration turned down these proposals, but the military insisted that an invasion of Cuba was the best alternative.

As a deterrent, Khrushchev sent nuclear missiles to Cuba, though maintaining that Russians and not Cubans would control them. This was regarded as a military threat against the United States, since the missiles would be able to destroy cities on the East Coast. The Pentagon urged an immediate invasion of Cuba, but President Kennedy wanted a diplomatic solution. Attorney General Robert Kennedy was sent to the Soviet embassy to have private discussions with the ambassador. Finally, a secret deal was made in which the Russians would remove the missiles from Cuba, and the United States would later remove Atlas missiles from Turkey. The world breathed a lot easier having missed the possibility of nuclear war.

A major area where difficulties were not resolved was Vietnam. The United States had supported a military government in South Vietnam to offset the Communist government in North Vietnam. This began a civil war between Communists in the North versus anti-Communists in the South, with a large population of Buddhists caught in the middle. Ho Chi Minh was the leader of the nationalists which had kicked out the French colonial rulers, and he was attempting to maintain a separate nation in spite of attacks from South Vietnam.

Ho Chin Minh (born Nyguen Sinh Cung) was a somewhat cosmopolitan figure. With natal Eris square Venus in the Second House, he had good prospects, starting out as a Confucian scholar studying the Chinese language. Yet, with Eris trine his Chiron in the Third House, he decided to expand his horizons as a scholar by leaving Vietnam and traveling to France, the United States, Great Britain, and finally the Soviet Union. He worked as a cook's helper, and performed other menial jobs. When transiting Eris was trine his Ceres, sextile his Sun and Moon, and quincunx his Saturn, he became involved in the Vietnamese independence movement, as well as socialist teachings.

In 1940, when Eris was sextile his Neptune, he adopted the name "Ho Chi Minh", which means "he who has been enlightened." He became leader of the Viet Minh Independence Force, a guerrilla force with about 10,000 members. They worked against the Japanese occupation of Indochina during World War II, and actually received support from the OSS, the forerunner to the CIA. At the end of World War II, Ho Chi Minh was an American ally, having helped in the defeat of the Japanese. However, the French were allowed to take control of Vietnam again, and American support for Vietnamese independence came to an end.

In 1946, Ho Chi Minh had transiting Eris sextile his Pluto, trine his Juno and Vesta, and quincunx his Pallas. He began a whirlwind of activities involving international deals, political purges, and strange alliances. According to some accounts, he cooperated with the French in killing off non-Communist nationalists so that the Viet Minh would be the only nationalist party fighting for independence. He tried negotiating independence with the French, but the negotiations failed and he ended up returning to guerrilla warfare. He was hesitant to ask for Chinese aid out of fear that the Chinese might annex Vietnam, but eventually he got an agreement that the Chinese would not send troops into Vietnam. In his strangest encounter, he met David Ben-Gurion, the future prime minister of Israel, and they developed such a rapport that Ho Chi Minh offered

Ho Chi Minh
May 19, 1890
5:00 LMT
Hoang Tru, Vietnam
Koch 18N41
105E34

David Ben-Gurion the chance to form a Jewish Homeland in Vietnam. Ben-Gurion turned it down because of the expectation that Israel would be formed in Palestine.

By the mid-1950's, when Eris was trine natal Mars and sextile the Midheaven in Ho Chi Minh's chart, he had defeated the French at Dien Bien Phu, signed the Geneva Accords which created two Vietnams, and rejected the idea of a national election to have one government. Militant changes began taking place in North Vietnam, with land reform and the persecution of old landlords. Those who did not accept the party line were isolated or executed. An attempt was made to infiltrate Laos, which supposedly ended when a neutral government was installed.

Ho Chi Minh

Yet, there was a secret pathway through Laos for smuggling weapons to insurgents in South Vietnam, which was nicknamed "The Ho Chi Minh Trail." There were rumors that he was secretly corresponding with South Vietnamese President Diem in the hope of a peaceful settlement.

On November 2, 1963, a group of Vietnamese generals assassinated President Diem, with the support of the CIA, and the new government was recognized by the American ambassador to South Vietnam. The Kennedy administration was shocked and embarrassed by this violent change in government. Unfortunately, Kennedy did not have much time to react to it, since his own assassination took place 20 days later. In Ho Chi Minh's chart, Eris was sextile his Jupiter, and he gained more attention from the world as violence in Vietnam escalated. However, after 1965, when Eris was sextile his Mercury, Ho Chi Minh was suffering from health problems, and he remained as a figurehead leader until his death in 1969.

The new USA president, Lyndon Johnson, inherited the problems that Kennedy faced in Vietnam. To complicate matters, Johnson was facing an election, and his Republican opponent, Barry Goldwater, was proposing a massive bombing campaign to subdue North Vietnam. Goldwater said that to bring victory in Vietnam the United States should use every weapon in its arsenal, including nuclear weapons. The Republicans championed Goldwater's stand with the slogan, "In your heart, you know he's right." The Democrats responded with the slogan, "In your guts, you know he's nuts." The Democratic strategy depicted Goldwater as a warmongering extremist who might get the country involved in a nuclear war.

Barry Goldwater was born with Eris squaring his Node axis and trine his Mars. He became noted for his strong values and his outspoken promotion of those values. The son of a department store owner, he took over the family business at age 21. As transiting Eris was passing over his Saturn, he supported the politics of Herbert Hoover at a time when the New Deal was growing in importance. Goldwater had a distinguished career in the Air Force during World War II, flying 165 different types of aircraft, and retiring as a Major General in the Air Force Reserve.

In the 1950's, when Eris was sextile his Juno, Goldwater was building up the Republican Party in Arizona, which had been a heavily Democratic state. His first public office was on the Phoenix city council, and he served as part of a bipartisan team to clean up gambling, prostitution, and other corruption in the city. In 1952, he was elected to the U.S.

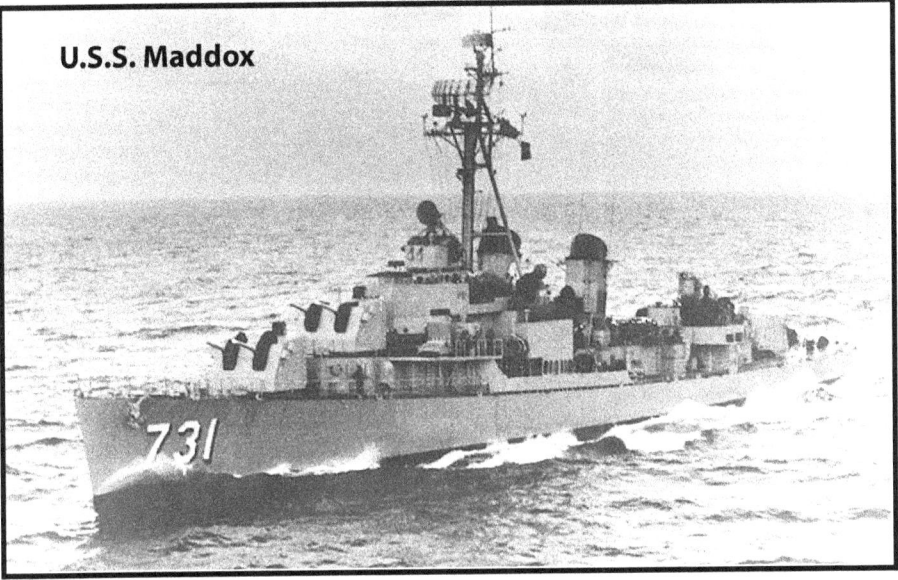

U.S.S. Maddox

Senate from Arizona during a national wave of support for Republicans. By the late 1950's, when Eris was trine his Pallas, people were calling him the "Grand Old Man of the Republican Party," although there were some who considered that his policies were too regressive.

In 1964, when Eris was square his Sun, Goldwater was a national figure and going after the Republican Presidential nomination. He managed to overcome more moderate candidates in the primaries, such as Nelson Rockefeller and Henry Cabot Lodge Jr. One platform of the campaign was States Rights, a controversial issue during this year when the Civil Rights Act was promoted and then passed. Goldwater's opposition to the Civil Rights Act was one of his greatest mistakes. In the election, he only carried five Southern states and his home state of Arizona.

Although Goldwater lost the election, his positions made him an inadvertent "grey eminence" behind the Vietnam policy. The Democrats had promoted "peace" but there was a fear of being attacked by Republicans as "soft on Communism." The Johnson administration began expanding America's role in Vietnam. Bombing missions on North Vietnam, which Goldwater had advocated, became part of the Johnson policy, though they did not use Goldwater's plan for tactical nuclear weapons.

With Eris quincunx his Vesta, Goldwater was out of office until 1968, when he was returned to the Senate, and he served three more terms. In 1974, when Eris was trine his Venus, he gained national attention by telling Richard Nixon he had to resign as President, because only a handful of Republican Senators would vote against Nixon's removal

Barry Goldwater
January 2, 1909
3:00 MST
Phoenix, Arizona
Koch 33N26'24
112W04'24

16 ♌ 52

14 ♍ 54

09 ♋ 18

♃ 14 ♍ 31 ℞

15 ♋ 50 ℞

25 ♊ 24 ♇
♊ 55 31 ℞

13 ♎ 19

09 ♊ 15

11 ♏ 23

☽ 21 ♉ 45

11 ♉ 23

⚴ 12 ♏ 20

♂ 24 ♏ 52

09 ♐ 15

☿ 09 ♐ 03

♀ 13 ♐ 20

☊ 25 ♐

08 ♐ 16 55

♄ ♀ 04 ♈
⊗ 24
21 ♓ 33 00
♓ 44

13 ♈ 19

☉ ♅ 11 ♑ 16
☿ 16 ♑ 52
⚷ 08 ♑ 33

☿ 20 ♒ 28

14 ♓ 54

09 ♑ 24 40

09 ♑ 18

16 ♒ 52

---

from office. That incident became en-shrined in politics as a "Goldwater mo-ment", when a President learns he can not even depend upon the support of his own party.

In the early 1980's, when Eris was quincunx his Jupiter and square his Nep-tune, Goldwater gained further praise when he told off Rev. Jerry Falwell and the members of the Moral Majority who were opposing the Supreme Court nom-ination of Sandra Day O'Connor. Fal-well had said that every good Christian should be concerned about O'Connor's opinions on abortion. Goldwater's re-

Senator Goldwater

sponse was that "Every good Christian ought to kick Falwell right in the ass." His salty rhetoric continued after his retirement from politics. In 1994, when Eris was square his Uranus and Mercury, he was warning against extremists in the Republican Party who were pushing a religious agenda. In his final years, he became a supporter for Gay Rights when his grandson came out as Gay. Yet, his legacy remained as a conservative who wanted to get tough on Communism by promoting a libertarian freedom from government control.

In August, 1964, Lyndon Johnson was presented with his opportunity to get tough on Communism, when an incident took place in the Gulf of Tonkin off the coast of North Vietnam. On August 2, the destroyer, U.S.S. Maddox, was on an intelligence mission, monitoring broadcasts from North Vietnam. At 3 pm, the Maddox reported it was under attack by North Vietnamese patrol boats. The Maddox gave its position as being 28 nautical miles from Vietnam, in international waters. Later reports would put the destroyer at 8 nautical miles, within the 12 nautical miles limit claimed by North Vietnam.

Daniel Ellsberg was the Pentagon official who received the report that North Vietnamese patrol boats were firing torpedoes and machine guns at the Maddox. Years later, in the Pentagon Papers, Ellsberg revealed that the Maddox had fired the first shots as warnings to the patrol boats. This contradicted the statements released by the Johnson administration that the North Vietnamese had fired first. The North Vietnamese also told some whopper tales, claiming that one of their torpedoes had hit the Maddox.

In the chart of the August 2 attack, Neptune is moving away from a Yod formation with Eris, leaving Pluto and Uranus quincunx Eris. In the past, Eris quincunx Pluto has represented a lopsided victory. In this case, North Vietnamese patrol boats only hit the Maddox with some machine gun bullets, and managed to escape without damage. However, what was to come would eventually bring a major victory for North Vietnam, though it took another 11 years to accomplish it.

On August 4, the Maddox was running another intelligence gathering mission, accompanied by another destroyer, U.S.S. Turner Joy. Both ships detected the patrol boats by radar. The Turner Joy opened fire against the patrol boats, claiming to have sunk two boats. No wreckage or bodies were ever found. Later, there was a question as to whether what was seen on the radar was the approach of real patrol boats or just freak weather glitches on the radar. Secretary of Defense Robert McNamara never told the president about the uncertainty of the second attack.

When Lyndon Johnson learned about the report of a second attack, he ordered a retaliatory air strike against North Vietnam. On the evening of August 4, the President interrupted programming on national television to make the announcement that the North Vietnamese had attacked U.S. Navy vessels which were in international waters. On August 7, Congress passed the "Gulf of Tonkin Resolution" authorizing Lyndon Johnson to take whatever means necessary to fight Communists in Vietnam.

The result of the resolution was that Lyndon Johnson was no longer seen as being "soft on Communism," but it placed him on a path which would ruin his political career. In 1965, Johnson began escalating the number of troops sent to Vietnam, just as the Uranus-Pluto conjunction was making its final quincunx to Eris. Over the years the troop total would eventually reach 500, 000 personnel. Air strikes continued against North Vietnam as political pressure to force them to peace negotiations. Johnson did not have a diplomatic solution to the war, but just kept following what his military advisors advocated.

In the real world, things were a bit more complicated. The "freedom" Americans were fighting for in Vietnam was represented by a corrupt and incompetent government. Two of the Vietnamese generals, Thieu and Ky, had seized control of the government, and American efforts were directed into creating a false economy to keep them in power.

In the United States, young men were starting to question why they were being drafted into the military to fight a guerilla war 10,000 miles away. By 1967, when Eris was conjunct Saturn, a peace movement was starting to form, as thousands of young people across the nation rallied and chanted slogans against the war—

One, two, three, four
What the hell are we fighting for?
Hey, Hey, LBJ,
How many kids did you kill today?

By 1968, Lyndon Johnson realized he could not win the election against a strong peace candidate. At the end of March, 1968, Johnson announced he was suspending the bombing of North Vietnam, and that he would not be a candidate for re-election. However, there was some effort by pro-war Democrats to give the nomination to Johnson's vice-president, Hubert Humphrey, in the hopes he would continue the fighting.

Anti-war Democrats started a "Dump the Hump" movement, which culminated in a horrific riot at the Democratic convention in Chicago. Humphrey ended up winning the nomination, but narrowly losing the election to Richard Nixon.

Instead of bringing peace right away, the Nixon administration continued the escalation, and moved the warfare into Cambodia and Laos. It was not until after Nixon's controversial re-election in 1972 that the war was ended and American servicemen came home. In 1975, the North Vietnamese began an offensive, which finally overthrew the government of South Vietnam, and placed the entire nation under Communist rule. This time the United States stayed out of the war, letting the Vietnamese accomplish what they had wanted to do for 20 years.

The result of the Gulf of Tonkin resolution was a humiliating decade for the United States. Only 50,000 Americans died, as opposed to millions of Vietnamese, but all those deaths galvanized the anti-war movement by showing the futility of war. North Vietnam suffered major destruction to its infrastructure, and some areas were said to look like "the surface of the Moon" after so much bombing. Yet, after years of struggle, a small Communist nation managed to come out as the victor in an encounter with the world's leading military power. In the early 1960's, with the Neptune-Pluto Yod pointing to Eris, the United States had created its own chimerical enemy, and spent billions on a failed campaign.

Since that time, relations between the United States and Vietnam have improved to the point that the "Communist" state regularly does business with capitalist America. Old veterans have gone back to Vietnam to make peace with the past. More cooperation has been made through financial aid than through military threats.

Ironically, the concept may have been predicted by the comedian Pat Paulsen, who ran a satirical campaign for President in 1968. When told that the war was costing the United States $600,000 for every Viet Cong killed, Paulsen responded,

"I say we could probably buy them off cheaper than that."

Bibliography - Chapter 21
Internet Sources

The Cold War
https://en.wikipedia.org/wiki/Cold_War

It's a Wonderful Life
http://www.openculture.com/2014/12/ayn-rand-helped-the-fbi-identify-its-a-wonderful-life-as-communist-propaganda.html

Kennedy-Khrushchev letters
http://history.state.gov/historicaldocuments/frus1961-63v06/comp1

False Flag operations for the invasion of Cuba
http://www.miamiherald.com/opinion/op-ed/article2263338.html

Berlin Wall
https://en.wikipedia.org/wiki/Berlin_Wall

Cuban Missile Crisis
https://en.wikipedia.org/wiki/Cuban_Missile_Crisis

The Vietnam War
https://en.wikipedia.org/wiki/Vietnam_War

Gulf of Tonkin Incident
https://en.wikipedia.org/wiki/Gulf_of_Tonkin_incident

Position of Laos
https://en.wikipedia.org/wiki/Operation_Barrel_Roll

Ho Chi Minh
https://en.wikipedia.org/wiki/Ho_Chi_Minh

Barry Goldwater
https://en.wikipedia.org/wiki/Barry_Goldwater

Operation Rolling Thunder
https://en.wikipedia.org/wiki/Operation_Rolling_Thunder

Vietnam War Casualties
https://en.wikipedia.org/wiki/Vietnam_War_casualties

Pat Paulsen's political campaign
https://www.youtube.com/watch?v=ntOuehGE_D8

Book Sources

Brugioni, Dino A., *MHQ: The Quarterly Journal of Military History* Winter 1992, New York, NY, Pages 92-101, The Invasion of Cuba.

Harriman, W. Averell & Abel, Elie, *We can't do business with Stalin*, American Heritage, New York, NY, Vol. 28, No. 5, August, 1977, Pages 16-21.

King, Larry L, Machismo in the White House: *LBJ and Vietnam*, New York, NY, American Heritage Vol XXVII, No. 5, August, 1976, Pages 8-13, 98-101.

McNamara, Robert S. & VanDeMark, Brian, *In Retrospect: The Tragedy and Lessons of Vietnam*, New York, NY, Times Books, 1995.

Mee, Jr, Charles L. , *Who started the Cold War?: A Good Way to Pick a Fight*, New York, NY, American Heritage, Vol. 28, No. 5, August, 1977, Pages 8-15.

Thomas, Hugh, *The U.S. and Castro, 1959-1962*, New York, NY, American Heritage, Vol. 29, No. 6, October/November 1978, Pages 26-35.

Zepezauer, Mark, *The CIA's Greatest Hits*, Tucson, AZ, Odonian Press, 1994.

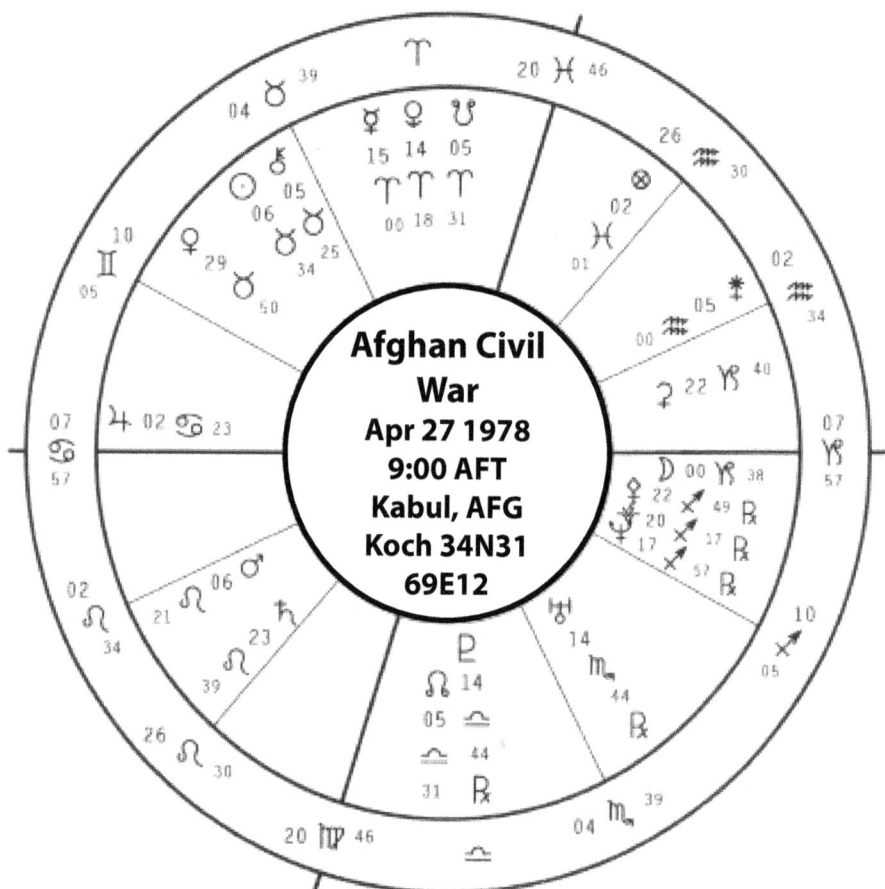

Afghan Civil War
Apr 27 1978
9:00 AFT
Kabul, AFG
Koch 34N31
69E12

Chapter 22

The Plan for Afghanistan?
Eris opposing Pluto

Afghanistan has developed a reputation as being "the graveyard of empires." In the 1980's, guerilla fighting against Soviet invaders created a military quagmire, which has been attributed to causing the break-up of the Soviet Union. In the 1990's, a power vacuum brought about the leadership of the Taliban (religious students) who imposed a repressive Islamic regime upon the country. After the 9-11 attacks, Afghanistan was invaded by the United States, which (at the time of this writing) maintains a military presence in the country.

Ironically, for part of the 20th century, Afghanistan was an area of stability and modernization. In 1933, King Zahir Khan came to the throne, and for the first years of his reign he relied on his politically experienced uncles to run the nation. It was after World War II that he realized Afghanistan needed to become a modern nation, and foreign advisors were brought in to help with the process. In this period, Afghanistan founded its first university. By 1964, during the Eris-Pluto quincunx, a democratic constitution was put into place, which allowed for free elections, women's rights, and universal suffrage.

One of the articles of the new constitution prevented members of the royal family from holding ministerial posts in the government. This excluded the king's first cousin, Mohammed Daoud Khan, who had served as Prime Minister during the previous decade. Although he was blocked from leadership, Mohammed Daoud Khan was busy developing his political base, particularly in working with the People's Democratic Party of Afghanistan, a pro-Marxist organization. His influence became so strong that in 1973, when the king was out of the country, Mohammed Daoud Khan organized a bloodless coup which overthrew the monarchy and established a republic, with himself as President.

With Eris conjunct Mars in his natal chart, Mohammed Daoud Khan was a force to be reckoned with. Eris and Mars were square Pluto, marking that time when nations were building up for World War One. Eris and Mars were trine his Sun, and Mohammed Daoud Khan was on the fast track to success as a member of the ruling family. He was educated in France, and showed great interest in political studies. While in his twenties he was made governor of the Eastern Province, and later governor of the Khandahar Province. When he was in his thirties, he became Lieutenant-General of the Kabul Army Corps. By the late 1940's, he had served as Defense Minister, Interior Minister, and Ambassador to France.

In 1953, when Eris was square his Mercury, Mohammed Daoud Khan was appointed Prime Minister by King Zahir Khan. Afghanistan continued its modernization, though the political leanings of Mohammed Daoud Khan were considered to be pro-Soviet. His term in office was marred by conflicts with Pakistan, because the Pashtun section of Afghanistan wanted to take more territory from Pakistan in order to bring in Pashtun tribesmen who had been displaced when the borders were drawn. Mohammed Daoud Khan supported the Pashtun tribes, but Afghan forces were defeated when they attacked Pakistan. The Pakistan border was closed, causing economic problems in Afghanistan, until Mohammed Daoud Khan was forced to resign as Prime Minister so that the conflict could be resolved.

By 1973 transiting Eris was quincunx his Jupiter and semi-sextile his Juno. His years of making political connections paid off when he announced the end of the monarchy and the establishment of a republic. From 1973 to 1978, Mohammed Daoud Khan, worked towards modernization in Afghanistan and better relations with the Soviet Union. He had to deal with Islamic uprisings, and contention with Pakistan over the Pashtun nationalism which threatened to create a "Pashtunistan state" inside of Afghanistan. By 1978, Mohammed Daoud Khan had decided to change foreign policy to become less dependent on the Soviet Union. A treaty was signed with Egypt to provide military training, and agreements were made with Saudi Arabia for financial aid.

This centrist policy was unacceptable for members of the People's Democratic Party of Afghanistan (PDPA). They wanted more Marxist control of the nation, and closer ties with the Soviet Union. On April 17, 1978, a prominent member of PDPA, Mir Akbar Khyber, was assassinated and factions in the organization then blamed Mohammed Daoud Khan for the killing. Street demonstrations were planned for protest during the

Mohammed
Daoud Khan
July 18, 1909
12:00 LMT
Kabul Afghanistan
Koch 34N31
69E12

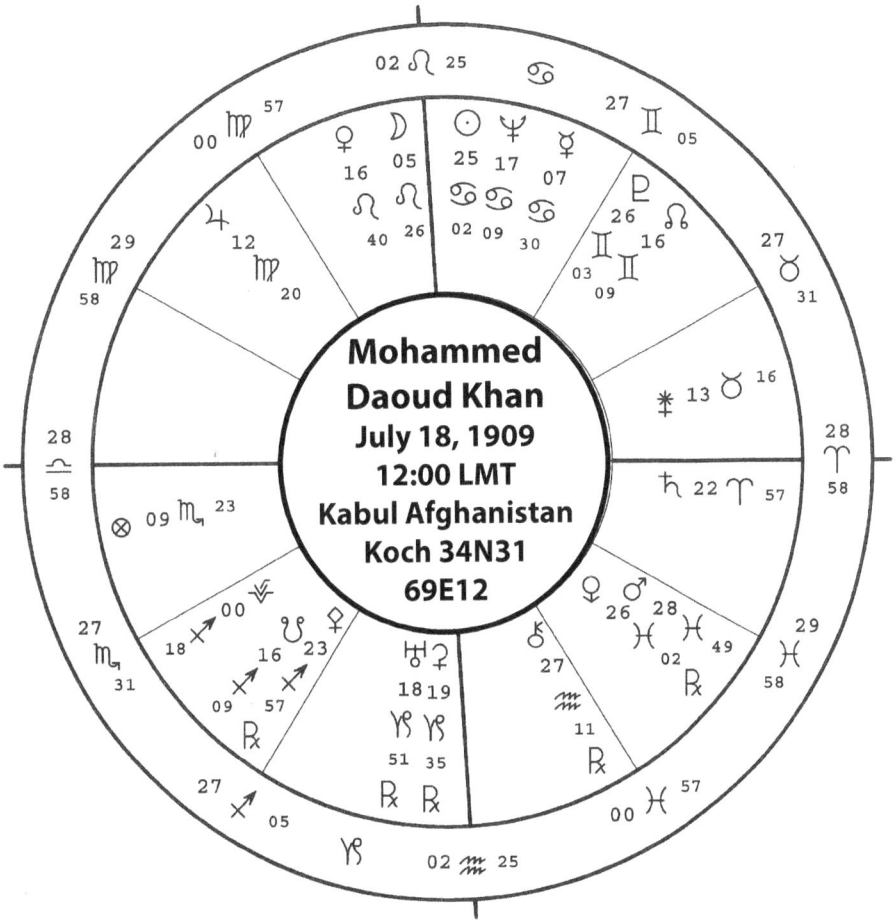

funeral. Leaders of the PDPA were put into jail, accused of stirring up the populace. This prompted the remaining members of the PDPA to attack before more were arrested.

On April 27, 1978, Eris and Pluto were in opposition, and this was when Afghanistan began its descent from a modern nation to a "banana republic." Eris was conjunct Mercury, trine Neptune and quincunx Uranus. Neptune trine Eris may have been an indicator of the religious fanaticism rising up at this time. In Iran, the government of the Shah was about to be toppled by Islamic fundamentalists. Also in America, a new religious political or-

Mohammed Daoud Khan

ganization, the Moral Majority, arose, that would end the career of Born-Again President Jimmy Carter.

It was said Mohammed Daoud Khan had hoped to destroy the PDPA by arresting its leaders during the funeral of Mir Akbar Khyber. Eris conjunct Mercury may have contributed to this master plan and Neptune trine Eris could have represented the fanatical will to defeat all opposition. Yet, with Uranus quincunx Eris, the President underestimated the number of PDPA members who had infiltrated the military. A cabinet meeting on April 27 was interrupted by a message that tanks were in the courtyard of the Presidential palace, and there was no chance for escape.

President Mohammed Daoud Khan and members of his family were gunned down by the military supporters of the PDPA. The announcement was made that the President had stepped down because of his health. The government was taken over by Nur Mohammed Taraki, a leader of the Khalq faction of the PDPA. In order to form a coalition, he brought in members of the Parchami faction of the PDPA. This party unity would only last a few months, as violent factions in the PDPA worked towards controlling all the power.

In the chart of Nur Mohammed Taraki, Eris is conjunct Chiron, and Taraki had a career as a reformer, though misguided. His path became clear when he was a teenager. Eris was trine his Saturn, and Taraki went to work as a clerk in Bombay, India. He met members of the Communist Party of India, who impressed him with talk of changes to be made. By 1937, when Eris was sextile his Jupiter, square his Pluto, and trine his Neptune, Taraki worked for the Afghan Minister of Economics, and he was introduced to Russian Communists. Soon, he was deputy head of the Bakhtrar News Agency, and he became famous for his books and poetry. His works on social and economic injustice were translated into Russian. The Russians called him the "Afghan Maxim Gorky."

In 1952, when Eris was conjunct his Vesta, Taraki was sent to work in the Afghan embassy in the United States. He was qualified for the position because of his language skills, but his job may have been a quiet attempt to get a radical out of Afghanistan. Yet, he kept writing against oppression in Afghanistan, and was dismissed from his embassy position.

When transiting Eris was sextile his Juno, Taraki actually worked as an interpreter for the United States Overseas Mission, but he soon quit that position to form his own translation service. In 1963, when transiting Eris was quincunx his Pallas and square his Node axis, he began working

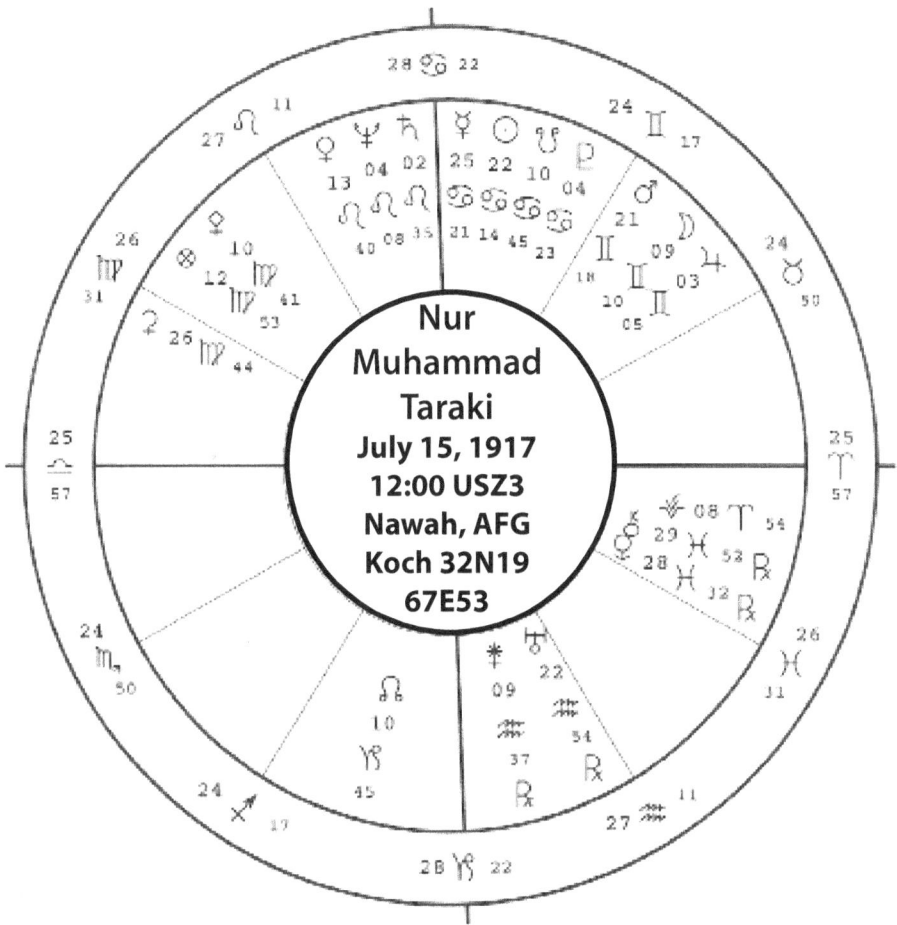

Nur Muhammad Taraki
July 15, 1917
12:00 USZ3
Nawah, AFG
Koch 32N19
67E53

for the new People's Democratic Party of Afghanistan (PDPA). In the 1970's, transiting Eris was trine his Venus, and he was a very popular political figure in Afghanistan, which resulted in his position as President once Mohammed Daoud Khan was out of the way.

The Taraki administration began as a progressive-Marxist regime with various reforms. Equality of the sexes was promoted, and forced marriages were prohibited. For the first time, women served in the Afghan government. Education was increased, with both sexes being allowed in schools. However, signs of repression

Taraki

became apparent when Taraki changed the flag of Afghanistan from green to red, making it closer to the flag of the Soviet Union.

A program of land reform was started, in which peasant farmers were given their own parcels of land, taken from the estates of wealthy landowners. No compensation was given to the previous owners. Peasant farmers who were burdened under crippling debt had their debts erased by the government. These policies to help the workers caused economic chaos in Afghanistan, since there was no way of telling who owed what in regard to land ownership and debt collection. Taraki tried to limit the policy when he found out how unpopular it was, but his efforts created a strong distrust of the central government, and prompted local leaders to prepare for a civil war. Taraki began arrests and executions of several thousand opponents of his regime.

While the rural leaders thought that Taraki was going too far, within the urban PDPA it was felt that he was not going far enough. The Parchamist faction of the PDPA began to assert more resistance against Taraki's Khalqi faction. Foreign Minister Hafizullah Amin, originally a supporter of Taraki, began to work against him and denounced the "cult of personality" that was growing up around Taraki.

Hafizullah Amin was born with Eris quincunx Neptune. He lost his father at an early age, but an older brother who was a teacher saw to his education. Amin was able to attend primary and secondary school while Eris was sextile his Ceres. Later, when Eris was square his Vesta, he attended Kabul University and graduated from a teacher's college. After serving as a vice-principal of the teacher's college, he went to the USA and attended Columbia University when Eris was trine his Sun and Mercury. At this time he took an interest in Marxism. He returned to Afghanistan for a few years more as a vice-principal, but then returned to Columbia University when Eris was conjunct his Uranus and sextile his Jupiter. This period marked a time when he became increasingly radical, to the point that he was neglecting his studies because of politics.

In the late 1960's, with Eris conjunct his Pallas and quincunx his Juno, Amin made more political contacts, both in the Soviet Union and Afghanistan. He became acquainted with Nur Muhammed Taraki, and he became a member of the PDPA central committee. He gained greater authority during the Daoud Khan administration, so by the time Daoud Khan was assassinated Amin had become one of the leading political figures. Eris was semi-sextile Amin's Chiron as the Daoud Khan regime ended. He may have felt that only he could rule Afghanistan well and heal its di-

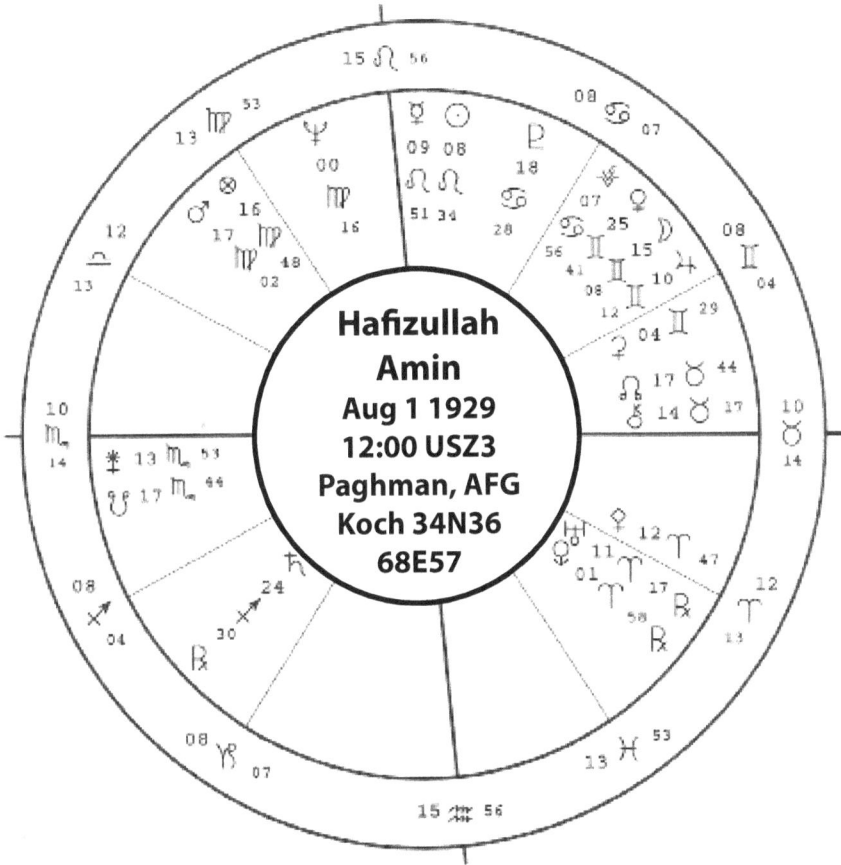

Hafizullah Amin
Aug 1 1929
12:00 USZ3
Paghman, AFG
Koch 34N36
68E57

Hafizullah Amin

visions. In September, 1979, when Taraki returned from a trip to Havana, Amin began pressuring him to resign. Taraki invited Amin to lunch at the Presidential palace on Sept. 14 to discuss the matter. When Amin and other Khalqi leaders arrived at the palace, they were fired upon by soldiers shooting from the windows. Amin survived, and summoned army leaders loyal to himself.

The Presidential palace was surrounded, and Taraki was taken prisoner. Amin telephoned Leonid Brezhnev, leader of the Soviet Union, and informed him of the regime change. He told Brezhnev that Taraki was in custody, and asked what should be done with him. Brezhnev responded with a non-committal statement that the choice was up to Amin. As a result, Amin ordered Taraki to be strangled, and word was put out that Taraki had died of natural causes.

Amin promoted a more collective leadership to prevent a cult of personality from developing. He ordered more purges, particularly with the army, to remove any personnel that were not loyal to the PDPA. The army of Afghanistan once had 100,000 members, but due to the purges and desertions to the rebellious forces in the countryside, the number dropped to less than 70,000 troops. Amin released the names of 18,000 people executed by Taraki's regime, but then he kept arresting people as well. PDPA members who opposed Amin, particularly the Parchamist faction of the PDPA, fled to the Soviet Union.

Amin's regime became so violent that even the Soviet leaders thought that he was giving Marxism a bad name. The KGB began an infiltration of the PDPA, which alarmed Amin. He started to move away from Soviet connections by conducting secret negotiations with Iran and Pakistan. For the Soviets, this was too much, and they began planning Amin's removal. In December, 1979, the Soviets informed Amin that they would send in troops to support his regime since he was unable to maintain order with the Afghan army. On December 27, 1979, the Soviet armed forces crossed the border into Afghanistan for what was supposed to be a simple regime change, but ended up being a nine-year stay for the Soviet military.

Amin had taken refuge in the Tajbeg Palace, which used to be the headquarters of the Central Army Command. It was a formidable fortress, and its walls were designed to withstand artillery fire. The KGB had made attempts against Amin by using poison and snipers, but he had the good luck to escape assassination. A special strike force, made up by KGB agents, was sent to attack Tajbeg Palace, though some Soviet officers thought such an attack was "crazy." The troops were whipped into frenzy with the propaganda that Amin was a "CIA agent" and "an American operative."

When the attack began, Amin refused to believe that it was an attack by the Soviets. He continued to believe that the Soviet forces had come to help him, but when he could not contact the leaders of the Afghan army, he finally guessed the truth. The Russian force killed Amin and his son, and seriously wounded his daughter. Amin's death was announced over national radio, and this time they did not say the President died of "natural causes." The Russians installed a new president, Babrak Karmal, who was an exiled leader of the Parchamist faction of the PDPA.

Rather than strengthen his base, Karmal started a series of purges in the PDPA, sending to trial the members of the Khalqi faction who had supported Taraki and Amin. The Soviets warned against this form of repressive action, but Karmal said it was necessary to purify the party. Karmal began increasing the military budget, promoting loyal officers, and organizing the army along Soviet military lines. With 100,000 Soviet personnel backing his regime, Karmal expected to be in power a long time.

Unfortunately for Karmal, the presence of so many Soviet troops gave the opponents of the regime a unifying factor. Previously, the Afghan tribes in the rural areas had been divided by religion, economic factors, and family feuds. The arrival of the Soviet troops gave everyone a common enemy, and the Afghans started to move away from the central government. Afghan refugees poured into Pakistan. Aid started to come in from anti-Soviet countries, which saw the conflict as a means to weaken the Soviet military without starting another World War.

This was the beginning of "Charlie Wilson's War," in which Russian weapons were purchased by Israel, sold to Egypt, then shipped to Pakistan by way of Saudi Arabia. Weapons were then smuggled from Pakistan into Afghanistan, where "mujahideen" (holy warriors) started using them against Soviet forces. With their helicopters, trucks, and tanks blown up, the Soviets suffered severe casualties, and back in the Soviet Union people started to ask if the war was necessary. By 1986, the Soviets were scapegoating Karmal for the failures of the war, and it was decided to remove him from office and replace him with Mohammed Najibullah, the head of the secret police. This time assassination was not part of the regime change, and Karmal was allowed to go into exile, although a decade later, in 1996, he died from cancer.

The Najibullah regime was not very popular, and made no headway in negotiating an end to the civil war. By 1987, the Soviet Union had decided to pull out of Afghanistan, and signed the Geneva Accords with Pakistan, Saudi Arabia, and the United States in an attempt to wind down the war. The Soviets did give more training and equipment to the Afghan army in the expectation that they would be able to maintain order once the Soviet Army had left. It was not until 1989 that the Soviet forces left Afghanistan, but it was too late to stop the turmoil and economic difficulties which brought about the collapse of the Iron Curtain.

Najibullah managed to hang on to power until 1992, when the Russian government under Boris Yeltsin refused to sell more supplies to Afghanistan. Once the Najibullah regime collapsed, there was an attempt at power sharing between the various factions. Different militias had risen up, with the backing of Pakistan, Iran, and Saudi Arabia. However, a new group called the Taliban (religious students) began to gain influence because they were not part of the provisional government, and they appealed to Afghan nationalism. The Taliban also appealed to factions who maintained a strict interpretation of Islam. Modern reforms for women were undone, and women were forced to wear traditional dress that hid their features.

The cruelty of the Taliban was especially evident by their treatment of former President Najibullah. Since his government fell, Najibullah had taken refuge in a facility run by the United Nations, and he had been trying to get asylum in India. On September 27, 1996, the Taliban raided the UN building and kidnapped Najibullah. They mutilated him and dragged his body through the streets behind a truck. His body, and the body of his brother, were left hanging near a traffic light.

Backed by recruits and funding from Pakistan, the Taliban fought against more moderate groups, like the Northern Alliance. The Taliban's strict interpretation of Sharia Law also appealed to Osama Bin Laden and his Al-Qaeda organization, which gave financial aid to the Taliban and set up a training center in Afghanistan. After the September 11, 2001 attacks, Afghanistan was the main target in the "War on Terror" (See Chapter 24) and the Taliban began to collapse under American intervention.

To this day, the situation in Afghanistan is still considered to be unstable. Yet, there was some appreciation for the old days of stability. In 2004, former King Zahir Khan was given the title of "Father of His Country." Although he did not play any part in Afghan politics, he was a respected figure until his death in 2007. In June, 2008, a mass grave was found near Kabul, containing the bodies of those assassinated on April 27, 1978. In December, 2008, the body of Mohammed Daoud Khan was officially identified. In March, 2009, when transiting Eris was square his natal Ceres, the former president was given a state funeral.

Bibliography for Chapter 22
Internet Sources

Afghanistan
https://en.wikipedia.org/wiki/Afghanistan

King Muhammed Zahir Shah
https://en.wikipedia.org/wiki/Mohammed_Zahir_Shah

Mohammed Daoud Khan
https://en.wikipedia.org/wiki/Mohammed_Daoud_Khan

Saur Revolution
https://en.wikipedia.org/wiki/Saur_Revolution

Nur Muhammed Taraki
https://en.wikipedia.org/wiki/Nur_Muhammad_Taraki

Hafizullah Amin
https://en.wikipedia.org/wiki/Hafizullah_Amin

Babrak Karmal
https://en.wikipedia.org/wiki/Babrak_Karmal

Muhammed Najibullah
https://en.wikipedia.org/wiki/Mohammad_Najibullah

Charlie Wilson
https://en.wikipedia.org/wiki/Charlie_Wilson_(Texas_politician)

Soviet Afghan War
https://en.wikipedia.org/wiki/Soviet%E2%80%93Afghan_War

Taliban
https://en.wikipedia.org/wiki/Taliban

Osama Bin Laden
https://en.wikipedia.org/wiki/Osama_bin_Laden

Book Source

Zepezauer, Mark, *The CIA's Greatest Hits*,
Odonian Press, Tucson, AZ, 1994

Chart labels:

Gulf War
August 2, 1990
2:00 BAT
Koch
29N20
47E59

Chapter 23

The Gulf War
Eris quincunx Pluto

The Gulf War of 1990-1991 resulted in the most decisive victory for the United States since World War II, but at the start there were some who questioned whether that outcome would take place. During the 1980's, the United States military did not see any major action. The stigma of retreat from Vietnam still hung over the military. In 1983, troops had been sent to Beirut as part of a peacekeeping force, but 241 Marines were killed by suicide bombers. The peacekeeping force pulled out of Beirut. Shortly after leaving Beirut, 7,300 troops were sent to the island of Grenada to overthrow a leftist government that had come to power after a coup. The invasion was promoted as a measure to prevent Marxist Caribbean forces from getting a stepping stone for attacking the USA. The last American military action of the decade was the invasion of Panama to capture General Manuel Noriega, an operation which took ten days.

In contrast, the nation of Iraq had been at war with Iran for the entire decade. In 1979, when the Iranian revolution was taking place, the Iranian military had been weakened by purges, executions, and desertions of capable officers. Saddam Hussein, leader of Iraq, saw this as an opportunity to capture territory. The Iraqis were mainly Sunni Muslims, as were the neighboring Arab nations, and there was fear that the Shiite revolution in Iran would spread to other nations. In the beginning, Saddam Hussein was seen as a champion of the Sunni cause, and he received support from Saudi Arabia and other nations.

However, Iran was not the only country without good military leadership. Because of his Stalinist-type control in Iraq, Saddam Hussein had purged military commanders who might have been a threat to him. Having no military experience, Saddam Hussein set himself up as the military leader of Iraq. The result was a stalemated war, comparable to World War One, with trench warfare, barbed wire, and poison gas. Although both sides had modern weapons, neither side had the strategic know-how to properly deploy the weapons in order to bring about a victory.

Saddam Hussein was born with Eris conjunct Saturn, and that could have represented his fanatical desire for control, even though that desire might cause upheaval. Eris-Saturn were trine Mars, and that might have accounted for his militant nature, always spoiling for a fight. (His true birth time is not known, but if he was born near Noon, the Moon would have been added to that mix, possibly giving emotional fulfillment for his actions.)

Fortunately for his opponents, Eris-Saturn was sextile his Pallas, and his rash behavior showed a lack of wisdom in provoking fights that were better left avoided. His early years, when transiting Eris was semi-sextile his natal Sun, were a combination of "school of hard knocks" with a "to the barricades" sense of revolutionary fervor. Through his family connections, he was brought into the radical Ba'ath (Arab Socialist) party, and instilled with rough political ideals.

When transiting Eris was semi-sextile his Uranus in 1959, Saddam Hussein took part in an assassination attempt against the Iraqi leader, General Qasim. Later propaganda films depicted Saddam Hussein as the leader of the plot, whereas he only played a small role in the assassination attempt. According to the versions from some observers, it was Saddam Hussein, himself who was most responsible for botching the killing by firing his weapon too soon. General Qasim managed to stay in power until 1963, when he was overthrown and killed by Ba'ath supporters in the army. His death brought in new Ba'ath leaders, and this brought Saddam Hussein even closer to the inner circles of government power.

By 1968, another coup brought to power President Ahmen Hassan Al-Bakr, and Saddam Hussein was appointed as his second-in-command, in charge of security. During the 1970's, a campaign of modernization was implemented in Iraq, using oil revenues to support a series of social services. The Ba'ath government received credit for the electrification program which lit up every Iraqi village, and the regime became noted for promoting the education and employment of women. Those who resisted modernization, or resorted to factionalism, were quickly wiped out by Saddam's henchmen.

President Al-Bakr started to weaken in health, and on July 16, 1979 he was forced to resign and proclaim Saddam Hussein as his successor. This took place as transiting Eris was trine Saddam Hussein's North Node, and sextile his South Node. The rise marked a change in his values, as he was no longer content with operating in the shadows, but wanted all of the glory of leadership. His drive for personal security was marked by

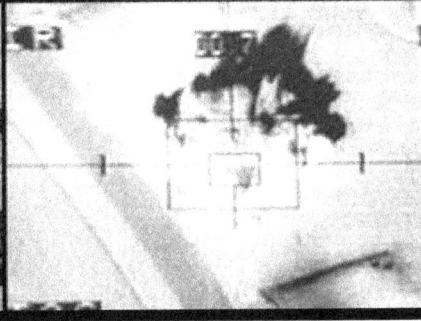

Scenes from the Gulf War

Eris square Vesta. He developed a ruthless sense of control which was shown during a conference of the Ba'ath party.

Saddam began by reading a letter about the "fifth columnists" who had infiltrated the party, and then security guards took away Ba'ath members who had been denounced by Saddam. It was obvious to the other delegates that these men were being taken out to be killed. The killing finally stopped when a lackey jumped up and declared that Saddam's greatest fault was that he was too merciful, and that more traitors should

If we're already melting now, what will happen when it's lit by war?"

Iraqi propaganda cartoons from the Gulf War

How long are we going to sit here pointlessly?
I want to go back before the cannons start firing.

be killed. For the sake of their own personal security, the Ba'ath delegates voted to support Saddam Hussein's purge of the party.

By the time Eris was sextile natal Neptune, Saddam Hussein had begun his disastrous war against Iran. Although Saddam Hussein was not a very good general, he managed to manipulate public opinion so that it looked like he was a great military leader. It was the start of a cult of personality, which brought in paintings, statues, and public declarations of love and devotion towards Saddam Hussein. He became a political chameleon, sometimes wearing a modern suit, or sometimes wearing robes while praying to Mecca. The goal was to attract as many factions as possible into his cult of personality, and then crush those who resisted.

The role of the United States in the Iraq-Iran conflict was ostensibly neutral. Yet, at the beginning of the war, there was support for Iraq as a bulwark against the Iranian revolution. There had been some concern that Iraq had been supporting terrorist groups, but Saddam Hussein ordered them out of Iraq in order to win Western support. This resulted in a shipment of supplies to Iraq, and a famous meeting in which Donald Rumsfeld shook hands with Saddam Hussein. At the same time, there were factions in the Reagan administration that wanted to establish better relations with Iran. This brought about Colonel Oliver North's dealings with Iran to sell spare parts to the Iranian military, the proceeds of which were used to fund the Nicaraguan Contras, leading to a major scandal in Reagan's second term.

By 1989, both sides were fed up with the war, and accepted a UN brokered cease fire. The war had proven to be a stalemate, with neither side gaining territory. For a decade, Iraq had been in a war economy, and the nation accepted conscription and military training for its youth. The war also bolstered the careers of Iraqi women, who were filling jobs that were vacated by men who had gone off to war. In the Arab world, Iraq was seen as the most modern state, and most liberal in its treatment of women. Still, that façade would soon crack as more military goals were sought.

Iraq began making threats against Kuwait, a small oil kingdom run by the Al-Sabah family. During the Ottoman Empire, Kuwait had been part of the Basra district of Iraq. After the war against Turkey, the British gave Kuwait to the Al-Sabah family in return for their support. For years, there were many in Iraq, including the late General Qasim and Saddam Hussein, who believed that Kuwait was still part of Iraq, and said the British had no authority to divide the country.

In July, 1990, the Iraqis complained that the Kuwaitis were overproducing their quota of oil for OPEC, thereby driving down the cost of oil, which hurt Iraq's exports. Of particular note was the complaint over the drilling near the Rumaila oil field, which was on the border of Iraq and Kuwait. Iraq complained the Kuwaitis were drilling at a diagonal angle, thereby tapping into the oil reserve that should have belonged to Iraq. For compensation, Iraq demanded $10 billion in payments, but the Kuwaitis would only offer to pay $9 billion.

A conference was convened in Jeddah, Saudi Arabia, with Egyptian President Hosni Mubarak acting as mediator. Saddam Hussein had a meeting with the American Ambassador, April Glaspie, in which she said that the USA had no interest in the conflict with Kuwait, and considered it to be a matter to be solved between Arab nations. In mid-July, there had been some saber-rattling, with 30,000 Iraqi troops moved to the Kuwaiti border. The start of the Jeddah conference eased tensions, and even the Kuwaiti army stood down, thinking there would be a diplomatic solution.

On August 2, 1990, the Iraqi army made its attack upon Kuwait. At first, it was assumed that they would occupy the Kuwaiti oil fields, but then their air force bombed Kuwait City and troops moved into the capital. The small nation was taken completely by surprise. A few Kuwaiti air force jets managed to get into the air, but not enough to be able to retaliate effectively against the Iraqis. The Al-Sabah family fled, and the entire country was subdued in 12 hours. The rapid conquest was a shock to the other nations, who had expected a diplomatic settlement.

In the chart for the invasion, Eris is quincunx Pluto in Scorpio, but is also square Venus and Pallas in Cancer and Saturn in Capricorn. This could represent the surprising and efficient elements of the invasion, which caught everyone off guard. The warmongering leading up to the invasion had been minor compared with the military propaganda of the previous decade. Although threats had been made against the Kuwaiti oil fields, no one expected that Saddam Hussein would conquer the whole country. In the chart, Eris was trine Ceres, and that has represented property loss. The Kuwaitis experienced significant property loss through looting by Iraqi soldiers. This would lead to a powerful, but misleading, propaganda story, about Iraqi soldiers confiscating medical equipment from hospitals, even to the point of tossing premature babies out of their incubators. (To be fair to the Iraqis, it turned out they did no such thing.)

The blatant aggression against Kuwait brought protests from the other nations, and there were a series of economic sanctions against Iraq to pressure the Iraqis into leaving Kuwait. The Iraqi government

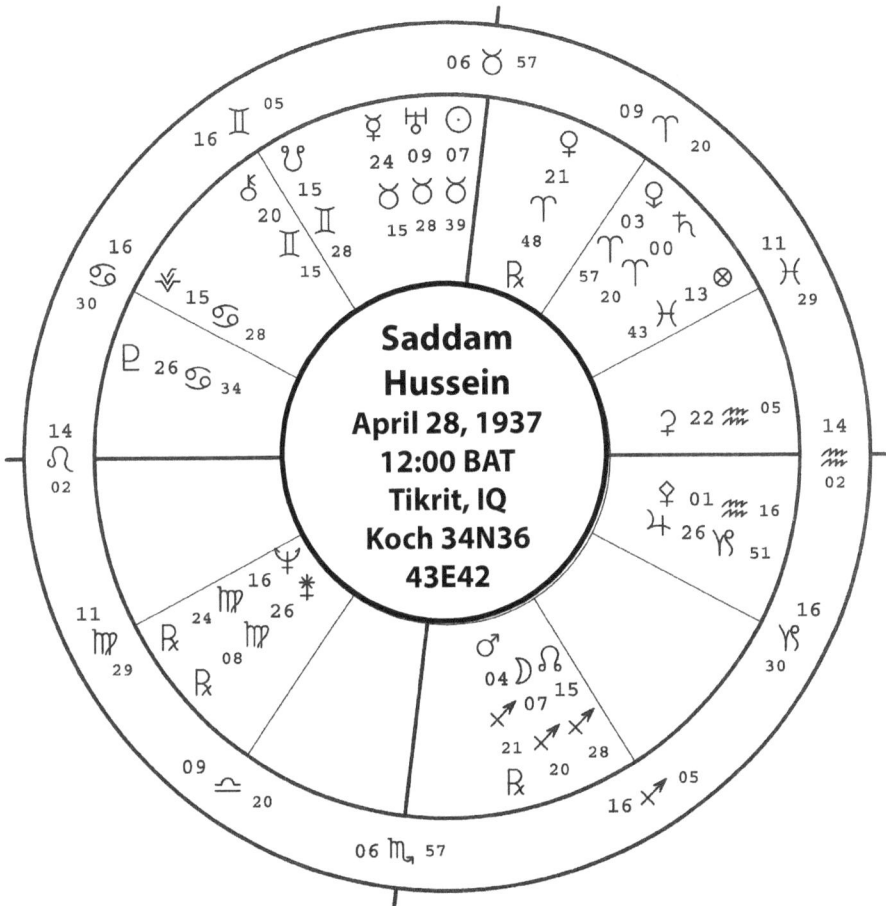

Saddam Hussein
April 28, 1937
12:00 BAT
Tikrit, IQ
Koch 34N36
43E42

responded by bringing out old maps which showed that a century earlier Kuwait had been part of Iraq. Therefore, in their mindset, Iraq was not an invader, but just reclaiming territory that had been taken away and given to someone else. The United Nations, the Arab League, and the United States all passed resolutions demanding an immediate withdrawal from Kuwait.

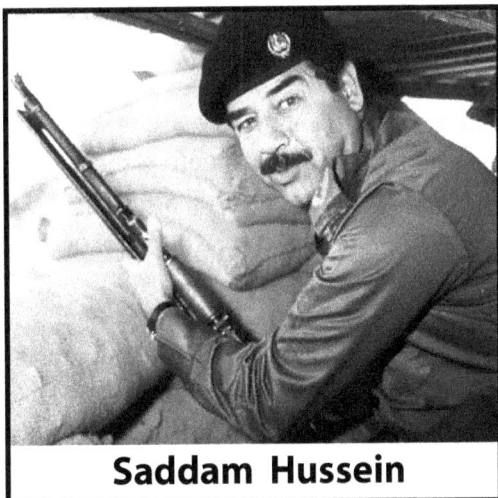

Saddam Hussein

During the autumn of 1990, fruitless negotiations were made with Iraqi diplomats, but they ended with the result that Iraq would go to war rather than give up Kuwait. In the meantime, the United States began Operation Desert Shield, which moved troops into Saudi Arabia to prevent further expansion by the Iraqi army. In addition to the American army, 34 nations sent troops to form a coalition army, which was placed under the command of General Norman Schwarzkopf.

When Norman Schwarzkopf was ten years old, transiting Eris was square his Part of Fortune and trine his Venus, and transiting Pluto was conjunct his Ascendant. He was attending the Bordentown Military Institute, and he posed for his class picture with a serious expression. The reason was, he said, "Someday when I become a general, I want people to know I am serious." This childhood dream came true after a lot of hard work. In the late 1940's, when Eris was square his Ceres, young Norman Schwarzkopf lived in various locations around the world because of the moves made by his father's military career. One significant visit was to Teheran, Iran, where Schwarzkopf developed an interest in Mid-Eastern culture, which would continue through the rest of his life.

In the 1950's, when Eris was sextile his Chiron, trine his Ascendant and South Node, and sextile his North Node, Schwarzkopf was on the fast track to a military career, driven by his desire to emulate his father, who had retired in 1953 as a Major General. Young Schwarzkopf graduated from the Valley Forge Military Academy, first in his class, and then went on to graduate from West Point when transiting Pluto was conjunct his Mercury and his Sun. After four years of service as a junior officer, he became a captain in 1961, studied engineering in Southern California, and was set to return to West Point as an engineering instructor when transiting Pluto passed over his Neptune. He felt that a tour of duty in Vietnam would increase his chances for promotion, and he delayed his teaching assignment for active service.

When Schwarzkopf went to South Vietnam, he was promoted to Major, and served with the Military Assistance Command. His first wartime experience came in August, 1965, when he joined South Vietnamese troops in breaking a siege at Duc Co Camp. Schwarzkopf helped rescue wounded South Vietnamese soldiers, and managed to hold off the North Vietnamese until reinforcements arrived. For this service he was awarded the Silver Star. In February, 1966, Schwarzkopf was wounded four times while leading a paratrooper attack, and he was awarded another Silver Star and a Purple Heart.

In 1966, Schwarzkopf returned to West Point, when Eris was quincunx his Neptune, and he met his future wife, Brenda, at a West Point football game. In 1969, he returned to South Vietnam for another tour of duty, where he impressed his men by leading from the front and sharing their risks. His heroism won him another Silver Star, a second Purple Heart, three Bronze Stars, and a Legion of Merit. Privately, he expressed concerns about U.S. foreign policy that would lead to such a war.

During the 1970's, Schwarzkopf served in Washington D.C., Alaska, Washington State, and Hawaii, gradually rising in rank. In 1983, when transiting Eris was semi-sextile his Pallas, he became a Major General and was placed in command of Fort Stewart, GA, where he instituted a tough training program and displayed an aggressive personality to the troops. It was also during this transit that Schwarzkopf took part in the invasion of Grenada, which he saw as helpful for building the morale of the military after the debacle in Vietnam. Although the invasion was short, it was hampered by communications problems between the different branches of service. Schwarzkopf became an advocate for joint commands and inter-service communication which helped for successful deployments in future campaigns, such as in the Gulf War.

The United Nations Security Council passed a resolution demanding Iraq's withdrawal from Kuwait by January 15, 1991. When that date passed without a response the coalition forces started Operation Desert Storm on January 17, 1991. The attacks began with a series of air raids against Iraq.

Saddam Hussein had promised that the war against him would be "the mother of all battles." As it turned out, he was on the losing side of that battle. In the preparation for war, it had seemed like the coalition forces were planning an amphibious landing, preparing to liberate Kuwait from the sea. The Iraqi forces had entrenched themselves along the Persian Gulf to prevent this invasion.

When the land battle began, it was discovered that General Schwarzkopf had tricked the Iraqis by sending coalition forces through the desert, attacking the Iraqi forces from the rear. Having dug in, the Iraqi army had no mobility to attack the coalition army. Trench warfare and barbed wire proved to be ineffective against modern tanks. In spite of the threat of chemical weapons, the coalition forces were not attacked with poison gas. Trapped in positions they could not defend, many Iraqi soldiers started to surrender.

It was during this part of the Gulf War that Neptune was square Eris, and there was an attempt to use religious conflict to break up the coalition against Iraq. Saddam Hussein ordered that Scud missiles should be fired against Israel. His rationale was that this would prompt Israel to declare war on Iraq, and the Muslim members of the coalition would quit rather than fight alongside Jews. Fortunately, diplomacy by the United States persuaded Israel to keep out of the conflict and to trust that the coalition forces would wreak vengeance upon Saddam Hussein.

In mid-February, 1991, when coalition troops moved into Kuwait, the Iraqi army put up a token resistance and then fled north. Tanks and trucks were jamming the six-lane highway from Kuwait City. The fleeing Iraqis were attacked by coalition aircraft and were easily massacred by the aerial bombardment. The area became known as "the Highway of Death", and the exact death count of Iraqis killed remains uncertain. There could have been as many as 10,000 or as few as 500 soldiers killed. It is certain that hundreds of vehicles were demolished in this area while fleeing from Kuwait City.

At the end of February, 1991, just as Pluto was separating from the quincunx to Eris, a cease fire was declared, and a free Kuwait was the result. At the same time, Saddam Hussein had to deal with two uprisings, a Kurdish rebellion in the North and a Shiite insurrection in the South. Iraqi troops that had survived the coalition attacks were sent into battle against the rebels, and managed to suppress them. The Iraqi rebels had hoped the coalition forces would support them in overthrowing Saddam Hussein, but the coalition only had a mandate to free Kuwait, not to invade and occupy Iraq.

The result of the Gulf War was that after being compared to Hitler and Stalin, Saddam Hussein was allowed to remain in power. A no-fly zone was imposed on Iraq, and sanctions prevented certain products from entering the country. In March, 1991, U.S. troops started moving out of the Persian Gulf region. The justification for not invading Iraq was stated by Secretary of Defense Dick Cheney, who said in 1992, "The question in my mind is, how many additional American casualties is Saddam (Hussein) worth? And the answer is, not that damned many." (A decade later, Cheney would have a dramatic change of mind.)

In spite of the military success, the Gulf War seemed to have a lack of closure, and the victory did not increase the popularity of the Bush Administration, which lost the election in 1992. Leaving Saddam Hussein in power brought a new set of worries, as stories came out in the 1990's about attempts to build chemical weapons, atomic weapons, and other weapons of mass destruction. Each story seemed to confirm that the United States had missed an opportunity by not bringing down his regime in 1991. The political result of these scare stories was a new

Norman Schwarzkopf
August 22, 1934
4:45 EDT
Trenton, New Jersey
Koch 40N1.01
74W44.36

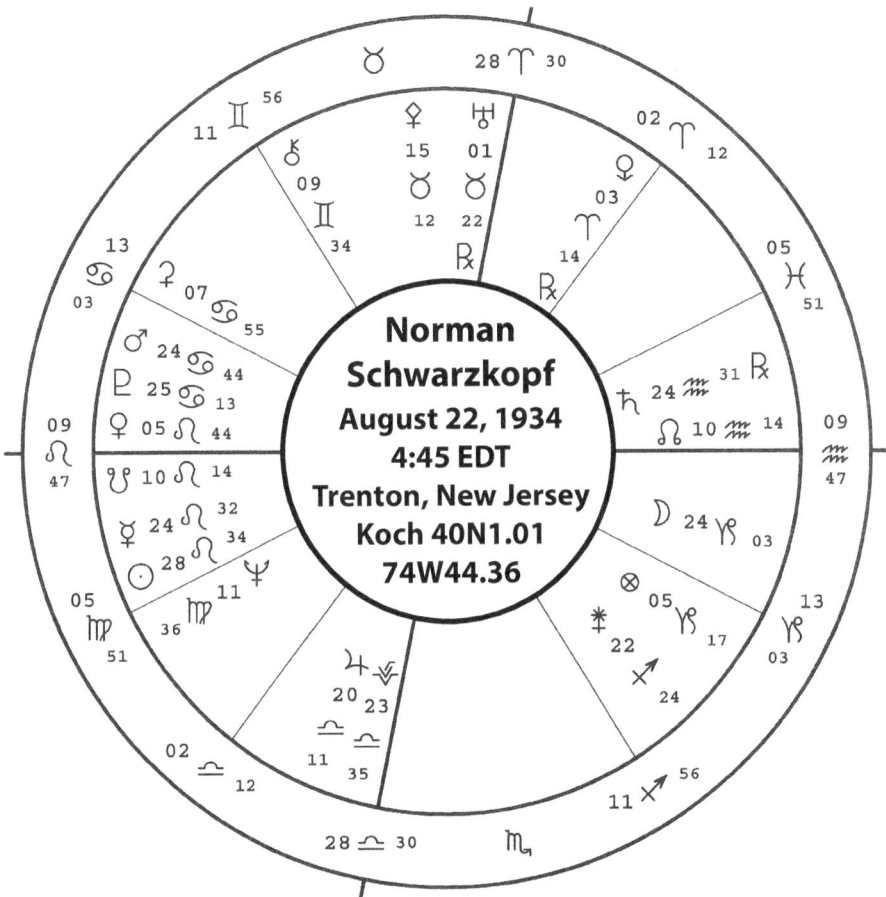

brand of "neo-conservatives" who would support an invasion of Iraq in the 21st Century.

Another unforeseen difficulty was the role of military forces in the Persian Gulf. To help protect Kuwait against future attack, Saudi Arabia allowed the United States to build military bases in that country. This action set off protests from conservative Muslims, who regarded Arabia as sacred land, and to have "non-believers" stationed so close to the holy city of Mecca was considered a sacrilege. Leading this opposition was an Arabian billionaire named Osama Bin Laden, who actually had been friendly

General Schwarzkopf

towards the United States during the 1980's when military aid was being sent to the guerilla fighters in Afghanistan. After the Soviets left Afghanistan, the United States did not want to send anymore aid. Osama Bin Laden stepped in with donations, and funded the Taliban. In the next chapter, we will see the outcome of his opposition to America's presence in Arabia.

Bibliography - Chapter 23
Internet Sources

Iraqi propaganda on American military effectiveness
http://www.psywarrior.com/iraqprop.html

Saddam Hussein
https://en.wikipedia.org/wiki/Saddam_Hussein

Iran-Iraq War
https://en.wikipedia.org/wiki/Iran%E2%80%93Iraq_War

Norman Schwarzkopf
https://en.wikipedia.org/wiki/Norman_Schwarzkopf,_Jr.

Invasion of Kuwait
https://en.wikipedia.org/wiki/Invasion_of_Kuwait

The Gulf War
https://en.wikipedia.org/wiki/Gulf_War

The Highway of Death
https://en.wikipedia.org/wiki/Highway_of_Death

Dick Cheney
https://en.wikipedia.org/wiki/Dick_Cheney

Book Sources

Bourque, Stephen A. & Burdan, John, *MHQ: The Quarterly Journal of Military History,* Autumn, 1999, Leesburg, VA, *A Nervous Night on the Basrah Road,* Pages 88-97.

Murray, Williamson, *MHQ: The Quarterly Journal of Military History,* Autumn 1997, Leesburg, VA, *The Gulf War as History,* Pages 6-19 .

Regan, Geoffrey, *Snafu: Great American Military Disasters,* Avon Books, New York, NY, 1993, *The Gulf War, 1991,* Pages 265-273.

Westwood, John, *The History of the Middle East Wars,* World Publications Group, Inc. North Dighton, MA, 2002.

Zepezauer, Mark, *The CIA's Greatest Hits,* Odonian Press, Tucson, AZ, 1994

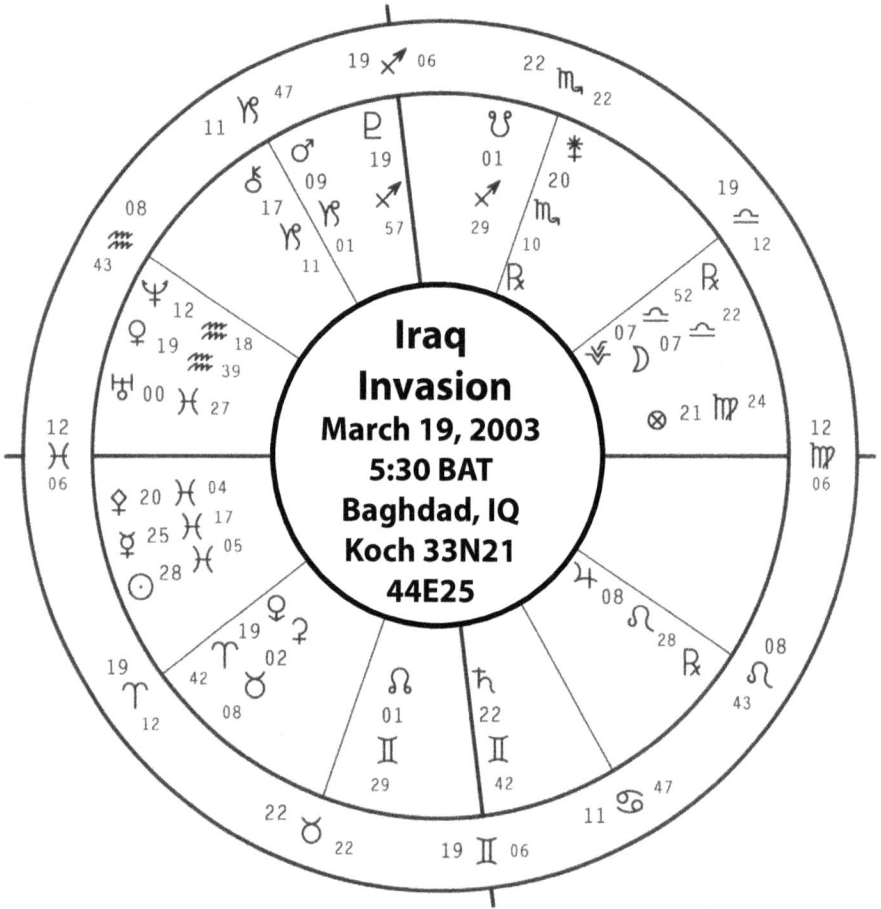

Iraq
Invasion
March 19, 2003
5:30 BAT
Baghdad, IQ
Koch 33N21
44E25

258. *Brother Pluto, Sister Eris*

Chapter 24

The War Against Dandruff:
Eris Trine Pluto

"It's like a war against dandruff. There's no such thing as a war against terrorism. It's idiotic. These are slogans. These are lies. It's advertising, which is the only art form we ever invented and developed." Gore Vidal

The conclusion of the Gulf War was unsatisfying for everyone. Saddam Hussein had his nation wrecked and isolated. The Kuwaitis got their country back, but there was the ominous presence of Saddam Hussein across the border. The Bush administration was turned out of office in the 1992 election, but the Clinton administration kept up with monitoring the international activities of Iraq. There were some efforts on the part of Iraq to produce chemical weapons, and the program was exposed when two sons-in-law of Saddam Hussein defected to Jordan. The program was shut down under international pressure, and the sons-in-law of Saddam Hussein were executed after they were tricked into returning to Iraq. In the late 1990's, the Clinton administration kept a watch on chemical weapons in Iraq, with the help of UN weapons inspectors. It gave the impression that something was going on, even though there was no evidence anything was going on.

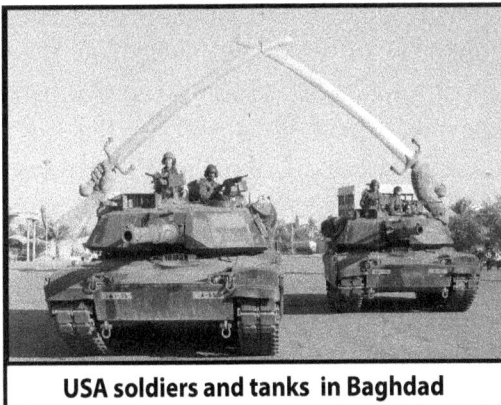

USA soldiers and tanks in Baghdad

In January 1998, a letter was sent to President Clinton from a neoconservative group, advocating the invasion of Iraq and the overthrow of Saddam Hussein. Donald Rumsfeld, Richard Perle, and Paul Wolfowitz were among those who signed the letter. Some of the signers would find positions in the administration of George W. Bush, and they would maintain that Iraq was the greatest threat to the United States. Yet, at the beginning of the Bush administration, they could not stir up public enthusiasm for a war against Iraq.

That attitude changed after the attack of 9-11-2001, in which the destruction of the World Trade Center and part of the Pentagon shocked the world. According to one account, even Saddam Hussein was shocked by the attack, and considered sending condolences to the United States, but he could not extend formal condolences to President Bush because of the Bush policy towards Iraq. The Bush administration wanted to believe that Saddam Hussein was behind 9-11, but investigation revealed it was the work of Al-Qaeda, a terrorist organization founded by Osama Bin Laden, the Saudi Arabian billionaire who wanted American troops off of Saudi soil after the Gulf War.

The Bush administration began an attack on Afghanistan, because the Taliban government had set up Al-Qaeda training centers in that country. Anti-Taliban militias were hired to track down Osama Bin Laden, but they lost him in the mountains of Tora Bora. He would remain free for another decade until finally tracked down in Pakistan. In the meantime, the invasion of Afghanistan was declared a success because it had overthrown the Taliban, and "neutralized" the influence of Osama Bin Laden. The result was that America felt avenged for the 9-11 attack.

Yet, the Bush administration still wanted a war against Iraq. Subtle hints were dropped that Iraqi agents had met with Al-Qaeda. Vice-President Dick Cheney said that the 9-11 ringleader Mohammed Atta had met with Iraqi agents in Prague, and the story circulated on news programs. The story was later discredited, and Cheney denied ever having repeated it, although there was film footage of him saying it.

New "evidence" started to appear that Iraq was building up "weapons of mass destruction," but it turned out that this "evidence" came from an Iraqi defector, code named Curveball, who had been spewing out nonsense to the German intelligence agency. The Germans did not believe the stories, but they were pushed as truth by the Bush administration, even though Secretary of State Colin Powell protested against their use.

The most outrageous fabrication was a report that Saddam Hussein had tried to buy "yellowcake" uranium from the African nation of Niger. Joseph Wilson, who had once been an ambassador to Niger, was sent on a fact-finding mission to determine the truth of the story. He discovered that the papers finalizing the purchase were a forgery, and one of the signatures was supposed to have been from a government minister who was no longer in office when the documents were signed. Joseph Wilson reported his findings, but they were dismissed by the Bush administration, which punished Wilson by leaking the information that his wife was really a CIA agent, making it look like Wilson had been on a pleasure junket paid for by the CIA. Ironically, Mrs. Wilson (Valerie Plame) had been part of an intelligence network, which was investigating foreign companies to keep Iran (not Iraq) from getting nuclear weapons, and this public outing ruined her efforts.

The Bush administration kept ramping up the rhetoric for a war against Iraq. In the 2002 State of the Union address, Bush referred to Iraq, Iran, and North Korea as an "axis of evil." This was a statement that did not make sense politically, historically, or even geographically. Iran still had resentment against Iraq because of the decade of warfare during the 1980's. North Korea was a politically isolated regime, constantly making threats against South Korea. During this period, there was agitation by North Korea, and talk of building an atomic bomb, but the Bush administration ignored them in favor of an attack against Iraq.

Adding to the war propaganda was a series of Bush speeches in which references to Saddam Hussein were juxtaposed with those of Osama Bin Laden. The plan was to create the idea in the public mind that these two were linked together. In reality, Osama Bin Laden despised Saddam Hussein as much as he despised the United States. Although a Sunni Muslim, Saddam Hussein did not practice the extreme Wahabi Islam that Osama Bin Laden and his followers promoted. Iraq under Saddam Hussein was a model of a modern Islamic nation, allowing women to wear western clothing and to take jobs that were usually held by men, a fact which outraged the Wahabi movement. Iraq had a death penalty against those who preached the Wahabi brand of Islam.

Another war justification was the idea that Saddam Hussein might give "weapons of mass destruction" to terrorist groups, although there was no evidence of his having any connection to terrorist groups, and there was also the probability that terrorist groups would use the "weapons of mass destruction" again Saddam Hussein. When Secretary of Defense Donald Rumsfeld was asked about this lack of terrorist connections, he responded with a masterpiece of obfuscation:

"Reports that say that something hasn't happened are always interesting to me, because as we know, there are known knowns; there are

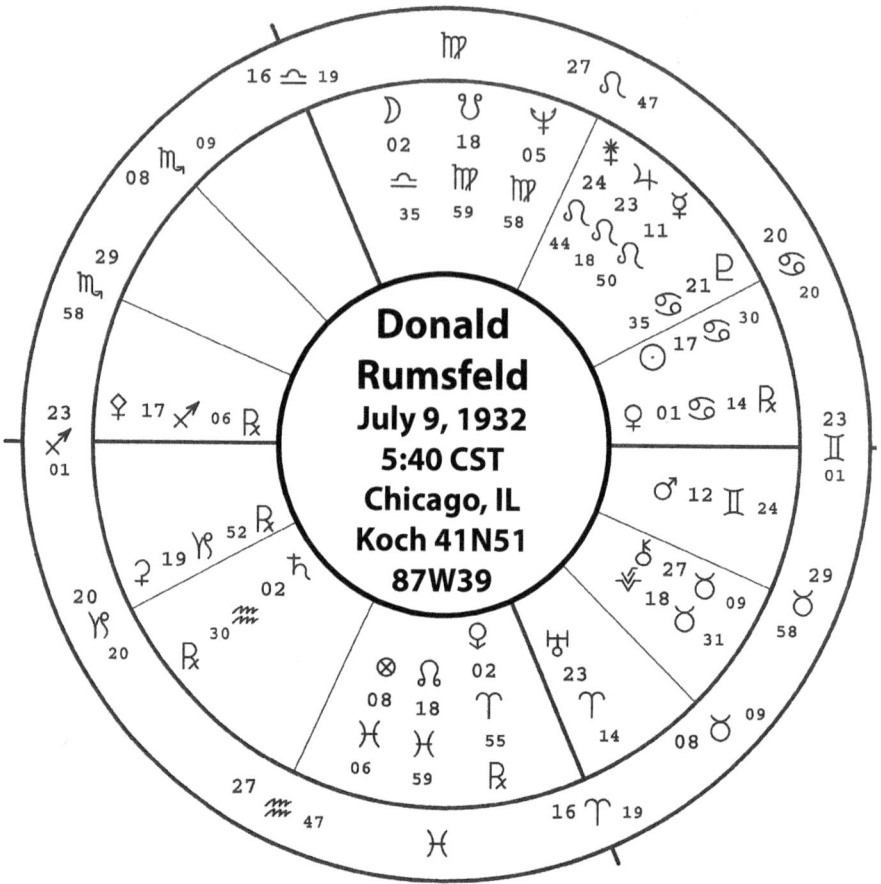

Donald Rumsfeld
July 9, 1932
5:40 CST
Chicago, IL
Koch 41N51
87W39

things we know we know. We also know there are known unknowns; that is to say we know there are some things we do not know. But there are also unknown unknowns — the ones we don't know we don't know. And if one looks throughout the history of our country and other free countries, it is the latter category that tends to be the difficult ones."

In facing reporters, Donald Rumsfeld started acting like Chico Marx in the movie "Animal Crackers," in which he would ask a question and then answer the question himself. As Groucho Marx noted in the same film,

Donald Rumsfeld

"Well it's pretty hard to be wrong if you keep answering yourself all the time." Yet, as the war progressed it was obvious that Rumsfeld and the others were coming up with the wrong answers to their own questions. The policy line of the administration was that the Americans would be greeted as liberators and the fighting in Iraq would not last longer than five days. The "weapons of mass destruction" would be found North-East-West-South in a circle around Baghdad and Tikrit. None of this happened, and people questioned the credibility of Donald Rumsfeld. Even the President's father, George H.W. Bush, questioned the capabilities of Rumsfeld, but these doubts would not be revealed until years later.

Donald Rumsfeld was born with Eris square Venus and opposing his Moon. He was blessed with rugged good looks, which helped him even in his later years. When he was sixty-nine, AARP dubbed him a sex symbol for the over-seventy crowd. However, with Eris sextile his Saturn, he spent his life following the straight and narrow path, having been brought up with the teachings of the Congregational Church. At age 17 he became an Eagle Scout, and later received awards from the Boy Scouts of America, such as the Distinguished Eagle Scout Award and the Silver Buffalo Award.

In the early 1950's, transiting Pluto was conjunct Rumsfeld's natal Jupiter and Juno, and trine his Uranus. This was a time of advancement for him when he attended Princeton University. He became captain of the varsity wrestling team, as well as captain of the lightweight football team. He made good contacts at Princeton, including a friendship with Frank Carlucci, who would also serve as Secretary of Defense. It was during this period that he met and married his wife, Joyce Pierson.

When transiting Pluto went into Virgo, it was conjunct Rumsfeld's natal Neptune, as well as sextile his Venus. He set out on a goal to become a member of Congress. He had worked on Congressional election campaigns, as well as serving as assistant to two Congressmen. In 1962, at age 30, Rumsfeld attained that dream by becoming a Congressman from Illinois. He was elected four times before leaving Congress to move further up in government.

In 1969, when transiting Eris was trine his Mercury, Rumsfeld was invited to join the Nixon administration as the head of the Office of Economic Opportunity. Rumsfeld was reluctant to take the OEO post, because he felt its purpose was at odds with his free market principles. Richard Nixon finally talked Rumsfeld into taking the post. By the end of 1970, when transiting Eris was sextile his natal Mars, Rumsfeld left the OEO and was given more authority in the Nixon administration. He was made a Counselor to the President and given his own office in the West Wing. Rumsfeld worked well with the leading men in the Nixon administration, and even Nixon praised him as a "ruthless little bastard."

In 1973, when transiting Pluto was conjunct his Moon and opposing his natal Eris, Rumsfeld was sent to Belgium as ambassador to NATO. Being away from Washington helped his career, since he was not caught up in the Watergate scandal that brought down the Nixon administration. He served well as a diplomat, helping to mediate a conflict between Cyprus and Turkey. In August, 1974, he returned to Washington, D.C. to serve as Chief of Staff for President Gerald Ford. When transiting Pluto was trine Rumsfeld's Mars and sextile his Mercury, he was appointed Secretary of Defense, the youngest man to hold that office. Thirty years later, he would set a record as the oldest man to hold the office. It was also during the Ford administration that Rumsfeld developed a working relationship with Dick Cheney, who took over as Chief of Staff.

After leaving the government in 1977, Rumsfeld served as CEO and later Chairman of G.D. Searle, a pharmaceutical company, which he helped to make prosperous, and then the company was sold to the Monsanto Group. G.D. Searle was the company that introduced the sweetener Aspartame, which had been banned by the FDA, but according to rumor Rumsfeld had used his government connections to get the ban lifted. During the Reagan administration, when transiting Eris was opposing his Midheaven, Rumsfeld was doing part time work for the government, which included a meeting with Saddam Hussein in 1983.

In the early 1990's, when Eris was trine his Pallas and square his Sun, Rumsfeld focused on the private sector again by becoming Chairman and CEO of General Instrument Corporation. This was a company that was developing broadband information and high-definition television. Rumsfeld put the company on a strong financial footing before departing in 1993.

By the time George W. Bush became President, Rumsfeld had transiting Eris square his Ceres. With the aid of his friend, Dick Cheney (now Vice-President), Rumsfeld was appointed Secretary of Defense. On Sept. 10, 2001, Rumsfeld gave a speech attacking the Pentagon bureaucracy, which he claimed could not account for 2.5 trillion dollars in transactions. The penchant for saving taxpayer money would be forgotten after Sept. 11, 2001, and the build up to the Iraqi war.

Donald Rumsfeld meets Saddam Hussein

On October 16, 2002, the Congress passed the "Authorization of the Use of Force Against Iraq Resolution", which was essentially a blank check for the Bush administration to go to war, and without having to go through the Constitutional measure of having Congress officially declare war. In the 2003 State of the Union address, President Bush stated that Iraq had mobile biological weapons labs. In February 2003, Secretary of State Colin Powell appeared before the United Nations, showed satellite pictures of tractor trailers in Iraq, and used the disputed "Curveball" stories about mobile weapons labs. Powell also claimed Saddam Hussein's intelligence service had connections with Al-Qaeda, even though an FBI investigation of 500,000 leads and interviews with 175,000 people could not turn up any evidence of a connection.

President Bush tried to make it seem the war was a personal vendetta, saying that Saddam Hussein had once tried to kill his father. This was in reference to a 1993 visit former President George H.W. Bush made to Kuwait, where he was to be greeted with a parade. On the parade route, security forces found a parked car packed with explosives. It was thought to be a ham-handed attempt by the Iraqi secret service to blow up the elder Bush. In retaliation, on June 26, 1993 an air strike was ordered against the Iraqi Intelligence Service headquarters, which killed six people. However, after the invasion of Iraq, a meticulous search of the files of the Iraqi Secret Service could not find any reference to an assassination plot against the elder Bush.

Although many Americans approved of a regime change in Iraq, nearly the same number wanted a diplomatic solution. In February, 2003, UN weapons inspectors issued a report saying that they could not find "weapons of mass destruction" in Iraq. Peace movements throughout Europe began protesting the American push for war. According to one estimate, 36 million people took part in 3000 rallies for peace, but the Bush administration was not paying attention to any of them. A "Coalition of the willing" was raised to send forces to Iraq from Great Britain, Australia, and Poland, while other nations like France, Germany, and New Zealand protested against the war.

The war began with an air raid on March 19, 2003. In the chart for the attack, Venus is sextile both Pluto and Eris. If Venus is the ruler of diplomacy, then it was being squeezed by death and the desire to go to war. Pluto on the Midheaven of the chart was in opposition to Saturn, and Eris was sextile Saturn. In the rush to war, the Bush administration had overruled older, wiser generals who had advocated sending more troops to support the occupation. They also did not prepare the troops with sufficient armor for their vehicles.

Pluto was squaring Pallas and Mercury, and Eris was semi-sextile Pallas and Mercury. A lack of intelligence and objective battlefield coverage were apparent on both sides of the struggle. American reporters were embedded in the U.S. Forces, thereby making it easy for the military to prevent reporters from seeing things they were not supposed to see. On the Iraqi side, news reports came from the Iraqi Information Minister, who was given the nickname of "Baghdad Bob." His statements about the invincibility of the Iraqi army were colorful and exaggerated, and he kept speaking about victory over the Coalition, even as American tanks rolled into Baghdad.

The military part of the struggle took a little more than a month, and at the beginning of May it was announced that combat operations had stopped in Iraq. What was not said was that there were still police actions going on, as looters, snipers, and guerilla forces were operating behind the scenes. Once the Iraqi army had surrendered, the soldiers were allowed to return home, but they were permitted to keep their guns. This would give them the means to take part in an insurgency. Millions of dollars of antiquities were stolen from Iraqi museums, because no one was guarding them. A bunker full of weapons was left unguarded and local insurgents made off with them for their own arsenal.

With Eris square Chiron in the attack chart, one thing the Bush administration could not hide was the casualties. Even though combat operations had stopped, casualties were taking place each day. There was an attempt to cover up the deaths by passing a law saying it was forbidden to photograph the flag-covered coffins being returned from Iraq. Yet, the walking wounded, the survivors of guerilla attacks served as living reminders that all was not going according to plan, if there ever was a plan.

No one wondered why the Iraqi military did not use the "weapons of mass destruction" on the invaders. Once combat operations had stopped, searches were made to find the "weapons of mass destruction." Some weapons were found, but they turned out to be chemical weapons the United States had sold to Saddam Hussein 20 years earlier. The result was that the expression "weapons of mass destruction" joined the lexicon of fanciful menaces like "Chimera", "Dragons", and "Martians." Billions of dollars and thousands of lives had been lost fighting a menace that did not exist.

In the attack chart, Eris is conjunct the Second House cusp, and financing became a major problem for the war. When the Bush administration came to power, there was a surplus in the government budget. The invasion of Iraq quickly turned that into a deficit. Major tax cuts for corporations, plus excessive spending on the war had the red ink flowing like a waterfall. It was baldly stated that Iraq's oil revenue would pay for the war, thereby proving it was a "blood for oil" military effort. Yet, even though Dick Cheney's old company, Halliburton, received no-bid contracts, they could not get the oil flowing fast enough to pay for the war. The main plan for post-war recovery was to send pallets filled with newly printed hundred dollar bills to Iraq as if the presence of money would stop the fighting.

In running post-war Iraq, L. Paul Bremer was given command. He was a career diplomat, but did not have any experience in the Middle East. He made the decision, supported by President Bush, to disband the Iraqi army, even though military leaders wanted to make the Iraqi troops into a security force. The dismissed soldiers ended up fighting in the insurgency, creating more problems for the American military. Instead of military reinforcements, private contractors like Blackwater were brought in to fight against the insurgents. The result was that there was no legal oversight and no code of military justice, which enabled the contractors to shoot at anyone they desired. Even in the military, discipline was hard to maintain, and shocking revelations came out when it was found that the guards of Abu-Ghraib prison were using the prisoners for their own sado-masochistic amusement. Stories of prisoner abuse came out of Guantanamo Bay, and later there would be reports of CIA torture

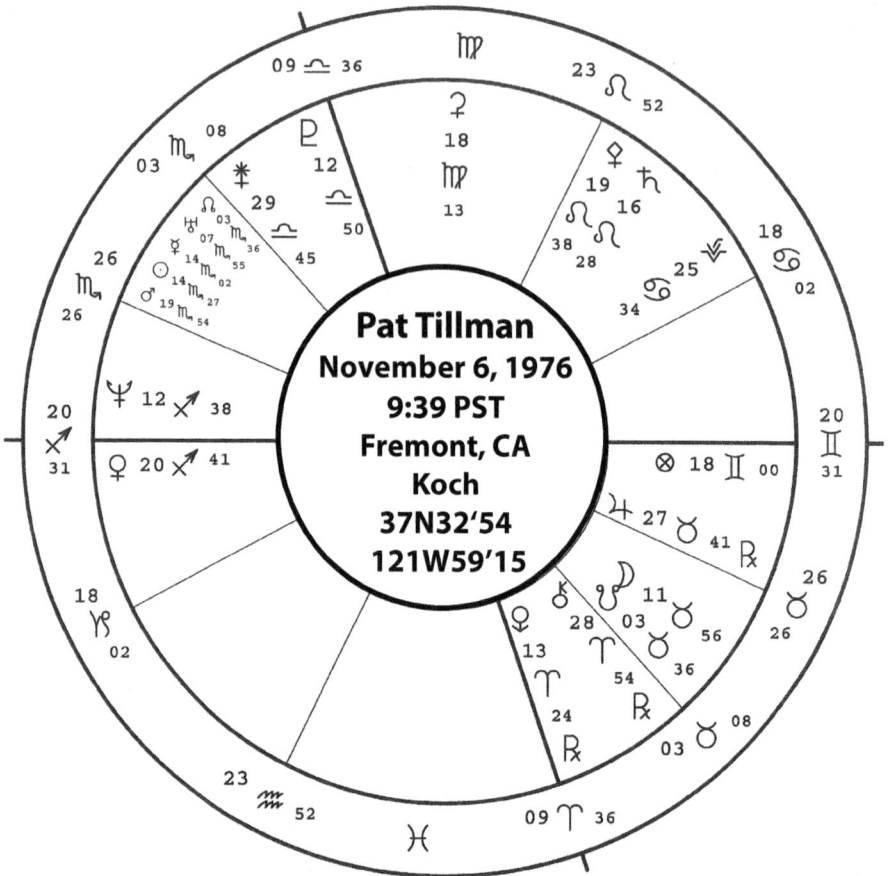

Pat Tillman
November 6, 1976
9:39 PST
Fremont, CA
Koch
37N32'54
121W59'15

Pat Tillman

(though they called it "enhanced interrogation.")

Attempts were made to set up an Iraqi government to take control of the country. Leaders of the Iraqi expatriate movement were brought in as consultants. Yet, there was a major scandal when it was discovered that one of the leaders, Ahmed Chalabi was working as a spy for Iran. It raised a question as to whether Chalabi was operating for the interests of Iran in getting the United States to depose Saddam Hussein. A destabilized Iraq would benefit Iran, and there was a possibility the Shiite revolution could spread there.

The only good news to come out of Iraq was the shooting of Saddam Hussein's sons, and finally the capture of Saddam Hussein himself, who was found lurking in an underground lair on December 13, 2003. He was put into prison, guarded by American soldiers, and questioned by the FBI. It was found that Saddam Hussein had spent most of his time writing trashy novels rather than planning terrorist attacks against the United States. Saddam Hussein was later put on trial by an Iraqi tribunal, and put to death by hanging on Dec. 30, 2006.

Meanwhile, the war in Afghanistan became "the forgotten war" as most of the military was engaged in Iraq. The world got a shocking reminder of the Afghan War on April 22, 2004, when Army Ranger Pat Tillman was killed. At first, the military said he had been killed by the enemy, but a month later the story changed and it was revealed that he had been killed by "friendly fire." The death started a series of investigations, some of which hinted at sinister motives for the cover-up.

Pat Tillman was born with Eris opposing Pluto, an aspect which was seen during the upheaval in Afghanistan in 1978. Eris was trine his Neptune and Saturn, while Pluto was sextile his Neptune and Saturn. Eris was also semi-sextile his Moon, and quincunx his Sun and Mercury. Tillman grew up with an intense devotion to his family, who were freethinkers and did not raise him with religious dogma. He also had a powerful love for football. In high school, he showed his championship skill, and helped bring Leland High School to the Central Coast Division Football Championship. From there he received a football scholarship to Arizona State University, where he excelled as a linebacker.

By 1998, as transiting Eris was sextile his Part of Fortune and quincunx his Ceres, Pat Tillman moved into the world of professional football. He joined the Arizona Cardinals, and moved to the position of safety. During his NFL career he made 238 tackles. He was making more than half a million dollars a year, and was ready to sign a contract for more than three million dollars when the 9-11 attacks made him reconsider his priorities. He gave up professional football to join the Army Rangers. Tillman enlisted in 2002 (along with his brother, Kevin) and underwent training in the Army Ranger indoctrination program in Fort Bening, GA. It was at this time that transiting Eris was trine Pat Tillman's Pallas and quincunx his Mars. Although his patriotism was applauded, there was a question as to whether he had made the right career decision.

In 2003, Pat Tillman was part of the invasion of Iraq, and he spent nearly six months in Iraq before being sent back to Fort Bening, GA for another Army Ranger course. It was during this time that Tillman expressed private doubts about the war in Iraq and whether it was necessary while the war in Afghanistan was going on. In 2004, he was redeployed to Afghanistan, when transiting Eris was trine his Ascendant and Venus. He was well aware of his notoriety, but even being a famed personality could not save his life. According to reports, when he was being shot by "friendly fire", he was screaming his name to the soldiers in an attempt to get them to stop.

Investigation revealed a cover-up attempt by some Army Rangers to conceal the fact that Tillman had been killed by his own troops. Tillman had died from three shots to the head. The Rangers burned his uniform and body armor to make it look like he had been in a more intense battle. Those responsible for the desecration were later dishonorably discharged from the Army Rangers. They even burned Tillman's private notebook, which may have contained his opinions about the war. Conspiracy theories were later put forward that Pat Tillman had been killed because he was going to speak out against the war, and he allegedly had an interview scheduled with an anti-war journalist for when he returned from Afghanistan.

A Congressional investigation was held into the circumstances of the death of Pat Tillman, and in 2008 it declared that a conclusion could not be reached due to the inability of personnel to recall the events. The only blame was that the Defense Department did not meet its obligations in providing accurate information to the Tillman family and the rest of the world. Supporters for the Tillman family still seek out the truth in the face of obfuscation. When political figures offered religious condolences for Pat Tillman, his brother, Richard, responded bluntly, "Thank you for your thoughts, but he's fucking dead!"

Stories of the incompetence in Iraq and Afghanistan were kept under wraps as the 2004 Presidential election approached. President Bush kept playing the warrior game by pointing out that Al-Qaeda was operating in Iraq, and it was better to attack them there than let them get to the United States. He sneered at the terrorists who were attacking American troops, making the statement of "Bring it on", although not thinking that he might be causing the deaths of Americans with his taunting. Bush mocked his Democratic opponent, John Kerry, as a flip-flopper, saying that he was "for the war before he was against it." Kerry was defeated by a slim margin of votes which carried the state of Ohio for Bush. To this day, there are still unresolved questions about the role played by electronic voting machines and whether the election was stolen.

In the second term of Bush, it was hoped that with new cabinet members there might be some improvement in the military situation. However, Bush's incompetence was exposed during the crisis caused by Hurricane Katrina, which resulted in the flooding of New Orleans. There was a lack of National Guard personnel to help the city because the National Guard units were fighting in Iraq. Bush's appointee to the Federal Emergency Management Agency, Michael Brown, was a political hack, who responded to the crisis with e-mail messages asking about the best places to eat in the area and making jokes about "drowning" with so much work. In spite of Brown's incompetence, Bush gave him a public show of support with the statement, "Brownie, you're doing a heck of a job." Brown's resignation in disgrace shortly afterward left Bush with egg on his face.

By 2006, as Eris and Pluto were separating from their trine, more people began to protest the management of the Iraq war. In particular, Donald Rumsfeld became a lightning rod for complaints. When asked by soldiers why they had not received the proper armor for their vehicles, Rumsfeld tried to blame it on the manufacturers, saying they did not have the means to produce more armor. The manufacturers responded, saying that they had been prepared to ramp up production by 22%, but no orders had been sent in. By the time of the mid-term elections in 2006, when transiting Eris was squaring his natal Pluto, Rumsfeld realized he had become a liability to the administration, and he sent in his resignation the day before the election. Bush did not formally accept the resignation until the day after the election, when the Democrats had already gained control of Congress. Some Republicans felt that the Rumsfeld resignation might have helped their chances in the election if announced earlier.

In 2006, author Gore Vidal was interviewed about the "War on Terror" and likened it to a "war on dandruff." At the time, there were threats about extending the war into Iran. Vidal was asked what it would take to prevent further war, and his response was a bit prescient:

"Economic collapse. We are too deeply in debt. We can't service the debt, or so my financial friends tell me, that's paying the interest on the Treasury bonds, particularly to the foreign countries that have been financing us."

Vidal's expectation of economic collapse came true in 2008, when Wall Street banks threatened to close. The Bush administration managed to get a government bail-out for the banks, which resulted in increasing the deficit. The new president, Barack Obama, had to deal with lowering the deficit, which his opponents blamed him for causing. No one blamed Bush for maxing out the government credit card, and whenever Bush's name was mentioned, Republicans would respond with the terse remark, "Bush isn't President anymore." In an odd sense, Bush became an "unperson", and while there were lavish praises for the days of Ronald Reagan, no Republican would mention Bush's name in a speech. (As for Bush himself, he retired to being an artist, doing paintings of various parts of his body.) President Obama moved troops out of Iraq, based on a timetable set by the Bush administration. A special mission was sent to kill Osama Bin Laden in Pakistan. Troops were sent to Afghanistan to help stabilize the situation in the forgotten war.

Some conservatives recently have made the suggestion that maybe it would have been better if the USA had not invaded Iraq. The most surprising statement came from Donald Rumsfeld, who expressed disagreement over George W. Bush's attempt to establish democracy in Iraq. With transiting Eris square his Pluto, Rumsfeld may be trying to resurrect his credibility, or perhaps trying to create a new reality. In 2002. Rumsfeld wrote a classified memo, encouraging the development of democracy in Iraq by organizing a political opposition to Communists, Shia militants, and Sunni fundamentalists. As it turned out, this opposition was ineffective, leading to more insurgency.

On October 17, 2004, the Sun was opposing Eris and sextile Pluto. Author Ron Suskind published a quote which became the explanation for the unrealistic and implausible policies for the "War on Terror." Quoting a White House aide (who may have been Karl Rove), Suskind wrote:

The aide said that guys like me were "in what we call the reality-based community," which he defined as people who "believe that solutions emerge from your judicious study of discernible reality."... "That's not the way the world really works anymore," he continued. "We're an empire now, and when we act, we create our own reality. And while you're studying that reality—judiciously, as you will—we'll act again, creating other new realities, which you can study too, and that's how things will sort out. We're history's actors...and you, all of you, will be left to just study what we do.

Of course, the aide failed to take into account that even "history's actors" can deliver a bad performance, and that people will be shocked by a presentation that delivers torture, mutilation, and death without some resolution. By the time the curtain came down on the Bush administration, the USA was left with the reality that Pat Tillman and thousands of other Americans were dead, more than a hundred thousand Iraqis were dead,

Iraq had not recovered as a nation, and the American economy was near collapse.

As of this writing, the war on terror has moved into Syria, with Al-Qaeda helping rebels against the repressive government of President Assad. Recently, an extremist faction broke away from Al-Qaeda, calling itself ISIS, and performing acts of terror even against Al-Qaeda members. The United States has made ISIS the main focus of attacks in Syria, which ironically gives aid and comfort to the former terrorist enemy, Al-Qaeda. It is enough to make one wonder, "who did win that war on terror?"

Bibliography - Chapter 24
Internet Sources

Aftermath of the Gulf War
http://www.indepthinfo.com/iraq/aftermath.shtml

Iraq chemical weapons
http://www.pbs.org/wgbh/pages/frontline/shows/unscom/experts/defectors.html

Rumsfeld autobiography review
http://www.theguardian.com/world/2011/feb/08/donald-rumsfeld-book-misstatements-wmd

Bush Senior Assassination Plot
http://www.huffingtonpost.com/2008/03/25/pentagon-report-shows-no-_n_93264.html

Saddam Hussein on 9-11
http://edition.cnn.com/2001/WORLD/meast/10/20/gen.iraq.letter/

Weapons of Mass Destruction in Iraq
http://nsarchive.gwu.edu/NSAEBB/NSAEBB80/

Intelligence Failures
http://prospect.org/waldman/myth-faulty-intelligence

Axis of Evil
https://en.wikipedia.org/wiki/Axis_of_evil

Misrepresentations About Saddam
http://www.wnd.com/2003/10/21119/

Colin Powell's UN Speech
http://www.cnn.com/2003/US/02/05/sprj.irq.powell.transcript/

Curveball
https://en.wikipedia.org/wiki/Curveball_(informant)

Ahmed Chalabi
https://en.wikipedia.org/wiki/Ahmed_Chalabi

Attacks on Joseph Wilson
https://consortiumnews.com/2015/08/16/neocons-to-americans-trust-us-again/

Valerie Plame Exposure
http://en.wikipedia.org/wiki/Plame_affair

Rumsfeld's Rhetorical Questions

274.   Brother Pluto, Sister Eris

http://rhetorica.net/archives/5733.html

Animal Crackers Review
https://www.youtube.com/watch?v=pdp7LKp796o

Rumsfeld Memos
http://gawker.com/5766225/the-pentagon-papers-that-donald-rumsfeld-doesnt-want-you-to-see/all

What Rumsfeld knew we didn't know about Iraq
http://www.politico.com/magazine/story/2016/01/iraq-war-wmds-donald-rumsfeld-new-report-213530#ixzz3yHs17C9e

Rumsfeld contradicted by Humvee manufacturers
http://www.seattlepi.com/national/article/Humvee-makers-dispute-Rumsfeld-remarks-1161662.php

Bush Senior criticizes Cheney and Rumsfeld
http://www.theguardian.com/us-news/2015/nov/05/george-bush-senior-iron-ass-cheney-arrogant-rumsfeld-damaged-america

Hurricane Katrina Criticism
http://en.wikipedia.org/wiki/Criticism_of_government_response_to_Hurricane_Katrina

Gore Vidal Interview
https://www.sharedhost.progressive.org/gore_vidal.html

Chemical Weapons in Iraq
http://www.nytimes.com/2014/10/24/world/middleeast/questions-answers-abandoned-chemical-weapons-in-iraq.html?_r=0

Iraq Study Group Report
http://en.wikipedia.org/wiki/Iraq_Study_Group

Dismissing the Iraqi Army
http://www.nytimes.com/2008/03/17/world/middleeast/17bremer.html

US Army Report on Iraq
http://www.theguardian.com/world/2008/jun/30/iraq.usforeignpolicy

Iraqi Reconstruction
http://usatoday30.usatoday.com/news/world/iraq/2007-04-29-us-funded-projects_N.htm

Reconstruction Failures in Iraq
http://pogoblog.typepad.com/pogo/2012/01/interview-foreign-service-officer-peter-van-buren-on-reconstruction-failures-in-iraq.html

Iraq Reconstruction Corruption and Waste
http://www.huffingtonpost.com/2013/03/06/iraq-reconstruction_n_2819899.html

Iraq Occupation Embarrassments
http://www.businessinsider.com/l-paul-bremer-was-embarrassed-on-first-and-last-days-in-iraq-2014-8

Abu Ghraib Torture
https://en.wikipedia.org/wiki/Abu_Ghraib_torture_and_prisoner_abuse

Iraqi munitions raided
http://www.nytimes.com/2004/10/25/international/middleeast/25bomb.html?_r=0

Blackwater
https://en.wikipedia.org/wiki/Academi

Rumsfeld 9-10-2001 speech
http://www.agovernmentofthepeople.com/2001/09/10/donald-rumsfeld-speech-about-bureaucratic-waste/

Pat Tillman
http://en.wikipedia.org/wiki/Pat_Tillman

2004 Election questions
https://en.wikipedia.org/wiki/2004_United_States_election_voting_controversies

Hurricane Katrina
https://en.wikipedia.org/wiki/Hurricane_Katrina

George W. Bush as an "Unperson".
http://www.huffingtonpost.com/2012/08/29/george-w-bush-republican-convention_n_1838248.html

Donald Rumsfeld on Democracy in Iraq
http://www.huffingtonpost.com/2015/06/09/woodward-rumsfeld-iraq_n_7543660.html

Rumsfeld Disagrees With Bush
http://www.msnbc.com/msnbc/donald-rumsfeld-george-w-bush-was-wrong-about-iraq

Rumsfeld Grilled on "Unknown Knowns"
https://www.rawstory.com/2016/01/stephen-colbert-makes-donald-rumsfeld-squirm-until-he-nearly-admits-iraq-war-was-a-mistake/

Art Work of George W. Bush

http://www.huffingtonpost.com/2013/02/08/george-bush-
selportrait_n_2648021.html

Reality Based Community
https://en.wikipedia.org/wiki/Reality-based_community

Book Sources

Bowden, Mark, *The Finish: The Killing of Osama Bin Laden,* Atlantic Monthly Press, New York, NY, 2012.

Carroll, James, *Crusade: Chronicles of an Unjust War,* Metropolitan Books, Henry Holt and Company, New York, 2004.

Chandrasekaran, Rajiv, *Imperial Life in the Emerald City:* **Inside Iraq's Green Zone**, Alfred A. Knopf, New York, NY, 2006

Goodman, Amy & Goodman, David, Static: *Government Liars, Media Cheerleaders, and the People who Fight Back,* Hyperion Books, New York, NY, 2006.

Hersh, Seymour M., Chain of Command: *The Road from 9/11,* Abu Ghraib, Allen Lane/Penguin Group, New York, NY, 2004.

Kegley, Charles W. (Editor), *The New Global Terrorism*: Characteristic, Causes, Controls, Prentice Hall, Upper Saddle River, NJ, 2003.

Miles, Steven H. (M.D.), *Oath Betrayed: Torture, Medical Complicity, and the War on Terror,* Random House, New York, NY, 2006.

Pitt, William Rivers & Ritter, Scott, *War on Iraq: What Team Bush Doesn't Want You to Know,* Context Books, New York, NY, 2002.

Weiss, Michael & Hassan, Hassan, Isis: *Inside the Army of Terror,* Regan Arts, New York, NY, 2015.

Westwood, John, *The History of the Middle East Wars,* World Publications Group, Inc. North Dighton, MA, 2002.

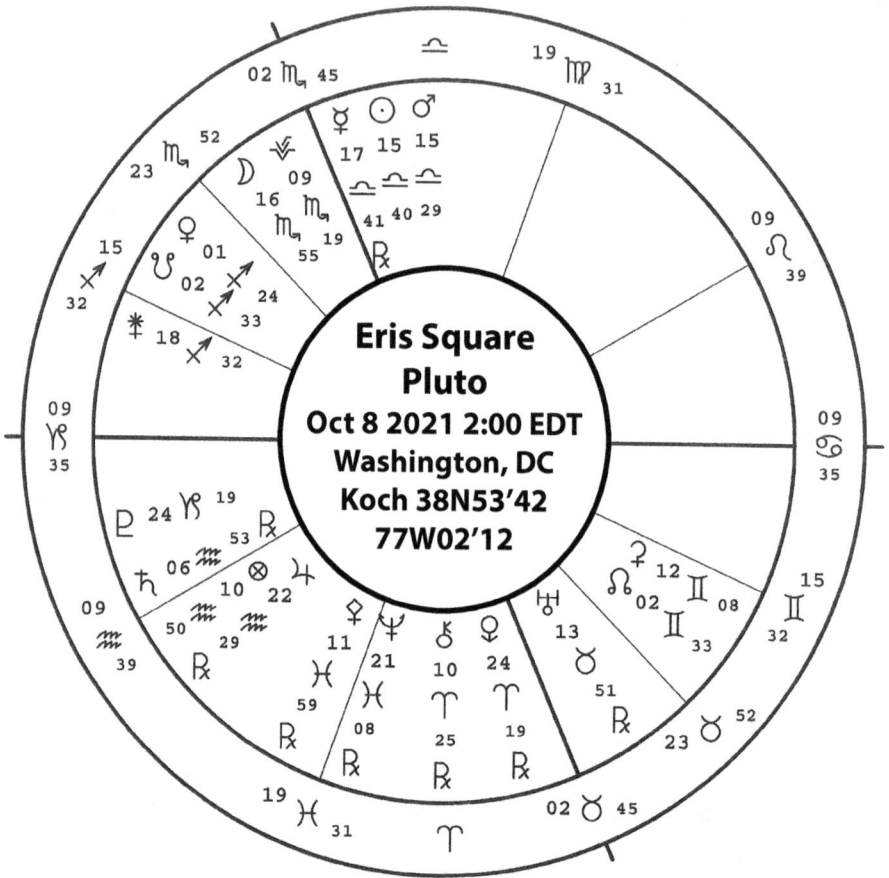

Eris Square
Pluto
Oct 8 2021 2:00 EDT
Washington, DC
Koch 38N53'42
77W02'12

Chapter 25

Conclusion—

1.   2021—Eris square Pluto

In the past 700 years, there have been just three Eris/Pluto squares. One common theme that came out of them was an event (or series of events) that "seemed like a good idea at the time", but ended up with unexpected results and long-lasting consequences:

In 1431, the burning of Joan of Arc was seen by the English as removing a charismatic figure in order to demoralize the French. What they did not expect was that they would make her into a martyr, a national heroine, and a Roman Catholic saint, and it was her sacrifice that inspired the French to kick out the English forces within 20 years.

In 1536, the Pilgrimage of Grace was an attempt to force the Protestant King Henry VIII into restoring the rights of Roman Catholics. The result was a persecution of Catholics, and an enmity toward Catholics by the monarchs of England, which lasted nearly 400 years.

In 1905, the diplomacy of Theodore Roosevelt ended the Russo-Japanese War, and subsequent diplomacy would end the Pig War, the Italo-Libyan War, and the two Balkan wars. Yet, nothing was done to end the increased militarism and ruthless competition between nations, which would erupt in World War One.

In 2021, Eris and Pluto will be square once again, and it could mark events that may seem like a good idea at the time, but which may end up as provoking a major backlash. It could be changes to the Constitution, or Supreme Court decisions that cause upheaval.

Possibly it could be a peace agreement, which may relieve the United States from involvement in the Middle East, which has been on-going since the time of the Eris-Pluto opposition in 1978. For more militant groups, both within the USA and without, the results of the peace might not be satisfying, and it could result in a new Cold War, with various factions making attacks instead of a large scale national war.

Another possibility, with Eris sextile Jupiter in the 2021 chart, is that there could be a trade agreement, which may satisfy the people in charge, but may not be satisfying for the general public.

After this square, Pluto will be moving into Aquarius, and the last time it was in that sign was during the American Revolution. Adding to the potential upheaval is that the United States will be experiencing its third Uranus return in 2027. Whatever agreement is made in 2021 may be the kindling for the later conflagration. It may not be a full-scale revolution, but a breaking apart of factions, possibly stirring up discontent and civil disobedience for the sake of working against the government.

Also in the chart for 2021 is that Eris will be semi-sextile Neptune, and it is possible that religious groups may play a major part in opposing any agreements. Certain churches do have a paranoid attitude against "world government", thinking that it will usher in the reign of the Antichrist. An international agreement, possibly brokered by the United Nations, may stir up those irrational fancies.

At the time of the 2027 Uranus return, there will be a Grand Trine in Air with Uranus, Pluto, and Mars. Neptune in Aries, opposing Mars, will be at the focal point of a Kite formation, suggesting that irrational Neptune might be playing a part in spurring on the upheavals.

2.   2042—Eris sextile Pluto

You know those bomb shelters that your great-great-grandparents built during the Cold War? Yeah, those funny structures in the back yard and in the basements of government buildings? Well, you might want to clean them up and put them to use. Put in some beds, chairs, and tables, if there is room. Be sure to stock up on bottled water, canned food, and a can-opener. A source of heat, like a woodstove, might not be a bad idea. It also might be a good idea to update those civil defense manuals.

It may seem totally pessimistic but history has shown that Eris/Pluto sextiles can be times of major loss of life, as was seen during the Sack of Haridwar, when the Ganges River ran red with the blood of 60,000 bodies. The Siege of Malta was less bloody, but it did mark the beginning of the end for the Ottoman Empire's naval power. The Glorious Revolution and Queen Anne's War marked 25 years of European warfare, which spilled over into the American colonies. The worst sextile may have been the decade that saw the Crimean War, the Taiping Rebellion, and the American Civil War, a time when warfare itself underwent major technological changes.

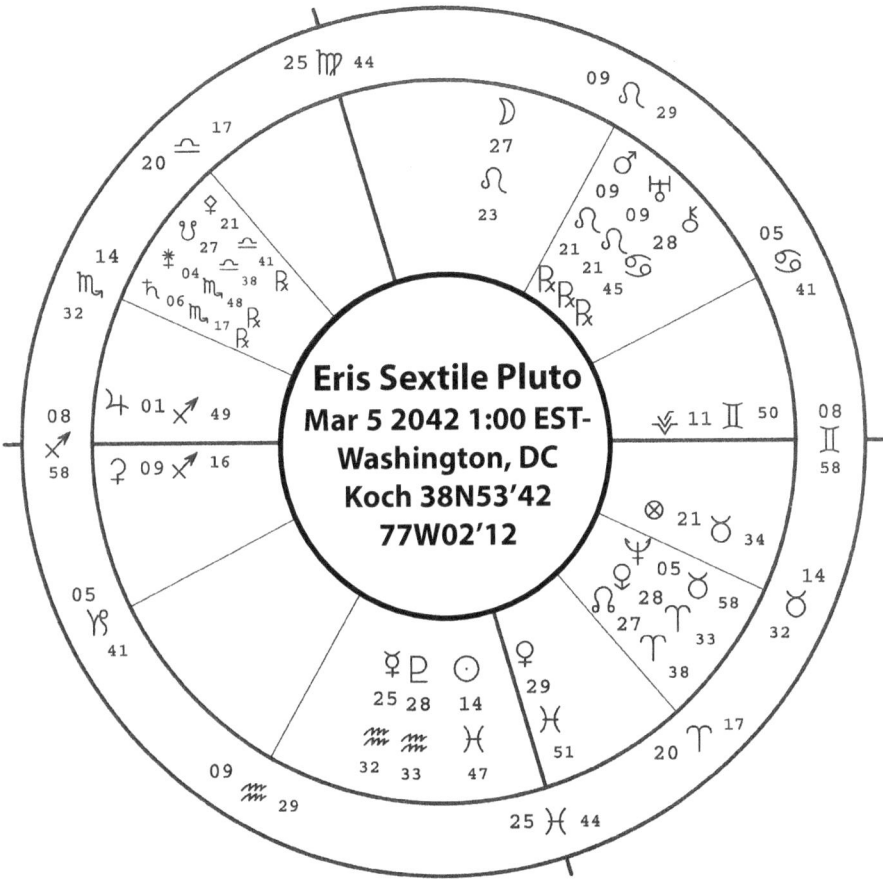

Eris Sextile Pluto
Mar 5 2042 1:00 EST-
Washington, DC
Koch 38N53'42
77W02'12

The upcoming conflict may last until 2046. The final resolution may come once Eris moves into Taurus. In the past, Eris moving into Taurus marked collapse of a great power, and a power vacuum filled by newcomers. The last time Eris went into Taurus was in 1519, when Cortez arrived in Mexico and brought about the end of the Aztec civilization, with the help of horses, smallpox, and Aztec mythology. It was also a time when the spark of the Protestant Reformation was lit by Martin Luther, which would end centuries of Roman Catholic spiritual domination.

About 550 years before that, the Norsemen had created a power vacuum in Western Europe, which they filled by creating the Duchy of Normandy on the coast of France. The Normans would eventually go on to conquer England, and set themselves up as the ruling class.

About 550 years before the Duchy of Normandy, the Goths, Visigoths, and Huns were battering at the remains of the Roman Empire, to bring about its final collapse. Also, Christianity was made the state religion of Rome, bringing about the end of "Paganism."

About 550 years earlier, the Roman legions were conquering Greece, and the other city states of Italy, breaking the power of local kingdoms to make their empire.

Do you get the picture? Outside pressure was placed on kingdoms which were already weakening within. I am not going to speculate which empire might fall in the 2040's, but it may not even be by an earthly power. If ever the Klingons are going to attack Earth, the timing of Eris going into Taurus may mark their effort. This is not to say they would be successful. Perhaps resistance would lead to a Klingon collapse. Sometimes it is the strongest empire that succumbs to the up-and-coming contender. Consider it hubris, or underestimating the resources of their opponents, overconfidence may lead to a destruction of the bigger state.

3. 2074—Eris semi-sextile Pluto

In the past, Eris semi-sextile Pluto has marked strange wars and unusual victories. The battle of Crecy saw the use of new weapons which would do away with the medieval methods of warfare, particularly by the use of cannons on the battlefield. The Thirty Years War started as a local religious conflict, but ended up bringing in the major countries of Europe, resulting in a shift in the power structure from the Southern European Catholic states to the Northern European Protestant states. The War of Polish Succession brought in outside political forces, and much of the war was fought in Italy instead of Poland. The French Revolutionary Wars saw the rise of Napoleon Bonaparte, and presented a war based on political ideology rather than religious or military motivations.

In the 2070's, this aspect will be returning again, and with some interesting companions. Jupiter in Leo will be trine Pluto and square Eris in Taurus. Uranus in Capricorn will be square Pluto and trine Eris. On the day of the exact aspect, the Moon will be conjunct Eris, bringing up deep, emotional stuff.

Uranus in Capricorn will be at the point of natal Eris in the USA chart. That aspect first happened in 1823, when President James Monroe and Secretary of State John Quincy Adams were preparing the "Monroe Doctrine," which set the American foreign policy to "protecting" the nations of this hemisphere from European intrusion. The Uranus return to the USA Eris point again was in the early 20th Century, just as President Theodore Roosevelt was implementing his "Big Stick" policy towards Latin American nations. In 1990, Uranus returned to the Eris point again, just in time for the Gulf War. This third aspect may have been an indicator

Eris Semi-
Sextile Pluto
Feb 3 2074 3:07 EST
Washingon, DC
Koch 38N53'42
77W02'12

that the United States was expanding its power into global conflicts, and maybe the Monroe Doctrine applied to the whole world. Perhaps with Uranus on the USA Eris point again, it may be that all of the countries "helped" by the USA over the past 200 years may want some retribution.

Coming up at this time will be the Tricentennial of the United States, and the USA may be on a war-time footing as preparations are being made to celebrate. Saturn rising in the chart of the semi-sextile may be an indication that only old-fashioned values may be appreciated. Saturn is forming a Grand Trine with Jupiter and Pluto, suggesting that the conflict may begin from a position of strength.

Yet, with Juno opposing Neptune, and both squaring Chiron, there may be problems with alliances, particularly over religious and moral issues. Self-righteous attitudes and fixed concepts may be in for an upheaval, or it may be a time of national questioning and an evaluation of the country's past. People may debate over what sort of nation the USA should be as the third century is coming to a close, and the fourth century is beginning.

4. 2115—Eris conjunct Pluto

The last two Eris/Pluto conjunctions were times of international upheaval. The Templars lost their order due to the collusion between the King of France and the Pope at Avignon. Although they lost their property and lives, they did become the leading secret society for conspiracy theory fiction, and were supposedly the spiritual ancestors of the Freemasons. By the 1750's, the rise of the Freemasons in England and other Protestant nations took a karmic twist with the Seven Years War against France. This time it was France on the losing side, and forced to give up most of her international empire.

Jupiter is rising in the Eris/Pluto conjunction chart for 2115, and might mark a time of new prosperity. The Eris/Pluto conjunction is semi-sextile the Sun and Chiron, trine the Moon, and quincunx Neptune. New ideas may be promoted which may upset feelings and bring a change in the world outlook, as well as religious and medical values. Neptune opposing Saturn could be a complete break with the past in regard to spiritual matters. Saturn and Uranus are forming a Yod pointing at the South Node. The technology of Uranus combined with the organization of Saturn could be a point of material advancement.

One thing science fiction writers have been speculating on is the concept of Technological Singularity, in which a day will come when artificial intelligence will advance beyond human intelligence, leading to a time when machines could wipe out human beings. Another variation on the singularity theme is also a time when human beings may be able to transfer their intelligence to machines, and thereby attain a new form of afterlife. These are two of the fantasy nightmares for the future, and the question then arises as to whether we would have machines of superior intelligence fighting against machines containing human intelligence?

Keep in mind that treachery was a major theme during the last two Eris/Pluto conjunctions. The Templars lost their order because of the treachery of the King of France. During the years of the 1750's, there was a generation of treacherous revolutionaries born, represented by men such as Danton, Robespierre, Barras, Talleyrand, and Fouche. The United States saw its own version of power-hungry giants in the forms of Alexander Hamilton and Aaron Burr, who ended up on the dueling grounds together.

The coming conjunction may bring forth another generation, but their power schemes may be directed into new areas of technology. Instead of the guillotine, perhaps they might even find a way to obliterate the soul of man.

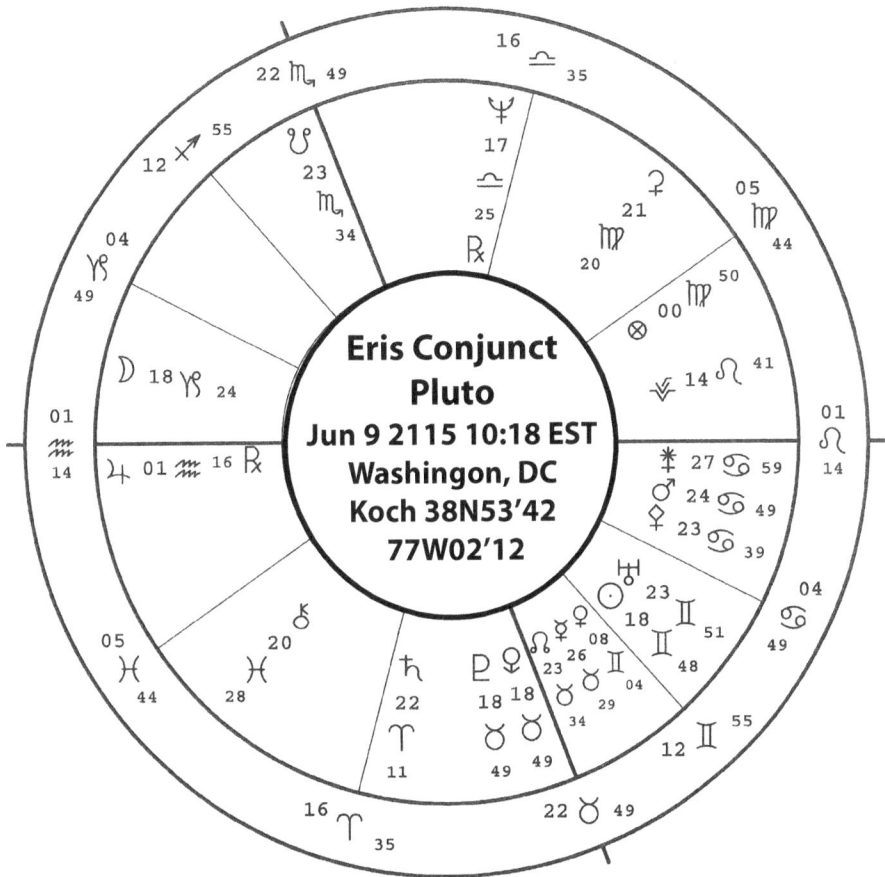

Eris Conjunct Pluto
Jun 9 2115 10:18 EST
Washingon, DC
Koch 38N53'42
77W02'12

So, to those in the 22nd century, it may be wise to take a look back on the times of Eris and Pluto, and watch how those periods played out in power and personal struggles. It was once thought the Templars were the best and most powerful group in Christendom, but their fortune was wiped out during the seven years of the Eris/Pluto conjunction.

In the 1750's, France was regarded as one of the most powerful empires in the world, but within seven years her fortunes declined dramatically.

Whatever institutions or organizations may seem to be a mainstay in the 22nd Century, do not be overconfident that they will be around forever. If there is one message that needs to be passed on to the next century it is the cautionary warning of...

"WATCH YOUR BACK!"

INDEX

A

AARP 263
Abercrombie, British General 142
Abu-Ghraib 267
Adams, John 162-163,
Adams, John Quincy 161, 282
Addington, Henry 159
Afghanistan 35, 233-242, 256, 260, 269-270
Africa 80, 213,214,260
Alexander I, Czar of Russia 164, 167
Alexander II, Czar of Russia 192
Alexander VI, Borgia Pope 46, 64
Alexandra (Czarina) of Hesse-Darmstadt 192
Al-Qaeda 6, 242, 260, 272-273
Al-Sabah 249-250
American Colonies 86, 114, 118, 123-124, 137-144,
American Revolution 86-87, 148
Amin, Hafizullah 238-241
Andros, Sir Edmund, 114. 118
Animal Farm 219
Anne, Queen of England 121-123, 125
Anne Boleyn 84
Anne of Cleves 87
Anne de Beaujeau (Regent of France) 61-62
Anne (Duchess of Brittany, later Queen Anne of France) 62-64
Ancona 51
Aphrodite 7
Aquitaine 27
Ares/Mars 7
Arthur, Prince of Wales 83
Aske, Robert 85
Asteroids 9
Astro Computing Services 9
Athena 7
Athens 49-51
Atta, Mohammed 260
Auchinleck, Field Marshal 214
Augustus II, King of Poland 130-131

Augustus III, King of Poland (Gus) 131-133
Austria 23, 62-64, 99-108, 131-133, 146, 152, 174-175, 197-200, 204, 206
Avignon 19
Axis of Evil 261
Ayutthaya 96
Aztecs 80

B

Bache, Benjamin Franklin 161-163
Baghdad 36, 38, 266
Baghdad Bob 266
Balkan League 198
Banking Collapse (2008) 6, 271
Baphomet 19
Barbarosa, Operation 38
Barras, Paul 153, 167
Battle Hymn of the Republic 185
Battle of Britain 208
Battle of Jena 196
Bay of Pigs 220, 221
Bayinnong, King of Siam 96
Beatrice 23
Beirut 245
Belarus 74
Ben-Gurion, David 222-223
Benedict XI, Pope 19
Berlin Wall 6, 221
Bethien, Gabriel 101
Bin-Laden, Osama 242, 256, 260, 261, 272
Bismarck, Otto Von 185, 195, 196, 200
Blackbeard (Edward Teach) 124
Black Death (Bubonic Plague) 31-32
Black Guard 69, 71-72
Blackwater 267
Boccaccio, Giovanni 22, 23, 38
Boer War 196
Bohemia, Kingdom of 99-101
Boniface VIII, Pope 19
Boxer Rebellion 196
Braun, Eva 203, 210

Braveheart (film) 27
Bremer, L. Paul 267
Brezhnev, Leonid 239-240
Brienne-le-chateau 155
Brittany 62-64
Brown, Dan (author) 23
Brown, John 183-185
Brown, Michael (astronomer) 8
Brown, Michael (FEMA) 270-271
Bulge, Battle of 210, 213
Burr, Aaron 148
Burma 96
Burney, Venetia 4
Bush, George H.W. 254-255, 259, 263, 265
Bush, George W. 259-260, 264, 265, 270-272

C
Calixtus III, Pope 45
Calvinism 99, 106
Cambodia 96
Cambridge 157
Caribbean 80
Carlucci, Frank 263
Carter, Jimmy President 235
Casmir (King of Lithuania) 57
Catherine of Aragon 83-84
Catherine of Braganza 107
Catherine (the Great), Czarina of Russia 164-165
Catherine Howard 87
Catherine Parr 87
Ceres (dwarf planet) 9
Ceres square Chiron 106
Chalabi, Ahmed 267
Chamberlain, Neville 206
Charles I, King of England 106, 107, 112, 115
Charles II, King of England 107-108, 112
Charles II, King of Spain 120
Charles V, Holy Roman Emperor 84
Charles VII, King of Sweden 41-42, 44, 129
Charles VIII, King of France 61-64
Charles XII, King of Sweden 126

Charlie Wilson's War 241
Chaucer, Geoffrey 38
Cheney, Dick 254, 260, 264, 267
China 38, 80
Christian IV, King of Denmark 101
Christina, Queen of Sweden 104
Church, Benjamin 124
Churchill, Sarah 122
Churchill, Winston 137, 213, 220
Civil War (USA) 6, 11, 171, 180-186
Clay, Henry 183
Clement V, Pope (Raymond Bertrand de Got) 19, 20, 22
Clinton, Bill 259
Cold War 5, 220, 215
Columbus 17
Constantinople 49, 50 77
Cortez, Hernando 80
Council of Mantua 50
Council of Vienne 21
Crecy, Battle of 27, 29-31
Cromwell, Oliver 107, 115
Cuba 220, 221
Curies, Marie & Pierre 36
Curveball 260

D
D-Day 6, 210, 213
D'Abret, Alain 62
Danzig 206
Dante 23
Da Vinci Code (novel) 23
Dayan, Moshe 214
De Bourienne, Louis 155
De Valette, Jean Parisot 92-93, 94
Decameron 32
Defenestration of Prague 100-101
Delhi , Battle of   35-36
Demeter/Ceres 2
DeMolay, Jacques 20-22
Denis, King of Portugal 21
Denmark 69-72, 101, 106, 126, 186

De Payens, Hugues 17
Diem, President 224
Dithmarschen 69, 71-72, 186
Djerba, Battle of 91-93
Don Garcia, Viceroy of Sicily 95
Douglas, Stephen 183
"Dwarf" Planet 9
Dysnomia ((Moon of Eris) 9

E

Ecole Militaire 155
Edison, Thomas 36
Edward I, King of England 27
Edward II, King of England 27
Edward III, King of England 26, 27-32
Edward the Black Prince 32
Eisenhower, Dwight 213, 214, 220
Elizabeth I, Queen of England 84, 93
Elizabeth, Czarina of Russian 164
England 27-32, 41-46. 49, 83-88, 105-106, 107, 111-126, 137-143, 157-
159, 174-179, 206-215, 265
English Longbow 30
Eris conjunct Ceres 214
Eris conjunct Chiron 63, 84, 164,194, 236
Eris conjunct Jupiter 105, 131 159,
Eris conjunct Mars 115, 196, 233-234
Eris conjunct Mercury 235-236
Eris conjunct Midheaven 121
Eris conjunct Moon 156, 194, 282
Eris conjunct Neptune 171, 196,
Eris conjunct North Node 132
Eris conjunct Pallas 92, 132, 238
Eris conjunct Pluto 12, 17-23, 28, 137-148, 153, 284-285
Eris conjunct Saturn 115, 165, 228
Eris conjunct South Node 157
Eris conjunct Uranus 142
Eris conjunct Venus 101
Eris conjunct Vesta 44, 181, 236
Eris opposing Chiron 152
Eris opposing Juno 78, 203
Eris opposing Jupiter 123

Eris opposing Mars 210
Eris opposing Mercury 124, 156
Eris opposing Midheaven 156, 264
Eris opposing Moon 157, 263
Eris opposing Neptune 50, 140, 145, 219
Eris opposing Pallas 105, 123
Eris opposing Pluto 13, 61-65, 235, 264, 269
Eris opposing Saturn 156, 161
Eris opposing Sun 272
Eris opposing Venus 155, 157, 161, 214
Eris opposing Vesta 157
Eris quincunx Ceres 112, 155, 161, 269
Eris quincunx Juno 28, 238
Eris quincunx Jupiter 182, 185, 226, 234
Eris quincunx Mars 156, 269
Eris quincunx Moon 159
Eris quincunx Mercury 155, 161, 269
Eris quincunx Neptune 58, 107, 132, 140, 157, 220-221, 253
Eris quincunx Pallas 155, 161, 178, 236
Eris quincunx Part of Fortune 157, 177
Eris quincunx Pluto 55-58, 69-72, 219-229, 245-256
Eris quincunx Saturn 185, 194
Eris quincunx South Node 155
Eris quincunx Sun 157, 161, 269
Eris quincunx Uranus 203, 227, 235
Eris quincunx Venus 156
Eris quincunx Vesta 140, 155, 161, 225
Eris semi-sextile Ascendant 185
Eris semi-sextile Ceres 94, 194
Eris semi-sextile Chiron 238
Eris semi-sextile Eris 105
Eris semi-sextile Juno 140, 210
Eris semi-sextile Jupiter 63, 87, 173, 177, 179, 203-204
Eris semi-sextile Mercury 94, 178, 181, 266
Eris semi-sextile Mars 72, 182, 194
Eris semi-sextile Moon 192, 269
Eris sem-sextile Neptune 87, 192
Eris semi-sextile North Node 178
Eris semi-sextile Pallas 94, 173, 181,185, 212, 253, 266
Eris semi-sextile Pluto 12, 27-33, 99-108,

129-135, 151-167, 173, 282-283
Eris semi-sextile Sun 173, 204, 246
Eris semi-sextile Uranus 174, 246
Eris semi-sextile Venus 84, 131
Eris semi-sextile Vesta 194
Eris sextile Ascendant 166
Eris sextile Ceres 28, 146, 173, 197, 238
Eris sextile Chiron 112, 115, 131, 155, 161, 174, 252
Eris sextile Juno 161, 181, 224, 236
Eris sextile Jupiter 83, 155, 161, 236, 238, 280
Eris sextile Mars 115, 143, 203, 263
Eris sextile Mercury 58, 143, 174, 177, 181, 185
Eris sextile Midheaven 118, 158
Eris sextile Moon 173, 178, 222
Eris sextile Neptune 177, 182, 204, 212, 249
Eris sextile North Node 252
Eris sextile Pallas 129, 196, 246
Eris sextile Part of Fortune 156, 269
Eris sextile Pluto 13, 35-38, 91-96, 111-126, 172-186, 192, 207, 212, 222,
280-282
Eris sextile Saturn 157, 263
Eris sextile Sun 116, 178, 222
Eris sextile Uranus 72, 159, 177, 197
Eris sextile Venus 140, 152, 182, 185, 203, 266
Eris sextile Vesta 115, 179, 197, 203
Eris square Ceres 140, 152, 242, 252
Eris square Chiron 212, 266
Eris square Eris 116
Eris square Juno 87
Eris square Jupiter 58, 101, 103, 140, 156, 282
Eris square Mars 124, 140, 165, 173
Eris square Mercury 87, 116, 227, 234
Eris-Pluto square Midheaven-Uranus 28
Eris square Moon 112 , 177, 210, 212
Eris square Neptune 115, 226, 254
Eris square Nodes 224, 236
Eris square Pallas 58, 83, 116, 205, 250
Eris square Part of Fortune 205, 252
Eris square Pluto 13 41-46, 83-88, 140,191-200, 234, 236, 271, 279-280,
Eris square Saturn 58, 87, 94, 103, 152, 183, 250

Eris square Sun 140, 165, 177, 182, 225
Eris square Uranus 83, 115, 124, 140, 156, 157, 227
Eris square Venus 46, 63, 115, 116, 196, 222, 250 263
Eris square Vesta 177, 238, 247
Eris trine Ascendant 87, 214, 252, 269
Eris trine Ceres 87, 115, 116, 118, 159, 204, 222, 250
Eris trine Chiron 116, 210, 222
Eris trine Juno 143, 194, 222
Eris trine Jupiter 45, 116, 165, 185, 210
Eris trine Mars 155, 157, 161, 246
Eris trine Mercury 105, 159, 212, 238, 263
Eris trine Midheaven 181, 207
Eris trine Moon 94, 196
Eris trine Neptune 45, 83, 133, 155, 161, 235-236, 269
Eris trine North Node 203, 247 269
Eris trine Pallas 124, 140, 157, 225, 264, 269
Eris trine Part of Fortune 166,173, 182
Eris trine Pluto 13, 49-51, 77-80, 116, 203-215
Eris trine Saturn 87, 181, 213, 219 236 269
Eris trine Sun 212, 234, 238
Eris trine Uranus 155, 192, 282
Eris trine Venus 107, 178, 192, 225, 236, 252, 269
Eris trine Vesta 165, 222
Eris/Vesta opposing Juno 44
Eris in Astrology 9-14,
Eris Mythology 2, 6-7
Eris/Planet 8-9

F

Falwell, Jerry 226-227
Ferdinand II, Holy Roman Emperor 99, 106
Ferdinand III, Holy Roman Emperor 106-107
Finland 122
First Crusade 17
Fleury, Andre-Hercule Cardinal 132
Fort Stewart 253
Fortress of Saint Elmo 92-94
Fouche, Joseph 153
Fox, Charles 157, 159
France 17-23, 27-32, 41-46, 51, 59-63, 99-105, 116, 124, 129-133,
137-143, 151-167, 174-177, 191, 197, 208, 223

Francis (Duke of Brittany) 62-63
Franklin, Benjamin 161, 162
Franklin, Deborah Read 161
Franz Joseph, Emperor of Austria 197
Frederick II, King of Denmark 72
Frederick the Great, King of Prussia 144-147,196

G

Gabrielle (sidekick to Xena) 8
Ganges River 36
Garbo, Greta 104
Gay Liberation 5
G.D. Searle 264
General Investment Corp. 264
Genoa 30, 38, 95
George II, King of Great Britain 132, 142-143
George III, King of Great Britain 157, 159, 160
George IV, King of United Kingdom 160
Gerasimov, Mikhail 38
Gessler 23
Gibson, Mel 27
Gilbert, W.S. 123
Glaspie, April 250
Glinski, Mikhail 79
Glorious Revolution 111-118
Golden Age of Piracy 120
Golden Apple of Discord 7
Goldwater, Barry 224-227
Great Depression 5
Great Northern War 126
Greece 49-51, 198-200
Grenada 245, 253
Guantanamo Bay 221, 267
Guillotin, Dr. Joseph 152
Gulf of Tonkin Resolution 228
Gulf War 245-256, 282
Gustavus Adolphus, King of Sweden 102-104

H

Halliburton 267

Hamilton, Andrew 130-131
Hamilton, Alexander 148, 160
Hanover, House of 122,
Haridwar 35-36
Harper's Ferry 185
Harvard College Observatory 3
Helen of Troy 7
Hemmingstedt, Battle of 69-72
Henry IV, King of England, 38
Henry VI, King of England 44
Henry VIII, King of England 22, 64-65, 83-88
Hera 7
Hercules 7
Hill, A.P. 181
Hirohito, Emperor 215
Hiss, Alger 220
Hitler, Adolf 74, 203-210
Hohenzollern family (rulers of Prussia) 124
Holy Roman Empire 95-101
Hossback Memorandum 205
Hugenberg, Alfred 205
Hudson Bay 125
Hudson, Rock 5-6
Humphrey , Hubert 229
Hundred Years War 28, 41, 45
Hungary 53-56, 101, 146
Hurricane Katrina 270-271
Hussein, Saddam 245-251, 254-255, 259, 260, 261, 268-269

I
Iceland 69
Illinois Central Railroad 181
India 35-36, 76
Innocent II, Pope 18
International Astronomical Union (IAU) 4, 8, 9
Iran 235, 245, 252, 261, 267-268
Iran-Contra Scandal 6, 249
International Banking 18
Iraq 245-256, 259-263
Isenbrand, Wulf 71
Israel 254

It's a Wonderful Life 220
Ivan the Great, Grand Duke of Moscow 77
Ivan the Terrible 79

J

James II, King of England 111-118
James III, King of Scotland 65
James IV, King of Scotland 65
Jane Seymour 87
Japan 80, 107-108, 186, 191-192, 209, 215
Jefferson, Thomas 160, 163
Jerusalem 17-18
Joan of Arc 40-46
Joan (bride of Louis, Duke of Orleans) 62, 64
John II, King of France 32
John IV, King of Portugal 107
John V of Saxe-Lauenberg 69, 71
Johnson, Lyndon 224, 227, 228, 229
Juno (asteroid) 9
Jupiter/Neptune conjunction 46

K

Kanagawa, Treaty of 186
Karmal, Babrak 241
Kazahkstan 35
Kennedy, John F. 219, 220, 224
Kennedy, Joseph 219
Kennedy, Robert 221
Kerry, John 270
KGB 240
Khan, Mohammed Daoud 233-236, 242
Khan, Zahir (King) 233, 234, 242
Khodynka Field 194
Khrushchev, Nikita 221
Khyber, Mir Akbar 234, 236
King Henry VI, Part 1 (play) 46-47
Knights Hospitaller 19, 20, 91, 165-166
Kore/Persephone 2-3
Kronos/Saturn 2
Kuiper Belt 8
Kursk, Battle of 209

Kuwait 249-256, 259, 265

L

Lafayette, Marquis de 152
Lake George 142
Laos 221, 224
Law, Bernard Cardinal 6
Lawless, Lucy 9
Leningrad 208
Leonowens, Anna 186
Lepanto, Battle of 96
Liberace 6
Lilah (Hindu deity) 8
Lincoln, Abraham 59, 181-182
Lindsay of Piscottie 65
Lithuania 73-75, 98
Lodge, Henry Cabot Jr. 225
Louis, Duke of Orleans (later King Louis XII of France) 61-65
Louis XIII, King of France 105
Louis XIV, King of France, 116, 118, 120, 122
Louis XV, King of France 131
Louis XVI, King of France 152
Lovejoy, Elijah 185
Lowell, Percival 3, 4
Lowell Observatory 3, 4
Luftwaffe 208
Luther, Martin 80, 99
Lutherans 99, 192
Lyons, Matthew 163

M

Mad War 61-65
Maddox, U.S.S. 225, 227
Magdeburg, Sack of 102
Maginot Line 208
Magnus of Saxe-Lauenberg 69-71
Malaysia 96
Malta 91-96 165-166,
Marconi 36
Manchuria 191
Mao Zedong 214

Marcy, Mary Ellen 181
Marlborough, Duke of 120
Marlowe, Christopher 27
Mars conjunct Chiron 145
Mars conjunct Pallas 145
Mars opposing Moon 146
Mars opposing Neptune 183-184
Mars opposing Saturn 146
Mars sextile Venus 145
Mars square Ceres 107
Mars square Mercury 183
Mars square Neptune 132
Mars square Pluto 234
Mars square Uranus 72
Mars trine Sun 234
Marx Brothers 262
Mary I, Queen of England (Bloody Mary) 83, 84,108
Mary II, Queen of England (wife of William of Orange) 114-117
Mary (sister of King Henry VIII) 64-65
Matthias Corvinus (King of Hungary) 53, 56
Maximilian I, Emperor of Austria 60-61
McNamara, Robert 228
Mehmed the Conqueror 49-52
Mein Kampf 205, 204
Menelaus, King of Sparta 7
Mexican War 181
Michael I, Czar of Russia 103
Minh, Ho Chi 222-224
Moldavia 55-58
Mongkut, King of Thailand 186
Monroe, Elizabeth 152
Monroe, James 152, 154, 282
Montcalm, General Louse-Joseph 138, 140-142, 144
Montgomery, Bernard (Monty) 210-215
Moon opposing Pallas 72
Moral Majority 235
More, Sir Thomas 84
Mortimer, Roger 28
Moscow 77, 156, 208
Mount Olympus 2, 3

Mount Vernon 11
Mubarak, Hosni 250
Muhammed, Prophet 51
Mujahideen 241
Mundane Astrology 9

N

Najibullah, Mohammed 241-242
Naples 95
Napoleon 78, 124, 152-156, 159, 196
Nazis 72, 204-210
Nebraska 183
Nelson, Lord Horatio 166, 167
Neptune (planet) 3, 9,
Neptune opposing Juno 72
Neptune opposing Pluto 107
Neptune/Pluto conjunction 36
Neptune sextile Venus 72
Neptune square Moon and Pallas 72
Neptune trine Saturn 72
Netherlands 69, 82
Newfoundland 126
Nicholas II, Czar of Russia 192-194
Nietzsche, Frederick 74
Niger 260
Nixon, Richard 219, 225, 229
Nobel Peace Prize 192
Noriega, Manuel 245
Northern Alliance 242
North Korea 261
North, Lord 157
North, Oliver 249
Nova Scotia 126
Novgorod 74
Nyx, Goddess of the Night 7

O

Oates, Titus 83, 108
Obama, Barack 272
OPEC 250
Operation Desert Shield 252
Operation Desert Storm 253

Operation Uranus 209
Orleans 41-42
Orsha, Battle of 77-80
Orwell, George 220
Oxford University 4

P
Paedomazoma 51
Pakistan 35, 234
Pallas (asteroid) 9
Palomar Observatory 8
Panama 245
Panic of 1837 185
Paris, Prince of Troy 7
Parma 95
Parthenon 50
Pashtun 234
Patton, George 213
Paul, Czar of Russia 164-167
Paulsen, Pat 229
Paulus, General Friedrich 209
Peace of Amiens 156, 159
Pearl Harbor 209
Pentagon 260
Perle, Richard 259
Peter the Great (Czar of Russia) 122
Peter III, Czar of Russia 146
Phillip of Anjou 120, 126
Philip the Fair (King of France) 18-21
Phillip II, King of Spain 91, 95-96
Philip VI (King of France) 28
Philippa, Queen of England 28
Pig War 197
Pilgrimage of Grace 85-88
Pitt, William (the Elder) 157
Pitt, William (the Younger) 157-159
Pius II, Pope 50-51
Pluto in Astrology 4-6
Pluto Mythology 1-3
Pluto (Planet) 3-6
Pluto conjunct Ascendant 213, 252

Pluto conjunct Chiron 131, 204
Pluto conjunct Juno 263
Pluto conjunct Jupiter 263
Pluto conjunct Mars 214
Pluto conjunct Mercury 252
Pluto conjunct Midheaven 266
Pluto conjunct Moon 264
Pluto conjunct Neptune 36, 252, 263
Pluto conjunct Pallas 204
Pluto conjunct Part of Fortune 204
Pluto conjunct Pluto 46
Pluto conjunct Saturn 213
Pluto conjunct Sun 252
Pluto conjunct Uranus 140
Pluto opposing Ceres 116, 215
Pluto opposing Chiron 143
Pluto opposing Mars 72
Pluto opposing Jupiter 116
Pluto opposing Uranus 152
Pluto quincunx Jupiter 63
Pluto sextile Chiron 116
Pluto sextile Jupiter 87
Pluto sextile Mercury 63, 264
Pluto sextile Neptune 63, 87, 212, 220-221, 227
Pluto sextile Pluto 116
Pluto sextile Saturn 58
Pluto sextile Sun 272
Pluto sextile Uranus 116, 214
Pluto sextile Venus 263, 266
Pluto square Chiron 46, 116
Pluto square Jupiter 214
Pluto square Mercury 266
Pluto square Pallas 46, 183, 266
Pluto square Pluto 214
Pluto square Sun 116
Pluto square Uranus 72
Pluto square Venus 63, 122
Pluto trine Jupiter 58, 116
Pluto trine Mars 130, 264
Pluto trine Neptune 104, 132

Pluto trine Pallas 58, 104
Pluto trine Sun 104 116
Pluto trine Uranus 46, 263
Poitiers, Battle of 32
Poland 54, 73-75, 95, 98, 122
Portugal 21,80, 105, 107, 131
Port Arthur 191
Portsmouth, Treaty of 192
Poseidon/Neptune 2
Pottawatomie 184
Pottenger, Rique 9
Powell, Colin 260, 265
PPDA (People's Democratic Party of Afghanistan) 233-242
Princeton 263
Protestant Reformation 80
Protocols of the Elders of Zion 194
Prussia 72, 124, 131, 144-147, 152, 179, 185, 196
Pskov 74
Puritan Rebellion 83

Q
Qasim, General 246, 250
Queen Anne's War 117-122
Qing Dynasty 167, 173

R
Rabinowitz, David (astronomer) 8
Rackham, John (Calico Jack) 124
Radu (brother of Vlad the Impaler) 55, 58
Rasputin, Grigori 192
Reagan, Ronald 264, 271-272
Reformation 76
Reign of Terror 152-153
Reims 42
Reis, Turgut 94
Renaissance 36
Rhodes 91
Richard II, King of England 32
Richelieu, Armand Cardinal 104-105
Roberts, Bartholomew (Black Bart) 124
Rockefeller, Nelson 225

Rommel, Erwin 213
Roosevelt, Franklin 162
Roosevelt, Theodore 191, 192, 282
Rosenbergs, Ethel & Julius 220
Rouen 42
Rove, Karl 272
Rumala oil field 250
Rumsfeld, Donald 249, 259, 261-265, 271-272
Russo-Japanese War 191, 194
Russia 77-80, 103, 126, 129-133, 156, 164-167, 174-177, 179-180,
 191-194, 197-200, 208-210, 219-221, 234, 236, 239-242
Ruthenia 73

S
Saturn conjunct Ascendant 210
Saturn opposing Sun 65
Saturn trine Mars 246
Saxony 122,
Schiff, Jacob 191
Schleswig-Holstein 69, 72, 186
Schwarzkopf, Norman 252-255
Scotland 27, 65, 107, 159
Second Balkan War 199-200
Second Opium War 185
Sejm (same) 125-129
Seltzer, Henry (Creator of the astro glyph for Eris) 9
Sepoy Rebellion 185
Shakespeare, William 32, 46-47
Shimbara Rebellion 103-104
Siam 96
Sicily 95
Simms, Maria Kay 9
Solomon's Temple 18
Spain 62, 80, 84, 95-96, 101, 105, 106, 120, 126, 147, 196, 198
Spanish-American War 11
Sputnik 220
Stalin, Joseph 4, 219
Stalingrad 208, 209
Stanislaw I, King of Poland (Stan) 129-133
Stephen, King of Moldavia 55-58
Stirling, Battle of 65

Suleiman Pasha 56-57
Sun conjunct Mars 140
Sun trine Neptune 132
Suskind, Ron 272
Sweden 102-105, 126, 179
Switzerland 23, 69

T
Tajbeg Palace 250
Taliban 233, 242, 256
Talleyrand, Charles Maurice de 153, 163
Tamerlane 35-38
Taraki, Nur Mohammed 236-240
Tartars 58
Tell, William 23
Telse the Virgin 72
Templar, Knights 16-23, 144, 284, 285
Tesla, Nikola 36
Thetis, Sea Goddess 7
Thirty Years War 99-108
Tillman, Pat 268, 269-270, 272
Tilly, Count of 102
Tombaugh, Clyde 3-4
Tora Bora 260
Tripoli 91
Trojan War 7
Trujillo, Chad (astronomer) 8
Tudor, Mary (sister of King Henry VIII) 62
Turkey, 38, 49-51, 55-58, 90-96, 101, 133, 174-176, 194, 198-200
Turner Joy, U.S.S. 227
Tuscany 95

U
UB-313 8, 9
Ukraine 73
Underground Railroad 185
United Kingdom 159
United Nations 6
United States of America 10-12, 135, 148, 153, 156, 160-163,

180-186, 205, 209, 213, 214, 215, 220-229, 249-256, 259-273,
United States Overseas Mission 236
Uranus 3, 6, 11,
Uranus Return (USA) 6
Uranus square Saturn & Moon 44
Urbina 95
Utrecht, Treaty of 125

V

Vasili, Grand Duke of Moscow 77-80, 83
Vaslui, Battle of 55-58
Vatican 19
Venice 38, 50-51, 69, 95
Venus square Chiron 63
Venus square Jupiter 101
Venus trine Neptune 101
Vidal, Gore 259, 271
Vietnam 222-224, 227-229, 245, 252-253
Virus, HIV 5
Vlad the Impaler (aka Count Dracula) 47 51, 56, 57, 58
Voltaire 96, 99, 145
Voorhees, Jerry 219
Von Wallenstein, Albrecht 102

W

Wahabi Islam 261
Wallace, William 27
War of 1812 11
War of Polish Succession 129-133
War of Spanish Succession 120-121, 123-124
War on Terror 6, 259-273
Washington, George 11, 76, 137-138, 140, 160, 161, 162, 163
Watergate Scandal 264
Weapons of Mass Destruction 260, 261, 263, 266-267
Westboro Baptist Church 6
Westphalia, Peace of 107-108
White Lotus Society 167
Wilhelm I, Kaiser 195, 197
Wilhelm II, Kaiser 192, 193, 194-197, 198, 199
Wilkinson, James 148
William III, King of England (William of Orange) 115-121

Wilson, Joseph 260-261
Witch Trials in Germany 103
Wolfe, General James 141, 142-144
Wolfowitz, Paul 259
Wolfstar USA chart 9, 10, 12
World Trade Center 260
World War One 4, 137, 144, 191, 194, 196, 200, 203-204, 245-246
World War Two 56, 202-215

X

Xena, Warrior Princess 8, 9

Y

Yankee Doodle Discord 12
Yekaterinburg 194
Yellow Cake 260
Yeltsin, Boris 242
Yorkshire 85
Yorktown, Battle of 10

Z

Zenger, John Peter 134-135
Zeus/Jupiter 2, 7

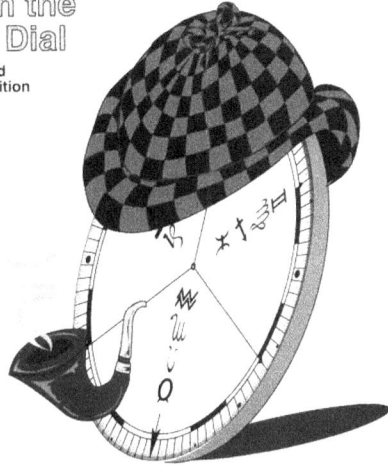

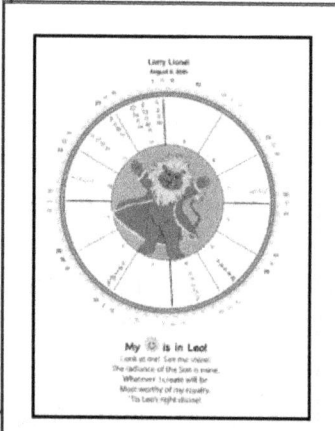

310. **Brother Pluto, Sister Eris**

www.ingramcontent.com/pod-product-compliance
Lightning Source LLC
Chambersburg PA
CBHW060041100426
42742CB00014B/2654